FINANCIAL MANAGEMENT FOR NONPROFIT HUMAN SERVICE ORGANIZATIONS

Second Edition

FINANCIAL MANAGEMENT FOR NONPROFIT HUMAN SERVICE ORGANIZATIONS

By

RAYMOND SANCHEZ MAYERS, Ph.D.

Rutgers, The State University of New Jersey
School of Social Work

CHARLES C THOMAS • PUBLISHER, LTD.
Springfield • Illinois • U.S.A.

Published and Distributed Throughout the World by

CHARLES C THOMAS • PUBLISHER, LTD.
2600 South First Street
Springfield, Illinois, 62794-9265

© 2004 by CHARLES C THOMAS • PUBLISHERS, LTD.
ISBN 0-398-07512-3 (hard)
ISBN 0-398-07513-1 (paper)
Library of Congress Catalog Card Number: 2004043798

With THOMAS BOOKS *careful attention is given to all details of manufacturing
and design. It is the Publisher's desire to present books that are satisfactory as to their
physical qualities and artistic possibilities and appropriate for their particular use.*
THOMAS BOOKS *will be true to those laws of quality that assure a good name
and good will.*

*Printed in the United States of America
GS-R-3*

Library of Congress Cataloging-in-Publication Data

Mayers, Raymond Sanchez
    Financial management for nonprofit human service organizations / by
Raymond Sanchez Mayers.--3nd ed.
        p. cm.
    Rev ed. of: Financial management for nonprofit human service agencies. c1989.
    Includes bibliographic references and index.
    ISBN 0-398-07512-3 -- ISBN 0-398-07513-1 (pbk.)
    1. Human services--United States--Finance. 2. Nonprofit organizations--
United States--Finance. I. Mayers, Raymond Sanchez. Financial manage-
ment for nonprofit human service agencies. II. Title

HV95.M33 2004
361'.0068'1--dc22

                                                                    2004043798

For Fontaine,
Jordan and Sara Caitlin,
and my parents, Esther and Arthur Bovero

PREFACE TO SECOND EDITION

This book is an update of the previous edition, formerly titled *Financial Management for Nonprofit Human Service Agencies*. We are grateful for the continued warm reception to the first edition. But many events have transpired since then. At the time of the writing of that first edition, nonprofit human service agencies were not regulated to the degree they are now. During the last few years many pressures have been brought to bear on nonprofits, not the least of which is the drive to make them more "businesslike", more "accountable", and more understandable to those outside of the nonprofit field.

This book attempts to provide nonfinancial managers in the nonprofit field with the critical knowledge needed to communicate with the "experts" they depend upon for financial decision making. It is not intended to be an entry-level text in accounting for nonprofit organizations. Rather, it is to familiarize the reader with the financial terms, concepts, required forms and procedures to be used in the nonprofit human service agency.

The central organizing theme of this book is the acquisition, distribution, and reporting of agency resources within a systems framework. Human service organizations take in resources that they convert to goods and services. To be accountable, they must record and report on the distribution and use of the resources they receive. This book attempts to present key concepts and skills in each of the major areas of the financial management process. The book is divided into sections relating to those parts of the process.

Section I is an overview that covers the historical and sociopolitical context of nonprofit organizations and financing as well as the systems concept and unique characteristics of nonprofits. Section II covers the planning and acquisition of resources by human service organizations. This involves planning and budgeting as well as marketing and grantwriting skills. Section III covers distribution of the acquired resources through internal control, budgeting, and investments. Section IV covers the recording and reporting of organizational financial activities. Included here are basic accounting techniques, fund accounting, financial reporting guidelines, and financial statement analysis.

Admittedly, there are some arbitrary distinctions made in the division of the topics. Real life is not so neat and tidy. Certainly those who work in nonprofit finance know that the activities of budgeting, recording, and fundraising go on simultaneously. The division of topics and the order in which they are presented are due to didactic attempts to show a logical flow from inputs (acquiring resources) to outputs (reporting of what happened to the resources), and to show the cyclical nature of the processes involved.

This book is still intended for students and practitioners in the human services, and new topics have been added to update the continual changes in nonprofit management. In addition to new topics, all of the sections have been revised and new features have been added:

Added Topics

New topics added in this edition include:
- Fees for services
- Purchase of service contracting
- Breakeven analysis for costing services and activities
- Third-party payments
- Internet resources
- A glossary

Revised Sections

There are updated sections to reflect changes in practice as well as in law. Major revisions are in the areas of:
- Financial Statements: The new Statement of Cash Flows, Statement of Financial Accounting Standards Nos. 116 and 117
- Audits and Financial Statement Analysis: Ratio analysis for Cash Flow Statements, audits for nonprofits receiving federal awards
- Fundraising: New guidelines for joint activities, unrelated business income tax
- Internal Control: COSO standards for internal control
- Investments: Socially responsible investing, Statement of Financial Accounting Standard No. 124.
- Grants: grants management and OMB Circulars A-110 and A-122

New Features

In order to serve the needs of both practitioners and students, the cases and exercises have been removed. Cases and exercises are now in a student workbook available from the publisher. This was done so the text could more readily serve as a reference tool for practitioners. The separate workbook allows students to complete exercises that facilitate a working knowledge of financial management principles. In addition, an instructor's manual is available from the author at the address listed below. Since this is a beginning text for the nonfinancial manager and others interested in aspects of financial management, those familiar with the more technical aspects of financial management such as accountants, Certified Public Accountants (CPA's), attorneys, and financial planners should always be consulted for technical expertise and the particular legal requirements of an organization's home state.

Raymond Sanchez Mayers
Rutgers University
School of Social Work
536 George Street
New Brunswick, NJ 08901

ACKNOWLEDGMENTS

I wish to thank all those who gave feedback and comments regarding the material in this book. Most of all, I wish to thank the many students in my fiscal procedures, financial management, grantwriting and fundraising classes who gave their views on each chapter. They helped make the topics covered here understandable to nonfinancial managers. I especially owe deep gratitude to Fontaine Fulghum who read and edited every chapter and gave important feedback and insights as an experienced human service administrator. Some of the illustrations were done by Darlene Mendez, others by the author. S.C. "Cat" Sanchez Mayers, Erin O'Brien, and Cathy Duzenski served as able research assistants. My heartfelt thanks also to those who reviewed certain sections of the book:

Philip Crunk, University of Alabama
David Hardcastle, University of Maryland
Richard Hoefer, University of Texas at Arlington
Jordan E. Mayers, Investment Banker
John McNutt, University of South Carolina
John Stretch, St. Louis University

Lastly, there are those who inspire us to professional excellence. I thank Dean Mary Davidson and Professor Paul Glasser of Rutgers University School of Social Work for their guidance, loyal support, and friendship.

I would appreciate any comments, suggestions, or other feedback from readers. Please e-mail me at: mayers@rci.rutgers.edu or visit my website at: http://crab.rutgers.edu/~mayers.

Faculty who would like an instructor's manual may send a letter on college/university letterhead to me at:

Rutgers University School of Social Work
536 George Street
New Brunswick, New Jersey 08901

To all those who gave their time, support, and ideas, I thank you, knowing that any errors or omissions are my own responsibility.

CONTENTS

FINANCIAL MANAGEMENT FOR NONPROFIT HUMAN SERVICE ORGANIZATIONS

I. OVERVIEW

Chapter One

THE SOCIAL CONTEXT
OF HUMAN SERVICES FINANCING

After reading this chapter you should be able to:

1. Understand the social context within which nonprofits operate;
2. Describe the human service organization in systems terms;
3. Have an understanding of the place of financial management within the nonprofit organization.

INTRODUCTION

This book is about the management of resources in nonprofit human service organizations. Using a systems approach, we will examine various aspects of financial management in the nonprofit organization, including budgeting, fundraising, financial statements, and agency accountability. However, before we begin a discussion of these topics, it is necessary to place the financing of human services in a larger context.

This chapter begins with a brief historical overview of nonprofits. Then a presentation of systems concepts as applied to the nonprofit will be presented, including the suprasystem, the sociopolitical environment in which such organizations operate, the nonprofit organization as a system, and its various subsystems.

HUMAN SERVICES: AN OLD ENDEAVOR

Care of the poor and others in unfortunate circumstances is a fundamental human impulse that goes back to the dawn of history as reflected in the Bible and other early writings. This concern flows through time and is embodied in the Elizabethan Poor Law of 1601, the Social Security Act of 1935, and the social welfare legislation of most world countries. Before the Middle Ages, organized religion had been the main source of support for the needy in the Western world. Religious groups, both Christian and Jewish, followed such teachings of the Bible as:

> For the poor shall never cease out of the land: therefore I command thee, saying, Thou shalt open thine hand wide unto thy brother, to thy poor, and to thy needy, in thy land (*The Holy Bible,* 1985, Deuteronomy 15:11).

With the passage in 1601 of the Elizabethan Poor Law in Great Britain, responsibility for the poor came under the aegis of small units of government, the local authorities representing the interests and resources of both Church and State. Many of the principles of social welfare regarding treatment of the needy in the 21st century can be traced back to the early 17th century. Some of these principles include the responsibility of local government for the needy in their jurisdictions; the idea that any monetary subsidies given to the poor should be lower than the lowest local wages; and the distinction between the "worthy" and the "unworthy" poor (Axinn & Levin, 1997).

When the first settlers came to the New World, they brought their values and some of their laws with them. These included laws regulating the provision of services to the needy. As more immigrants came, voluntary societies were formed to meet the needs of their members. Many of these voluntary societies, some of which are still with us today, were formed based on some special characteristic of the members, such as ethnic group, religion, or nationality (Sanchez Mayers, 1980). For example, the Scots Charitable Society was set up in Boston in 1657; a Friends Almshouse for poor Quakers was established in Philadelphia in 1713 (Axinn & Levin, 1997). Unlike many European countries that had some type of social welfare legislation in place in the nineteenth century, the United States had no national social welfare system until rather recently. Not until the middle third of the twentieth century did the federal government become involved in the provision or funding of social services, except for such groups as seamen, military personnel, and veterans. Up until the passage of the Social Security Act of 1935, social services were provided by private local nonprofit agencies, religious organizations, municipal authorities, or those states that had passed "mother's aid" legislation. The 1935 Act was passed in response to the tremendous needs brought on by the Great Depression and the inability of local agencies to fill these needs.

The passage of this Act and its subsequent amendments, as well as other major legislation in the 1970's, 1980's, and 1990's, has had a significant impact on the funding of social services in the United States.

Over the years since 1935, human service organizations have depended more and more on federal funding for the operation of their programs. This is true to the extent that many programs could not continue functioning without such funding, and some did not continue when funds dried up due to the vagaries of the economy and shifting political currents.

Because of the tradition of local responsibility assumed from the Elizabethan Poor Law, and our American espousal of "states rights," the administration of social welfare programs in this country has varied greatly. Even major federal programs under the Social Security Act, such as the former Aid to Families with Dependent Children (AFDC), have been administered differently in each state. That is, the amount of subsidy to eligible families has been based on an amount decided by each state. Other federal programs, such as the Social Security pension system, are administered uniformly throughout the states. Many social programs, however, are left largely to the province of the individual states. The federal government as well as state and local governments often elect to purchase services from voluntary agencies rather than providing the services themselves (Abramovitz, 1986).

The Great Society programs of the 1960's and early 1970's saw a tremendous increase in the funding of human services programs. Despite many criticisms and attacks from some quarters on such programs, particularly the traditional social welfare program (formerly AFDC), funding for many programs has increased over time. Such funding will probably continue to increase, especially to certain populations and certain targeted social problems. For example, with the aging of the huge cohort of baby boomers, many programs and services to the elderly are expected to expand.

As can be seen from Table 1-1, federal aid to state and local governments increased tremendously from 1970 to 1996. For example, payments to states for family support activities went from $81 million in 1970 to $953 million in 1996. This was an increase of 1,077%. Alcohol, drug abuse, and mental health payments to states (including grants for payments to individuals) went from $146 million in 1970 to $2,083 million in 1996, an increase of 1,327%. Some of this money, especially large portions of social services block grants to states, was paid to nonprofit human service organizations in the form of contracts and grants to provide services. These changes can be compared to the Consumer Price Index (CPI), an index used to chart the relative change in the cost of goods and services over time. The over-

Table 1-1
FEDERAL AID TO STATE AND LOCAL GOVERNMENTS: 1970 TO 1996*
(In millions of dollars)

Program	1970	1980	1990	1993	1995	1996	Percent Change 1970–1996***
Social Services block grants	574	2,763	2,749	2,785	2,797	2,484	333%
Payments to states for Family Support Activities (programs)	81	383	265	736	953	953	1077%
Alcohol, drug abuse, and mental health	46	679	1,241	1,994	2,444	2,083	1327%
Family support payments to states**(programs & benefits)	4,142	6,888	12,246	15,628	17,133	16,670	302%
Food stamps -administration	559	412	2,130	2,611	2,740	3,030	442%
Child nutrition and special milk programs**	380	3,388	4,871	6,589	7,387	7,757	1941%
Housing assistance**	436	3,435	9,516	14,100	18,416	16,762	3744%

*Source: U.S. Census Bureau, Statistical Abstract of the United States: 1997.
**Includes grants for payments to individuals.
***Note: During this same period the Consumer Price Index (CPI) increased 298.8% (Bureau of Labor Statistics, 1999); These program increases were well in excess of the CPI.

all CPI increased only 298.8% from 1970 to 1996 in contrast to the much larger increases in human services funding previously cited (U.S. Department of Labor, 1999). Thus we can see that increases in Federal Aid have increased dramatically over time, much faster than the average cost of living. Nevertheless, funding shifts from one program to another have left many organizations feeling pinched.

The ways in which funds have been received from the federal government has changed over time as well, from direct allocations in the form of grants to individuals and specific organizations to block allocations to states and local governments which then decide how the monies are used (Stoesz & Karger, 1993). The impetus for block grants was to give state and local governments more control over ways such monies would be spent, the assumption being that local communities are more aware of local needs than is an impersonal central government in Washington. But another factor has been the desire of political conservatives to reduce the role and scope of the federal government in social service provision (Jansson, 1997).

There are advantages and disadvantages to block grants. A major advantage to block grants is that more decisionmaking power is vested in local governments that are presumably more aware of the needs in their communities. A major disadvantage to block grants is that they are often at the mercy of local politics and politicians, who may use the funds for political patronage. Moreover, as different locales have different values and beliefs regarding the appropriateness of some federally mandated social legislation, the goals as originally intended in some legislation become subordinated to, or distorted by, local political agendas.

While government spending has become an increasingly important source of revenue for nonprofits, private dollars also continue to provide important support for social services. It is this mix of revenue and support from so many sources that makes the nonprofit experience so rich, and nonprofit fiscal management so complex. These sources of support will be more fully discussed in the next chapter and throughout this text.

As seen above, nonprofit organizations have existed for quite a long time. Most have come into existence to meet human needs whose resolution is often not seen as the province of government, or as a way to provide publicly mandated services using the less costly, and often better informed, delivery approaches characteristic of the private sector.

THE HUMAN SERVICE ORGANIZATION AS A SYSTEM

Systems theory has pervaded the physical and social sciences over the last decades and has provided a framework with which to view many different types of processes. Concepts and techniques of systems theory are important in financial management for a number of reasons. First, they are the bases for the development of computerized information systems found in all types of organizations today. An organizational systems analysis is an integral part of the planning and development of a computerized information system. Systems techniques, such as flow-charting, are used in programming. Further, modern auditing today includes in its evaluations a systems review (Bodnar, 1980; Bodnar & Hopwood, 1995). Thus, systems concepts are very important for accounting and auditing functions. Finally, systems concepts have been employed in social work (as has the related eco-systems approach) for several decades and help give us a way to look at the human service organization, its subsystems, and its processes in some kind of totality (Germain, 1978, 1981; Payne, 1997).

"A system is composed of interacting parts that operate together to achieve an objective or purpose. Systems are not random collections of objects. Systems consist of coherent, patterned, purposeful sets of elements" (Bodnar, 1980, p. 26). The concept of open systems holds that energy and resources flow across permeable boundaries. Material resources, technologies, and values may be seen as flowing into (as inputs) and out of organizational boundaries (as outputs). The environment of the human service organization (the suprasystem) is a complex net of social values and events, economic conditions, political constraints and facilitating factors, including federal and local laws and regulations.

The Suprasystem

It should be clear from the brief historical overview provided above that approaches to caring for the needy in our society are influenced by historical precedent, politics, public attitudes, religious beliefs and so forth. Thus human service organizations do not exist or operate in a vacuum, but rather in a complex socio-political environment that is influenced by many factors (see Figure 1-1 below). This environment we term the suprasystem. Thus, ". . . the suprasystem is comprised of those external individuals, groups, and other social systems that have an identifiable direct and ongoing pattern of relationships with the subject sys-

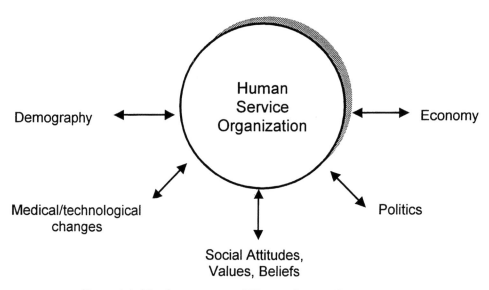

Figure 1-1: The Suprasystem of Human Service Organizations

tem (Norlin & Chess, 1997, p. 68). These external forces do not exist in isolation, but dynamically interact to influence each other. Some of these factors include: social attitudes, values, and beliefs; the economy; politics; demographic changes, medical and technological changes.

Social Attitudes, Values, Beliefs

Societal attitudes towards the needy and other vulnerable populations change over time and influence legislation regulating services to various groups (Groskind, 1994). For example, negative public attitudes toward the AFDC program prompted major welfare reform in the late 1990's.

The Economy

The degree of health of the economy influences the amount and type of human needs expressed and the different population groups experiencing such needs. When demand for workers is high, more people in the workforce tends to result in less demand for certain type of basic survival services, such as food and housing. When there are many unemployed, demand for basic services increases and other problems may become manifest, for example, increased substance abuse and/or child abuse

The nature of our economy also impacts our populace and its needs. Most acknowledge that the market economy cannot accommodate all citizens, and that those who are less able to compete in the marketplace should receive assistance within a just society.

Politics

The political process may be seen as a set of disparate forces vying to affect the distribution of goods and services within a society. Politics influences social legislation and is a reaction to needs and issues perceived by the electorate, as well as a jockeying for power by different interest groups (Rubin, 1993). Social legislation results in appropriation of funding for human services.

Demography

Demographic changes influence nonprofits as these organizations try to remain sensitive to the needs in their communities. For example, the aging of the baby boom generation means that there will probably be increased demand for home health care, transportation and other services for the elderly. Increased numbers of new immigrants from non-Western countries means increased need for services that are culturally compatible with these new groups, and so forth.

Medical/Technological Changes

Medical and technological changes affect how we view problems and create the need for new services, as well as create new technology for delivering services. For example, twenty years ago, HIV/AIDS were unknown problems. Twenty years ago, most premature babies less than a certain weight and age did not live. Twenty years ago, very few people had personal computers (pc's). Medical advances have helped new-borns survive, have made us aware of, and responsive to, the problems of persons with HIV/AIDS even though there is as of yet no cure, and those in our society who are without pc's are at a significant disadvantage. All of these developments, and many others, impact on human service organizations. Let us now turn to the human service organization, examining it in systems terms.

Characteristics of Open Systems

If we take a systems view of the human service organization, we may be able to see more graphically the place and function of the financial management aspect, or subsystem, as well as the overarching suprasystem within which such organizations must operate. First, let us look at the concept of the *open system*. Human service organizations are open systems because they are in interaction with their environments; there is a two-way exchange of energy and resources between the agency and its environment. Each influences and affects the other.

There are a number of characteristics of open systems that apply to nonprofit organizations (Katz & Kahn, 1978; Norlin & Chess, 1997):

Input

As no organization is self-contained, every organization must take in energy in the form of resources from its external environment. In the human service organization, these resources are called inputs. Inputs are material in the form of money, supplies, equipment, and so forth. Inputs may also be human resources in the form of personnel for the agency, and the clients the agency is to serve (see Figure 1-2).

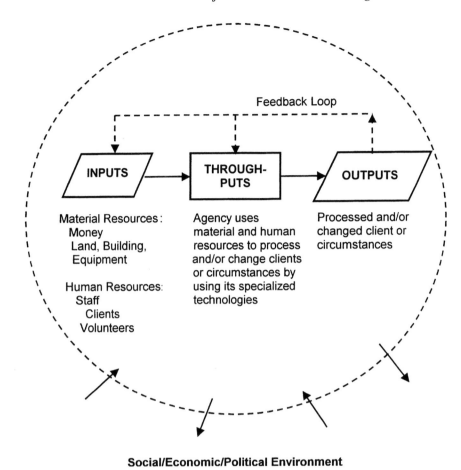

Social/Economic/Political Environment

Figure 1-2: A Systems View of the Human Service Organization

Conversion Operations

Open systems transform or convert the energy they take in. This means that some process occurs in the organization for the conversion to take place. In human service organizations, material and human resources are used to process and/or change clients or their circumstances (Hasenfeld, 1974; Vinter, 1974). The processes or technologies used are varied and include assessment, diagnosis, casework, and groupwork, to name just a few.

Output

After conversion operations have taken place, the result of the processing is returned to the environment. In the case of the human service organization, this output is the processed and/or changed client or changed client circumstance. For example, in a home for delinquent youth, the youth may be seen as an "input" into the home's system; the treatment he receives in the home is the "conversion operation", and the changed, presumably, non-delinquent youth who leaves the home is the "output". For a homeless family, the apartment located and secured for them by agency staff is the output. The outcome for the family is their changed circumstance (no longer homeless). You will note here that an output is the product of the organization's throughput, often the completion of a service. An outcome, on the other hand, reflects a quality of life change for the client (Netting et al., 1998).

Feedback

Inputs into an open system are not just of a material nature; there are informational inputs as well. These informative inputs (feedback) may come from the outputs of the organization and thus are cyclical in nature. They tell the organization about its environment and its own functioning in relation to that environment. The information that the agency receives regarding the results of its processes may be used to alter the process itself. In the example of the home for delinquent youth, if the youths discharged from the home are again involved in delinquent acts soon after leaving, the home may receive "feedback" in terms of complaints by parents, teachers, police, courts, and the general community. If the home wants to continue to treat delinquents, it uses the feedback as a basis for re-evaluating and modifying its program.

Cycles of Events

The exchange of energy (resources and information flowing through the agency) is, as demonstrated above, cyclical in nature. That is, the output from the system may provide the resources for the cycle of activities to continue. If the outputs of the human service organization are seen as successful, this information is relayed to funding sources and the community, which in turn means that a continuing supply of clients and funds will be channeled to the agency.

Negative Entropy

Entropy is a process by which all forms of organization move toward deterioration, even death. Open systems must try to retard or reverse this process by acquiring negative entropy. The open system can do this by taking in more resources from its environment than it uses, thus storing up additional energy and keeping it in reserve. How do human service organizations do this? Since they do not make a profit, in many instances they cannot store up reserves of funds. For example, if they have received government grants, all unexpended funds must usually be returned to the funding agency at the end of the fiscal year. However, sometimes human service organizations do have a surplus, an excess of revenues over expenses, that can be invested or put into new or ongoing programs. Another thing that most nonprofits have in abundance is human resources in the form of clients and volunteers. Most human service organizations have long waiting lists of clients. By keeping these long waiting lists, the nonprofit demonstrates the need and demand for its services. Many nonprofits also utilize volunteers whose services represent potential capacity, in addition to funded capacity, for service to clients.

Steady State and Dynamic Homeostasis

The process of importing resources into the human service system, transforming these resources, and exporting them back into the environment requires that the level of energy and relations between parts of the system remain somewhat constant. This is what is meant by a "steady state" and helps us understand why organizations at times commit acts that appear on the surface to be irrational or confusing. If there are disruptions to the system either internally or externally, the system moves rapidly to restore itself to its previous state or a new steady state. Through dynamic homeostasis, the system may attempt to preserve its character by growth and expansion.

Human service organizations try to maintain a steady state and homeostasis in many different ways. Some may look to their history and emphasize service approaches consistent with their beginnings and their mission. Others may seek to move in new directions in response to changing needs. Most seek to keep a steady flow of clients and resources into the agency and to maintain a stable source of revenue. Those organizations too dependent on one type of funding source have found themselves in precarious positions in times of cutback and retrenchment.

Differentiation

Open systems move from simple organizational structures to more complex ones by taking on elaborate and specialized roles. A human service agency that may have started with one social worker responsible for all tasks in a small office may grow to a large agency with very specialized professional staff such as intake workers, case workers, art and music therapists, group workers, clerical and support staff, and administrators.

Equifinality

A system can reach the same goal from different initial situations and by a variety of means. This is called equifinality. There are obviously more ways than one of reaching any given objective. For human service organizations this means that, while we tend to think one therapeutic method is superior to others according to our own theoretical orientations, there are many methods and strategies for helping clients to become healthy and lead productive lives. Equifinality also means that there are myriad strategies that the nonprofit may apply in planning for, acquiring, and utilizing the resources potentially available to it. However, some choices may lead to more efficient and effective delivery of services than others.

Subsystems

A system is often made up of *subsystems*. "Conceptually every system is a subsystem of a larger system to which it is connected through input/output exchanges" (Norlin & Chess, 1997, p. 322). Even a small human service nonprofit may be made up of a number of subsystems. The primary subsystem is one whose activities encompass the main goals and objectives of the organization. This is usually the client subsystem, which exists to help clients (see Figure 1-3). The agency may also have support subsystems that pursue activities to help the primary subsystem achieve its goals. A typical agency will have a personnel subsystem and a financial subsystem, but a larger agency may have even more subsystems. The personnel subsystem is concerned with recruiting, hiring, training, and evaluating employees. The financial subsystem is concerned with the activities that are the focus of this book, the economic activities of the agency.

Subsystems are in constant interaction with each other, so the activities in one subsystem have an impact on the other subsystems of the agency. There are a myriad of ways in which the client subsystem and the personnel subsystem produce voluminous data about activities going on in the agency. When these activities involve either the accumulation and/or the expenditure of agency monies, then these are recorded and/or distributed through the financial subsystem.

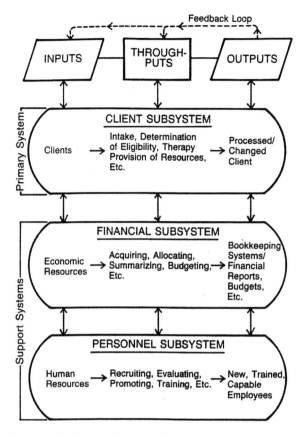

Figure 1-3: Human Service Organization Subsystems

Obviously, organizations are of many different sizes; the larger the agency, the more specialized it tends to become through the process of differentiation. For example, a very small agency may only have a part-time bookkeeper, an accountant who periodically comes in on a fee-for-services basis to prepare financial reports, and an auditor who comes in once a year to audit the books. A larger agency may have a full-time bookkeeper and an accountant who comes in more frequently. A very large agency may not only have an accounting department, but the whole financial subsystem may be divided into separate units such as payroll, travel, and so forth. Although the title of the department may vary according to the size of the agency, the principles are the same, the purpose is the same. A large part of what goes on in the human service agency involves the receipt of, and the disbursement of, money. It is the job of the human service accounting department to record these events, to disburse monies when necessary, and to be able, in a coherent manner, to account for all monies received and disbursed.

For example, when an employee provides an hour of service this involves the personnel subsystem, the client subsystem, and the financial subsystem. The hour of work may be entered on a time sheet (personnel subsystem) and sent to the accounting department (financial subsystem) for payroll purposes. When a client either receives or pays a bill for services rendered (client subsystem), a copy of the bill or the money itself is sent to the accounting department (financial subsystem) for recording, billing, and or depositing.

When a caseworker makes a home visit, a travel form is usually filled out and sent to the accounting department so that the worker can be reimbursed. The recruitment of staff also affects different subsystems. It may entail the expense of having an ad printed in the newspaper, or the printing of flyers to post as announcements. The bill for the newspaper ad, or the flyers and the paper used for the flyers, goes to the accounting or bookkeeping department. Similarly, the forms used in client intake are printed and paid for by sending a bill or purchase voucher to the accounting department. The receptionist who first greets the client, the intake worker who interviews the client, and the worker subsequently assigned the case are all salaried employees who are listed on the payroll account in the accounting department. They are paid by checks drawn up in that department and signed by the director of the agency or other authorized individuals.

Every human service organization has responsibility for large sums of money allocated to it from various funding sources, public as well as private. Every time monies are received from a different source, the transaction is (or should be) entered into a separate fund account. The organization, through the accounting department, has a checking account to enable it to pay for supplies, bills, payroll, and the like. This checking account gets a monthly statement just as a personal account does, and someone in the department has to do the job of reconciling the statement, or 'balancing the account'. In accepting financial resources from outside funding organizations, the agency has a public, professional, legal, and moral obligation to be able to account for the disposition of the resources in a way that is understandable to resource providers, as well as other interested third-parties, and in a manner consistent with *generally accepted accounting principles* (GAAP).

The average human service worker does not usually think of, or care about, this interaction between subsystems for s/he may have very little personal contact with the accounting department except for routine chores, such as filling out a W-4 form or submitting requests for travel reimbursement. For the human service administrator, however, what goes on in that department has just as much relevance as the services provided. The daily transactions recorded by the accounting department form the basis of the annual financial reports that are submitted to funding sources at budget review time. The administrator will have to work closely with his or her chief financial officer not only for budgeting, but also to aid in planning and decision-making. While the administrator is not expected to do the bookkeeping, s/he should know the basic principles of financial management to be able to converse intelligently about it, and most importantly, to be able to use the financial management subsystem as a tool for providing more efficient and effective services. In the next chapter we will look more closely at the financial management process.

REFERENCES

Abramovitz, M. (1986). The Privatization of the welfare state: A review. *Social Work,* 31(4):257–265, 1986.

Axinn, J. & Levin, H. (1997). *Social Welfare* (4th ed.). White Plains, NY: Longman.

Bodnar, G. H. (1980). *Accounting Information Systems.* Boston: Allyn & Bacon.

Bodnar, G.H. & Hopwood, W.S. (1995). *Accounting Information Systems* (6th ed.) Englewood Cliffs, N.J.: Prentice-Hall.

Germain, C. (1978). General systems theory and ego psychology: an ecological perspective. *Social Service Review,* 52(4):534–550.

Germain, C. (1981). The ecological approach to people-environment transactions. *Social Casework,* 62(6):323–331.

Groskind, F. (1994). Ideological influences on public support for assistance to poor families. *Social Work,* 39(1): 81–89.

Hasenfeld, Y. (1974). People processing organizations: an exchange approach, pp. 60–71 in Y. Hasenfeld & R. A. English (Eds.). *Human Service Organizations.* Ann Arbor: The University of Michigan Press.

Jansson, B. (1997). *The Reluctant Welfare State* (3rd ed.). Pacific Grove, CA: Brooks/ Cole.

Katz, D. & Kahn, R.L. (1978). *The Social Psychology of Organizations* (2nd ed.). New York: John Wiley & Sons.

Netting, F. E., Kettner, P.M. & McMurtry, S.L. (1998). *Social Work Macro Practice* (2nd ed.). New York: Addison Wesley Longman, Inc.

Norlin, J. M. & Chess, W. A. (1997). *Human Behavior and the Social Environment: Social Systems Theory.* Boston: Allyn & Bacon.

Payne, M. (1997). *Modern Social Work Theory* (2nd ed.). Chicago: Lyceum Books, Inc.

Rubin, I. S. (1993). *The Politics of the Budgetary Process* (2nd ed.). Chatham, NJ: Chatham House Publishers, Inc.

Sanchez Mayers, R. (1980). Self-help groups: An overview, pp. 53–57 in R. Wright (Ed.). *Black/Chicano Elderly: Service Delivery Within a Cultural Context.* University of Texas at Arlington: Proceedings of the First Annual Symposium on Black/Chicano Elderly.

Stoesz, D. and Karger, H. J. (1993). Deconstructing welfare: The Reagan legacy and the welfare state. *Social Work,* 38(5): 619–628.

The Holy Bible (1985). Authorized King James Version. Nashville: Homan Bible Publishers.

U.S. Bureau of the Census. (1997). *Statistical Abstract of the United States: 1997* (117th Edition). Washington, D.C.

U.S. Department of Labor, Bureau of Labor Statistics. (1999). *Consumer Price Index.*

Vinter, R. D. (1974). Analysis of treatment organizations, pp. 35–50 in Y. Hasenfeld & R. A. English (Eds.). *Human Service Organizations.* Ann Arbor: The University of Michigan Press.

Chapter Two

THE FINANCIAL MANAGEMENT PROCESS

After reading this chapter you should be able to:

1. Compare and contrast nonprofit and for-profit organizations;
2. Be familiar with both public and private funding streams;
3. Be familiar with the variety of oversight bodies governing non-profits;
4. Define the functions of financial management.

INTRODUCTION

This is an age of accountability; an age in which the impulse to charity is viewed in terms of unit costs, managed care, third-party payments, and financial statements. It is a time when human service professionals are expected to be efficient as well as effective in delivering services. In order to do so, they need to be familiar with the financial aspects of human service management. Unfortunately, due to the traditional nature of career advancement in the human services, very few human service professionals who rise to administrative positions are equipped to deal with financial matters in their organizations.

In the tradition of social work and other human services, a nonprofit administrator usually starts his or her career as a line worker. With increasing experience and demonstration of competence, the worker moves up the hierarchy of the organization to supervisory positions such as unit supervisor or casework supervisor. With each successive rise in administrative duty, the worker moves into areas where tasks and functions are unrelated to previous training and experience. The popular notion is that these new tasks, such as supervising, planning, budgeting, and so forth, involve skills that can be learned on the job. However, what often happens is that the effective caseworker is promoted to his or her level of incompetence. Most "muddle through" with varying degrees of success.

Another reason for the lack of skills in financial matters among nonprofit personnel has to do with the nature of nonprofits themselves. "Unfortunately, the combination of unique governance structure, heavy reliance on volunteers, and industry-specific tax and accounting rules often makes it difficult for nonprofit leaders to understand and adapt to their critical role in the financial management process" (Langan, 1998, p. 1). The lack of skills in the area of financial management has been particularly detrimental to human service organizations and the human service professions in general.

The inconsistent reporting and lack of formal evaluation characteristic of some, but certainly not all, such organizations have left human services open to criticism as being inefficient and unaccountable. One response from the field in the past has been that the human services deal with the qualitative, and that quantitative analyses and reports do not provide an accurate picture of the work done with clients. While it is true that the human services do have a definite qualitative aspect, there are other areas that can be quantified, indeed, must be quantified. Further, good qualitative reporting methods can also serve to provide a partial account, or to supplement, a quantitative account, of how clients are being served. Those who work in the human services are stewards of the public trust, and as such are accountable to their constituencies—clients, boards and committees, colleagues and peers, funding sources, the community, and the public at large. Not only is this a legal imperative, it is an ethical one as well as reflected in the National Association of Social Workers *Code of Ethics:*

> Social workers should be diligent stewards for the resources of their employing organizations, wisely conserving funds where appropriate and never misappropriating funds or using them for unintended purposes (1999, Section 3.09 (g)).

FINANCIAL MANAGEMENT DEFINED

One measurable way that agencies can be accountable is in the recording and reporting of their financial transactions. Financial management is a term that denotes a wide range of activities that take place in an organization. Some of these activities are fund raising, budgeting, grantwriting, and accounting. Therefore, financial management may be defined as planning for the use of the financial and material resources of an organization, the acquisition, allocation, control, recording/reporting of such resources as well as a periodic evaluation of these actions. You can see that financial management involves a number of diverse activities as defined below:

Planning: the use of a rational anticipatory approach to short- and long-term strategies to be employed by the organization to ensure its fiscal solvency.

Acquisition: the gathering in of human, material, and economic resources by the agency using such means as fund raising, grant writing, contractual arrangements, charging of fees, purchase of merchandise, hiring of staff, and the like.

Allocation: the distribution of resources imported into the organization. This distribution may be internal, that is, through budgeting a specific amount of money is apportioned to each department for expenses such as salary and other overhead. It may also be external, for example, contracting for services with an outside agency or consultant and paying for those services.

Internal Control: the establishment of standardized policies and procedures relating to all transactions and events involving monetary items. Such control ensures that generally accepted accounting principles and procedures are followed by the agency, that contractual and grant obligations are adhered to, and that all record keeping is in compliance with requirements of funders.

Recording/Reporting: the use of some sort of manual, automated or computerized system to list and classify all transactions of a financial nature in journals and ledgers and to generate periodic financial statements and reports.

Evaluating: the periodic review of financial activities in order to assess their efficiency and effectiveness in meeting agency and funder requirements for fiscal accountability. Periodic evaluation is done to check that the control system established by the agency is working as it was intended to do. Evaluation may also entail a review of agency activities to make sure that they are in the furtherance of stated agency goals and objectives.

While the human service administrator does not need to be an accountant, he or she is responsible for the total management and operations of the nonprofit. This responsibility includes having enough understanding of the fiscal arena to oversee financial staff and fiscal operations. Other agency staff, such as program or project directors and supervisors, are often called upon to write a budget for their program or unit, or serve on a budgeting committee. Therefore, it is incumbent not only upon the administrator, but also supervisors and program or project leaders to have some working knowledge of financial management.

THE FINANCIAL MANAGEMENT PROCESS

This book has been arranged to provide the student with a systems view of the financial management process. In the systems framework, the human service organization takes in resources as inputs; converts or processes them for its use; and has outputs in the form of clients, goods, or services. The foci of this book are the various stages of the process. Obviously, all the activities to be discussed may go on simultaneously in organizations. Also, the process is iterative and looping; each part is dependent on the other, and reflects a continuous cycle of events. However, for learning purposes these activities are broken down into small, discrete units.

In the first stage of the financial management process, the agency is concerned with the acquisition of resources (see Figure 2-1). To acquire

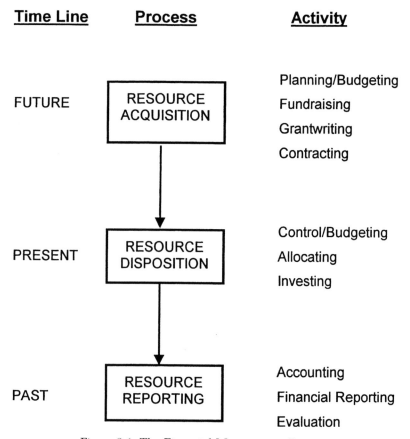

Figure 2-1: The Financial Management Process

resources effectively, the organization must have a clear idea of its mission, goals, and objectives. From its goals, the organization can develop a plan of operation that includes projections of amounts of resources needed over a specific time period. Developing short- and long-term plans are an integral part of budgeting as well as fund raising. The first stage of the financial management process, then, is concerned with the future. The agency needs to answer such questions as: How much money and material resources will we need to fulfill our mission? How can we raise this money most successfully? What potential contributors are available? How do we find them? How can we write grants and seek contracts that will be funded? How can we ascertain an appropriate fee schedule?

The second stage of the process begins at the point that the money or other resources are acquired. This stage is concerned with present time events, with the control and disposition of agency resources. Questions confronting the agency at this stage are: How do we develop good cash management systems? How can we ensure that we fulfill our stewardship responsibility in the most efficient manner possible? What shall we do with the endowment funds given us? How can we make sure that monies allocated for programs are used most efficiently? How do we build in a good control system?

The third stage of the process entails an historical perspective. It looks at what the organization has done with its resources. In this stage every financial transaction that takes place in the agency is recorded and then periodically summarized and reported. This forces the organization to evaluate its activities and answer questions such as: What has the agency done with the resources given it over the last year (or other designated time period)? How much has the agency spent for fundraising as opposed to services? What is the ratio of the agency's program costs to its administrative costs?

Now that we have viewed the financial management process, let us turn to some of the similarities and differences between not-for-profit (here called *nonprofit*) and for-profit organizations that have implications for the funding and administration of nonprofits. Current systems of financing for nonprofits, that is, all of the various possible streams of funding that can flow to the nonprofit, are also viewed. Indeed, it is the complexity of these possibilities and the myriad of regulations and oversight bodies to be dealt with that can make financial resource management a challenging art for the nonprofit manager and board.

NONPROFIT AND FOR-PROFIT ORGANIZATIONS

Nonprofit organizations are a special type of organization recognized in law, usually private entities set up as corporations under a charter granted by a given state and regulated by that state's nonprofit corporation act. They are specifically exempt from corporate taxes if they meet the requirements of the federal tax code. Local and state governments are also nonprofits, but they are public ones. In this book, private nonprofits that are subsumed under Section 501(c)(3) of the United States Internal Revenue Code are the focus of our discussion. They are defined as follows:

> Corporations, and any community chest, fund, or foundation, organized and operated exclusively for religious, charitable, scientific, testing for public safety, literary, or educational purposes, or to foster national or international amateur sports competition . . . or for the prevention of cruelty to children or animals, no part of the net earnings of which inures to the benefit of any private shareholder or individual. . . (United States Internal Revenue Code, Title 26, Sec. 501, 2000).

Thus the focus of this text is the nonprofit, especially those organizations designed to provide a service to human consumers or clients, regardless of ability to pay. Throughout this book, the term *nonprofit organization* will be used synonymously with *human service agency or organization*. While human service organizations are a type of nonprofit organization, they are not the only type. Municipal, state, and federal governmental units are nonprofits, but they are public entities financed by tax dollars and governed by elected and appointed officials and civil servants. Arts organizations and community redevelopment corporations may also be nonprofits, but, as with governmental entities, they are excluded from this discussion. Not all human service organizations are nonprofit, as some operate on a for-profit or commercial basis, but the only type that will concern us here is the nonprofit organization. Therefore, nonprofit human service organizations are defined here as private voluntary organizations whose mission is to meet a "socially desirable need of the community or its members" rather than to make a profit (Gross et al., 1995).

Similarities Between Profit-Oriented and Nonprofit Organizations

There are many similarities between profit-oriented business enterprises and nonprofit organizations (Financial Accounting Standards

Board, 1980; Freeman & Shoulders, 1999). Some of these similarities are:

Both Acquire External Resources

Although they vary in size, complexity, and goals, both types of organizations have to compete for, and acquire, valuable and scarce resources from their environments. Some of these resources include skilled, qualified personnel, money, and customers ("service recipients" or "clients"). Both types of organizations are part of the same economic system and use the resources they acquire to reach their stated goals.

Both Produce and Distribute Goods or Services

Both for-profit and nonprofit organizations are in business to produce and/or distribute goods and services. In order to do this in an efficient manner they must set up organizational structures that enable them to scan their environments, develop channels of distribution, sources for raw materials and supplies, networks of support, and means to reach consumers of the products or services. So a food bank, an emergency shelter, a battered women's shelter, and a clinic all have problems similar to the cereal manufacturer who must interest consumers in the cereal, find wheat and other materials at the lowest cost, have means to bring the product to market, and so forth.

Both May Provide Similar Goods or Services

Profit-oriented businesses and nonprofits may sometimes offer essentially the same goods or services. For example, there are profit-making marriage and family guidance clinics, for-profit home health services, counseling services, adoption services, and child care facilities. Previously, those clients with money went into the market place and purchased the goods or services they needed, thus a two-tiered system of social service provision resulted. The poor used public social services and those with means purchased services privately. Now accessing services is much more complex: a number of funding mechanisms are presently available whereby individuals as well as the government may contract for public or private services that may be paid with third-party or public monies (Kamerman, 1983).

Both Incur Financial Obligations

In order to acquire the resources needed to accomplish its mission, the nonprofit organization may incur financial obligations in much the same way that any business enterprise does. Both need to obtain labor, material, and facilities, and must pay for them in the present or at a future time. In paying for the goods and materials acquired in the course of operations, both types of organizations may borrow funds through loans or mortgages from creditors who must evaluate their financial viability.

Both Must Stay Financially Viable

In order to continue operations, both types of organizations must stay financially viable by taking in more resources than they use. While governmental entities and public utilities may function on deficit budgets, neither private for-profits nor nonprofits can stay in business long under those conditions. The goal of the nonprofit is to use its available resources for providing services and in doing so to: 1) break-even financially or 2) have a surplus that could be carried over into a new fiscal period to provide a cushion for on-going programs, or even seed money for new programs.

Both Have Limited Pools of Resources and Resource Providers

Obviously, all organizations do not have unlimited access to the resources in their environments. There are other organizations competing for some of the same resources. There are resource providers who may be interested in one type of organization and not another, and vice versa. Also, there are only finite amounts of money, skilled personnel, and potential consumers, or clients potentially available to any number of organizations.

Both May Charge Fees for Services

While the two types of organizations may charge a fee for the services they provide, the purpose of the fee is different for the two types of entities. Most profit-oriented companies try to sell goods or services at a price that exceeds their costs, thus making a profit. Nonprofit human service organizations typically offer their services at, or less than, cost. Often the service is provided at no cost to the customer or client, or on a sliding-fee scale to those served. In many cases the purpose of the charge is not to make a profit, but rather it is seen as a motivating factor for the client. Nonprofit organizations are generally not expected to cover all or even a large proportion of their costs from clients as they are providing a useful and necessary service that may not be obtainable anywhere in the market economy at a price that the client is willing or able to pay. Rather, human service organizations tend to rely on other sources of funding for a significant part of their budgets to pay for the services rendered to clients.

Both Must Employ Marketing Techniques to Attract Resources

For-profits spend millions of dollars a year to attract customers, or to convince them to buy newer and "improved" products or services. This marketing cost is seen as a cost of doing business. Not-for-profits also engage in marketing activities, although they do not usually refer to it as such. In the human services, the term often used to describe such activities is "outreach".

Both types of entities must develop marketing strategies to attract a specific client population. In the case of the human services, although many times clients have few other alternative sources for the good or service, there is still the problem of utilization. Underutilization of services sometimes occurs because all those eligible for a service may not know about it, may associate it with stigma, or may prefer informal networks of family and friends. The human service agency must learn to market and distribute its goods or services to its target population in much the same way business does. Some nonprofits are obviously more sophisticated than others at doing this.

Not only must the nonprofit use marketing techniques to attract clients, it must also use marketing strategies to create a positive corporate image in the community to attract resources such as donors. Marketing will be discussed further in Chapter Five, Marketing and Fundraising.

Characteristics of Nonprofit Human Service Organizations

While there are many similarities between the two types of organizations, nonprofit human service organizations differ from business or profit-oriented enterprises in many ways (Anthony & Herzlinger, 1980; Freeman & Shoulders, 1999; Langan, 1998; Sarri, 1971). This is why accounting procedures for the two types of organizations differ. Some of the distinguishing features of nonprofit human service organizations are:

Meeting Socially Useful Needs

The mission of a nonprofit human service agency is to meet a socially desirable need, as defined by the community, rather than to make a profit. Because the organizations are not concerned with profit, the financial statements of nonprofits have a different emphasis. There may be an excess of revenue over expenses, but this surplus is to be used for programs, not to enrich the owners.

Clients are Both Inputs and Outputs

A profit-oriented business such as a manufacturing firm takes in raw materials such as steel, plastic, aluminum, to make a new product such as a car. In contrast, the nonprofit agency takes in clients with problems or needs, processes and/or changes them so that one of the "products" of the human service agency is a changed and/or processed client.

Little Dependence on Clients/Consumers for Revenue

Many clients served by human service organizations cannot afford to pay for the services they receive. The purpose of the alternative sources of funds used by the nonprofit is to be able to provide the service without worrying about whether the client has the ability to pay. Even if a nonprofit has a sliding fee schedule, in most cases its major source of income is not the client.

Reliance on Human Relations Technologies and Professionals

Human service organizations rely on technologies that are based on theories and assumptions about human nature. Some technologies used by agencies may include behavior modification, biofeedback, gestalt therapy, and psychoanalytic therapy. The human service agency is also, in many cases, staffed and run by professionals. For-profit organizations may use the expertise of professional staff, but in many cases human relations professionals are in adjunct or consultative positions, performing tasks peripheral to the main goals of the organization. For example, a nursing home or hospital is in the health care business. The provision of social services is seen as an important but not central part of the hospital's mission, especially since the social services provided bring little revenue to such organizations.

High Proportion of Nonroutine Events

The human services deal with people and their problems. It is therefore almost impossible to routinize the nature of the tasks that must be performed to alleviate the problems. It is possible to routinize forms and procedures, but organizations must also cope with a myriad of emergencies that arise with people in trouble. And these emergencies have to be dealt with immediately; for example, someone has to be on call at the child welfare office to place children found abandoned in the middle of the night.

Resources are not Loans

Nonprofit organizations receive vast amounts of resources available only to them in the form of gifts, bequests, donations, allocations, and grants. The provider(s) of these resources do not usually expect economic gain or repayment for their contributions. Rather, these resources are to be used for the public good without tangible economic benefit expected in return. There are, of course, some direct and indirect benefits to those who wish to take advantage of them in the form of tax deductions for charitable expenses or increased status in the community.

Accountability and Stewardship

The goal of human service nonprofits is to meet a socially useful need; resources accrue to them on this basis. These organizations have a public responsibility to account for the funds they have received. Human service organizations are stewards or managers of public funds, therefore they should not only account for funds given for specific projects, but they also have a duty to use all the resources of the organization toward the "public interest" and in the most efficient and effective manner possible. Thus, nonprofits are held to a higher standard of accountability than for-profits.

Outside Constraints

While all organizations are somewhat constrained by governmental and legal regulations regarding their activities, there are other constraints placed by funding sources on the goals, policies, plans, and implementation strategies of human service organizations. Often nonprofits must abide by complex regulatory requirements that seem to be increasing.

Many times human service organizations have to provide services as dictated by an outside agency. For example, to obtain funds for a children's shelter an organization may have to have a certain number of staff with specified qualifications. In some cases, a nonprofit may also be constrained from offering other services that a funding source does not approve of, for example, abortion counseling. The old saying "Money rules–who has the money makes the rules" is nowhere more true than in the human services. No matter whether the funder is a government agency, United Way or other allocation body, these outside constraints are many times more powerful than nonprofit management or the governing board.

No Stockholders

There are no stockholders nor is there owner's equity in the nonprofit organization. This means that there are no ownership interests that can be bought and sold as in a profit-oriented company where stock may be issued or proprietorship passed or transferred to others. In the nonprofit agency, control rests with a board of directors who are supposed to represent the community, and with a professional administrative staff.

Blurred Lines of Responsibility

In many nonprofit organizations the line of responsibility is not often very clear. Outside agencies often dictate goals and activities of the nonprofit organization. In addition, the governing boards of nonprofits may be less influential in decision-making than the boards of profit-oriented companies. Although the governing board is ultimately responsible for the agency, members are not usually paid for their services. Their work on a board is seen as a public service and is done on a volunteer basis. They tend to be recruited from the elites in the community to help give the agency an aura of legitimacy, to help in fund raising, to provide a particular perspective or a particular expertise, and so forth. Many times elites prefer to sit on boards as a badge of prestige and community service. While they supposedly represent the public interest, in many cases they are the organization's largest contributors. Although they are legally responsible for the agency, they rarely, except in extreme cases of crisis, get involved in the day-to-day running of the agency.

Services or Goods May Be Monopolistic

Services or goods offered by nonprofits are often monopolistic in nature, that is, there are no consumer choices as to provider organization or type of service to be offered. For example, a battered woman seeking shelter from an abuser may find there is only one battered woman's shelter in her town or even her county, a person without health insurance seeking drug or alcohol treatment may find there is only one public facility in his county, and so forth. There are reasons for the monopolistic nature of some services. Regional planning bodies, local politicians, and funding sources try to avoid duplication of services so that funding for specific services can be spent most efficiently. One result of this is that there is no open market for the services in which their value may be objectively appraised. In addition, no competition may result in lack of quality, that is, "clients must take what they can get." The lack of rigorous evaluation as to the outcomes of some services contributes to the poor quality some clients may experience; too many agencies are still just reporting the number of clients seen.

Tax Treatment

As previously mentioned, nonprofits are classified as tax-exempt organizations under Section 501 (c) of the tax code. This means that they are generally exempt from federal, state, and local corporate income taxes on any excess of revenue over expenses. Most nonprofits, those with revenues over $25,000 per year, are required to file an annual information return, Federal Form 990 (see Chapter 12), in order to maintain their nonprofit status. This form asks the nonprofit to describe its operations, revenues, expenses, and other activities to demonstrate that it is in compliance with IRS requirements.

These then, are the major similarities and differences between the nonprofit and for-profit organization. These differences significantly affect the financial management systems of nonprofits, as has been briefly mentioned here and as will be illustrated throughout this book. For example, the accounting and reporting of nonprofit financial operations is somewhat different than for-profit accounting and reporting. These differences are related to the need for accountability of such a myriad of resources that accrue to nonprofits. Nonprofits receive many resources that for-profits do not, as for example, material and in-kind contributions. They also have available to them a wider range of funding options.

FUNDING OF NONPROFITS

In this section we will look at two aspects of the funding of nonprofits. The first aspect of funding has to do with the mechanisms of funding, that is, the sources from which nonprofits receive resources necessary to meet socially desirable needs. This is an important issue given the fact that many of the clients of nonprofit human service organizations are unable to pay for the services. These mechanisms may be seen as streams of funding flowing to the nonprofit. The second aspect of funding has to do with the types of resources obtained by the nonprofit.

Funding Streams for Nonprofits

Basically, there are four major funding streams for nonprofits. These are: governmental, for-profit corporations, nonprofit corporations, and public (non-governmental) (see Figure 2-2 below).

Governmental

Many governmental departments at the federal, state, and local (county and municipal) levels fund human services. At the federal level, Congress passes legislation, with monies attached, to provide certain types of services. Some of these monies go to states in the form of block grants or entitlements. Other monies may be made available through a competitive grants or contract bidding process. And still other monies are provided in the form of third-party payments for services, such as Medicaid and Medicare. States and counties may also provide funding for human services through a grants process, a competitive bidding process, or even allocations. These topics will be discussed in Chapter Six, on grantwriting, and Chapter Seven, on contracts.

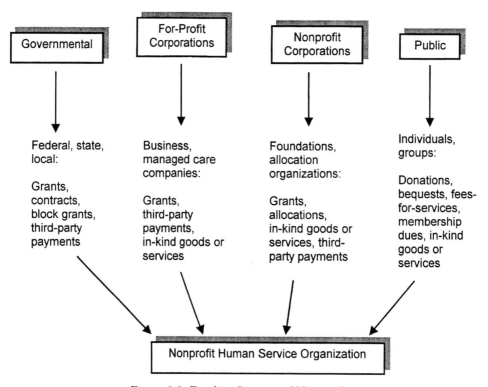

Figure 2-2: Funding Streams of Nonprofits

For-profit Corporations

Large for-profit corporations often have staff whose purpose is to maintain and improve community relations. Such corporations often contribute equipment and grants to nonprofits in their communities. Also included in this category are profit-making organizations, such as managed care companies, that pay nonprofits for the provision of services such as alcohol and drug counseling, marriage counseling, health care and so forth.

Nonprofit Corporations

Private nonprofit corporations are included under the 501(c)(3) rubric. These include community foundations. Some foundations have large endowments that are invested and the interest used to fund nonprofits through a grants review process. All foundations are required to distribute a minimal amount yearly to maintain their nonprofit status. In addition to the foundations, there are other nonprofit corporations actively involved in the acquisition and distribution of funds to nonprofits. These are the federated allocation organizations such as the United Way, Catholic Charities, Jewish Federation, Black United Fund, Women's Way, and others. These organizations play a major role in the provision of social services in this country, as will be discussed in this text.

Public

Individual donors and groups make up this category of funding. This source may be the result of specific solicitations by agency staff and volunteers. It may also result from the goodwill the agency enjoys in the community. It may also reflect concern on the part of contributors regarding the population the agency serves. This will be discussed more fully in the fundraising chapter.

Sources of Funds for Nonprofits

The most common sources of funds for a nonprofit organization, discussed below, are the following: 1) fees and third-party payments; 2) contracts; 3) allocations; 4) grants; 5) contributions; 6) vouchers.

Fees and Third-party Payments

Fees are earned revenues for the agency. That is, the organization receives money in return for providing a good or service. The client receiving the service may pay fees directly to the agency, but many times the client is unable to pay. In these cases, third parties such as Medicaid, or Medicare, Blue Cross/Blue Shield, other health/managed care plans, or other federal or state human service entities may pay for the services.

Contracts

Contracts between public and private agencies are frequently negotiated to provide mandated services such as foster care or adoption. This is often done because it may be easier and more cost-effective for a public agency to use the services of a private nonprofit that has demonstrated expertise in the service area. In these cases, the public agency refers the clients to the private agency and the contractee is paid for delivering the service. Recently, nonprofit agencies have begun to provide such contractual services as employee assistance programs to corporate clients, or counseling services to school systems that have no social workers.

Allocations

Allocations are the funds supplied by federated fundraising and allocation organizations such as the United Way, Jewish Federation, Catholic Charities, Black United Fund, and Women's Way. In these cases, the agency must submit a request for funds along with a budget and justification for the request. Then the request is reviewed by the funding agency's lay allocation and budgeting board which makes the final decision as to amount of allocation. Usually organizations that are recipients of allocations have passed rigorous screening criteria that render judgment on their credibility, legitimacy, stability, and solvency before they are accepted as members.

Grants

Grants are sums of money given for the agency to perform a specific task or to develop a specific program. Public agencies, private foundations, or corporations may dispense grants. In order to receive a grant, in most cases an agency must write a grant proposal spelling out in detail what it intends to do with the grant money. Writing grant proposals will be discussed more fully in Chapter Six.

Contributions

Contributions are sums of money donated by individuals or groups to support the work of the agency. Usually, the money is obtained without the agency having to exchange something tangible in return. That is, the agency does not provide a specific service to obtain the funds. Contributions may be in the form of money or in-kind goods or services. The contributions may be solicited as part of a regular, organized campaign, or by special events that are planned as a one-time occasion for a specific purpose or goal.

Vouchers

Vouchers are similar to script, that is, they represent a promise to pay. They are not given to the organization directly, but rather to clients. The client can then choose where to go for goods or services for which they give the agency a voucher. The agency then sends the vouchers it receives to the funding source that issued the voucher. The agency is thus reimbursed for the service it provided.

All these various types and sources of resources that fund nonprofits must be accounted for in some manner. There are a wide variety of organizations and structures in place to oversee the nonprofit and its fiscal activities.

ACCOUNTABILITY OF NONPROFITS AND THEIR REGULATION

Nonprofits are generally considered to be broadly accountable to society as a whole, operating as they do within the sphere of the "public interest". More narrowly, they are accountable to their boards of directors and to their funders. One of the implications of such a variety of funding sources is the plethora of "strings", or restrictions, attached. Not only are there many strings, but also in the last few years there has been a major movement to try to make nonprofit accounting and financial reporting more understandable and more "businesslike." This has resulted in more guidelines for nonprofits. The major regulators of nonprofits are: government (federal, state, and local); standards-setting bodies for the private sector, including the American Institute of Certified Public Accountants (AICPA), the Financial Accounting Standards Board (FASB), and accrediting and standards-setting bodies specifically for the private nonprofit human services sector, such as the United Way of America, Family Service Association of America, Child Welfare League of America, Better Business Bureau and others.

Federal Government

Different branches of the federal government have different requirements of nonprofits, depending on the department's responsibility (see
Figure 2-3). For example, nonprofits are required to submit annual returns to the Internal Revenue Service (Form 990) if they have revenue
over $25,000. The Form 990 is detailed as to an organization's activi-
ties and is used to make sure that it is fulfilling its tax-exempt role (see
Chapter 12). The IRS requires Form 990 to be available to the public
upon request. Many nonprofits have complied by allowing financial
statements and Form 990's to be posted on an internet website, a sort
of central repository of nonprofit information (Guidestar, 2000).

The Internal Revenue Service also looks closely at fundraising and

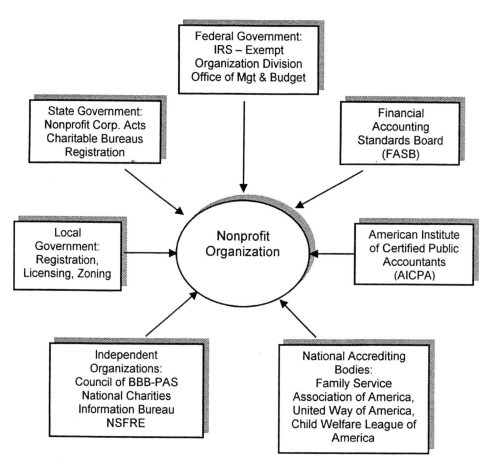

Figure 2-3: The Accountability Sphere of the Nonprofit Organization

other revenue-generating activities of nonprofits and may tax them if the IRS believes the organization is engaged in unrelated business activity. This tax is known as the unrelated business income tax (UBIT) and will be discussed further in Chapter Five on marketing and fundraising.

If a nonprofit receives a grant from the federal government, it must follow guidelines promulgated by the Office of Management and Budget (OMB) regarding allowable costs, allocating costs, and reporting. These guidelines are found in *OMB A-122: Cost Principles for Non-Profit Organizations* and *OMB A-133: Audits of Institutions of Higher Education and Other Non-Profit Organizations.*

State Government

Most states have laws incorporating and regulating nonprofits as well as laws regulating fundraising. Each state's requirements for nonprofits may be somewhat different, so it is advisable for the reader to check with his/her state Attorney General's office. If a nonprofit receives a grant or negotiates a contract with a branch of state government, there may be additional reporting requirements by that body. If a nonprofit desires to offer certain types of services or products, it may have to meet state licensing requirements regarding the facility to be used and the staff to be hired. For example, children's homes, day care centers, nursing homes, and other types of care facilities have to be licensed. There are also often requirements regarding staff/client ratios and qualifications of staff.

Local Government

Many counties and municipalities regulate nonprofits through registration, licensing, and zoning laws. For example, a group home may have to pass local zoning requirements as well as state licensing ones. Local governments also often regulate fundraising activities through registration and licensing.

Financial Accounting Standards Board (FASB)

The FASB is responsible for promulgating standards of accounting for private organizations, both for-profit and nonprofit. The standards for nonprofits include: Statement of Financial Accounting Standard *(SFAS) No. 116: Accounting for Contributions Received and Contributions Made; SFAS No. 117: Financial Statements of Not-for-profit Organizations;* and *SFAS No. 124: Accounting for Certain Investments Held by Not-for-profit*

Organizations. These standards will be discussed more fully later in this book.

American Institute of Certified Public Accountants (AICPA)

The AICPA also has standards for nonprofits, especially relating to requirements for audits. This is important since most state laws and funding sources require nonprofits to have an annual audit. The AICPA standards of relevance here are *SOP (Statement of Position) 98–2: Accounting for Joint Activities of Not-for-profit Organizations and State and Local Entities; SOP 98–3: Audits of State, Local Governments, and Not-for-profit Organizations Receiving Federal Awards.* Accounting and financial reporting will be more fully discussed in Chapters Ten, Eleven, and Twelve.

National Accrediting Bodies

Many national organizations such as Family Service of America, Child Welfare League of America, Planned Parenthood of America, United Way of America, YMCA, Boys and Girls Clubs, and so forth, have local affiliates that must meet national standards in order to be recognized as part of the parent organization. These standards include financial management and reporting. Some national organizations have published guidelines for nonprofits. The best known is the *Standards of Accounting and Financial Reporting for Voluntary Health and Welfare Organizations,* first published in 1964 and last updated in 1998. It was a joint effort of the National Health Council, the National Assembly of Health and Human Service Organizations (formerly the National Assembly of National Voluntary Health and Social Welfare Organizations) and the United Way of America. It was one of the first publications to give guidance on fiscal reporting to nonprofit human service organizations.

In addition, some organizations screen nonprofits on certain financial and organizational criteria so that potential donors can be informed about an organization of interest. Both the Philanthropic Advisory Service (PAS) of the Council of Better Business Bureaus and the National Charities Information Bureau have promulgated standards and issue information about charitable nonprofits to the public.

As can be seen by the above discussion, the environment for nonprofits has become increasingly complex. Thus it is important for nonprofit administrators, board, and staff to keep up with the regulatory changes taking place that influence financial management of these organizations.

In this chapter, characteristics of nonprofit human service organizations, as compared to for-profit organizations, were discussed. In addition, the financial management process as a framework for the presentation of topics and materials in this book was discussed.

In this book, methods of nonprofit accounting and reporting, as well as other tools and techniques such as fundraising, grantwriting, and investing will be explained. Tools and techniques needed for efficient management of organizational resources will be described within the context of the ethical and legal requirements that face nonprofits today. Chapters are arranged around the three main aspects of the financial management process—acquisition, disposition, and reporting of resources. The chapters on resource acquisition include planning and budgeting, fundraising, grantwriting, contracts, fees for services, and third-party payments. Those chapters on disposition of resources include topics such as budgeting and internal control, allocation of joint costs, and investments. Chapters on reporting of resources are comprised of the areas of accounting, financial statements, and financial information software, for both reporting as well as fundraising purposes.

REFERENCES

American Institute of Certified Public Accountants. *SOP (Statement of Position) 98–2: Accounting for Joint Activities of Not-for-profit Organizations and State and Local Entities.* New York: Author.

American Institute of Certified Public Accountants. *SOP 98–3: Audits of State, Local Governments, and Not-for-profit Organizations Receiving Federal Awards.* New York: Author.

Anthony, R.N. & Herzlinger, R.E. (1980). *Management Control in Nonprofit Organizations* (Revised ed.). Homewood, IL: Richard D. Irwin.

Financial Accounting Standards Board. (1980). *Objectives of Financial Reporting by Nonbusiness Organizations.* Statement of Financial Reporting Concepts No. 4, Stamford,CT: Author.

Financial Accounting Standards Board. (1993). *Statement of Financial Accounting Standard (SFAS) No. 116: Accounting for Contributions Received and Contributions Made.* Stamford, CT: Author.

Financial Accounting Standards Board. (1993). *Statement of Financial Accounting Standards No. 117: Financial Statements of Not-for-profit Organizations.* Norwalk, CT: author.

Financial Accounting Standards Board. (1994). *Statement of Financial Accounting Standard (SFAS) No. 124: Accounting for Certain Investments Held by Not-for-profit Organizations.* Stamford, CT: Author.

Freeman, R.J. & Shoulders, C.D. (1999). *Governmental and Nonprofit Accounting: Theory and Practice* (6th Ed.). Upper Saddle River, NJ: Prentice-Hall.

Gross, M.J. Jr., Larkin, R.F., Bruttomesso, R.S. & McNally, J.J. (1995). *Financial and*

Accounting Guide for Not-for-profit Organizations (5th ed.). New York: John Wiley & Sons, Inc.

Guidestar. (2000). www.guidestar.com

Kamerman, S. (1983). The new mixed economy of welfare: public and private. *Social Work,* 28(1):5–10.

Langan, J. P. (1998). Understanding nonprofit management. *Association Management,* 50(1):75–76.

National Association of Social Workers. (1999). *Code of Ethics.* Approved by the 1996 Delegate Assembly and Revised by the 1999 Delegate Assembly. Washington, D.C.: Author

National Health Council, the National Assembly of Health and Human Service Organizations & the United Way of America. (1998). *Standards of Accounting and Financial Reporting for Voluntary Health and Welfare Organizations.* New York: National Health Council, Inc.

Office of Management and Budget, *OMB A-122: Cost Principles for Non-Profit Organizations.*

Office of Management and Budget, *OMB A-133: Audits of Institutions of Higher Education and Other Non-Profit Organizations.*

Sarri, R. (1971). Administration in social welfare. *Social Work Yearbook, 16th Edition, Vol. 1.* New York: National Association of Social Workers.

United States Internal Revenue Code, Title 26, Subtitle A, Chapter 1, Subchapter F, Part I, Sec. 501, 2000.

INTERNET RESOURCES

American Institute of Certified Public Accountants (AICPA). http://aicpa.org

Financial Accounting Standards Board. http://www.fasb.org

National Association of Social Workers. http://naswdc.org

U.S. Department of the Treasury, Internal Revenue Service. http://www.irs.gov

U.S. Office of Management and Budget. http://www.omb.gov

II. RESOURCE ACQUISITION

Chapter Three

THE ROLE OF PLANNING IN BUDGETING

After reading this chapter you should be able to:

1. Understand the relationship of planning to the budget process;
2. Understand approaches to the budgeting process;
3. Explain the different types of budgets.

INTRODUCTION

The key to an organization's financial management system is a well thought-out, well-documented plan. An organizational master plan is the guide for the financial plan that will then be developed to implement the organization's long- and short-term goals. A master plan is the result of overall organizational planning and should reflect the mission, goals, and objectives of the organization. While a goal is a broad statement of a desired future state, a *budget* is an expression of a desired future state described in monetary terms.

Budgeting is one of the singular most important activities that takes place in the human service organization. As an activity, budgeting involves planning for the acquisition and allocation of resources for current and future programs. The outcome of the process is one or more budget documents that not only delineate resources assigned to personnel, materials, and programs, but also to a large extent reflect organization goals and priorities. Thus the budget is more than "a plan set forth in financial terms" (Abels & Murphy, 1981, p. 148), it is ". . . a summary of organizational process, policy, and program. It is a statement of goals, priorities, political trade-offs, decisions, authority structures. . ." (Miringoff, 1980, p. 115).

In systems terms, the planning and budgeting process may be viewed as one in which the organization scans its environment, takes in resources in the form of data and information, processes these data, and produces a plan that includes a budget (see Figure 3-1). The information used by the organization may be historical in nature and include such things as past budgets, financial statements, records of client flow, and so forth.

43

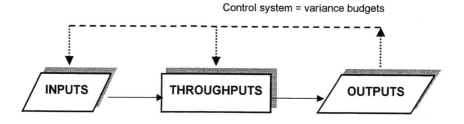

Historical Information:
- Past Budgets
- Financial statements
- Client flow trends
- Volume, revenue, expense trends

Projections:
- Demographic trends
- Economic trends
- Service volume
- Revenues/expenses
- Staff needs

Current Information:
- Unit costs
- Operating expenses-fixed/variable
- Budget variances

Budget Process: Decisions on:
- Structure
- Mission
- Goals
- Long & short-term plans
- Programs
- Services

Budget Documents:
- Annual Budget
- Quarterly/monthly budgets
- Cash flow budgets

Figure 3-1: A Systems View of the Budgeting Process

Data may also include projections of demographic trends, client flow, and future social problems. Current information that may be used by the organization includes figures on operating expenses, unit costs, break-even costs, as well as information on client needs. The organization takes in this information and has to process it in a meaningful way. The planning/budgeting process involves a number of crucial decisions on the part of the organization planning team. Key decisions involve the structure of the planning committee, positions of authority and responsibility, the mission, goals, and objectives of the organization, and the necessary tasks to implement them. Decisions are also involved in developing time frames to complete tasks, and formulate desirable, measurable outcomes. Finally, the outputs of the process may be short-term (up to one year) plans, long-term (3–5 year) plans and the budget documents that accompany them.

At the organizational level, there are a variety of approaches used in the preparation of the budget. Some of the most common approaches to the budgeting process are incremental budgeting, zero-base budgeting, and planning-programming-budgeting.

BUDGETARY PROCESSES

The type of approach used by an organization to develop a budget is sometimes mandated by the major funding source of that organization, or by the organization's board. For example, agency guidelines may specify that zero-based budgeting or some other specific approach will be used. This has implications for both the process and the documents needed. In many other instances, no specific approach is mandated, only forms to be completed as mandated by a funding source. It becomes quite cumbersome for an organization when it must fill out a myriad of different forms for a variety of funding sources. This section will present an overview of the most common types of budgeting processes used by nonprofit organizations today.

Incremental Budgeting

The budgeting process is an opportunity for organization administrators and staff to re-evaluate and re-order goals and priorities, to use the budget as a means of planning, control, and accountability. Unfortunately, many times this opportunity is not taken. Instead, previous years' budgets are looked over, an increase to account for inflation is tacked on to the previous figures, and the budget is re-submitted to funding sources as a reflection of the "status-quo". This is known as the *incremental* approach to budgeting. This approach is also commonly used in the reverse, for budget reductions when necessary. This is known as *decremental* budgeting.

One of the reasons that the incremental approach is so common is that it is so easy to do. It involves very little calculation beyond the initial decision as to what the incremental amount or percentage of increase or decrease should be. Another reason for the persistence of incremental budgeting is that it does not demand analysis of goals or policies (Wildavsky, 1982).

Some problems associated with this incremental approach are related to underlying assumptions regarding the ongoing activities of the organization. The incremental approach, typically involving cost-of-living or some other standardized increase, assumes that the programs and activities in the previous year's budget are essential to the accomplishment of organization goals and should be continued; that they are being performed in an effective, efficient manner; and that they will be cost-effective in the next year (Letzukus, 1982). These assumptions may not necessarily be valid, and they need to be examined.

Zero-Base Budgeting

While incremental budgeting starts with an established base of the previous year's operating levels and seeks to justify changes in the current year, zero-base budgeting (ZBB) attempts to provide some accountability by starting from a base of zero. In ZBB each proposed expenditure must be justified; this encourages the analysis of competing claims on resources and reduces the possibility of continuing obsolete, inefficient programs. ZBB is not new; it has been implemented at the state and federal levels as well as by some voluntary human service agencies. In principle, the ZBB system can be integrated with other ones such as the Planning, Programming, Budgeting System (PPBS) to be discussed below, although it may entail much more paperwork and time than some agencies are willing to spend.

Essentially, the ZBB system is a highly rational approach to planning and budgeting. It forces administrative staff to rationalize the existence and funding level for every program of the organization. It can give decisionmakers a choice of options along with the cost of each option. The ZBB process entails five main stages (Kugajevsky, 1981):

1. **Designating the Decision Units.** A decision unit is a department, program, or some other designated part of an organization that will develop the decision packages. ZBB is output and results oriented, so in choosing the decision units for the decision packages, it is most logical to pick those that can be tied to the organization's mission or long-range objectives. In most cases, these units will be the separate programs that make up the organization's primary activities. An important criterion for choosing a decision unit is that each unit have its own budget and an identifiable manager with authority to establish rules and allocate resources. If these programs have separate budgets, this enables the organization to identify the costs of delivering the specific service by that unit.

2. **Formulating the Decision Packages.** The decision package is the key to ZBB. It identifies "... a discrete activity, function, or operation in a definitive manner for management evaluation and comparison with other activities" (Pyhrr, 1973, p. 6). The decision package is usually

a one-page sheet that lists and describes a program activity in terms of its objectives, methods, alternative methods, consequences of not delivering the service or activity, performance measures and outputs, and cost/benefits. The decision packages may be prepared at three different levels of expenditure: high, medium, and low, so that decision makers can compare outputs and costs at various levels of expenditure (see Table 3-1 for a sample decision package form).

3. **Ranking the Decision Packages.** After formulating the decision packages, they are then ranked in order of perceived importance by the manager or team working on the budget. The ranking process continues as the packages move up the hierarchy of the organization from the project or program level to key administrative staff to board of directors.

4. **Consolidating the Decision Packages.** As the decision packages move through the organization, they are combined and compared with decision packages from other units.

5. **Preparing the Budget.** After decisions have been made as to the most important and necessary activities for the organization, the ZBB

Table 3-1
SAMPLE DECISION PACKAGE

Program: Family Counseling   *Rank:* 1

Purpose/Objective: To provide professional counseling services to families of children at risk of being abused.

Method of Performance: Individual, group, and family counseling on cases referred from Child Welfare and other sources; case management, follow-up and evaluation.

Expected Results: Reduction in the number of children neglected and abused in Metro County.

Consequences of Not Approving: Inadequate provision of services to at-risk families may lead to increase or continuation of current trends in child abuse and neglect.

Work Load Measures	FY 01	FY 02	FY 03
1. Number of children seen	251	265	282
2. Number of groups (includes separate childrens', mothers', and fathers' groups)	20	26	28
Unit Cost of Service	$40	$42	$43
Positions required	10	12	12
Estimated Expenses for Services			
Personnel	$300,000	$320,000	$326,000
Other Expenses	168,000	181,600	185,680
Total Estimated Expenses	$468,000	$501,600	$511,680

decision packages and budgets are then converted to the traditional functional budget

ZBB has been most useful for short-term planning and budgeting. In addition, it has been combined with other systems such as PPBS. Some advantages of ZBB are that it identifies and evaluates alternative costs for a program; it focuses on the high priority goals and objectives of an organization; it also encourages participatory budgeting in that middle managers are able to formulate the initial decision packages. Some disadvantages of ZBB are that it takes a few years for the system to be fully operational; it creates extra paperwork; organization staff may be resistant to changing old budgeting habits; and there may be intangible reasons why old programs or activities are carried over that are difficult to rationalize. Staff, and perhaps board members, who have a vested interest in continuing pet programs will be resistant to ZBB. Even staff without a vested interest in a program may find the ZBB process too time-consuming and disruptive to the organization (Stretch, 1980).

Planning Programming Budgeting System (PPBS)

The Planning Programming Budgeting System (PPBS) process tries to encourage agencies not to think of their programs as ends in themselves. Instead, programs are to be seen as one means of reaching desired goals and objectives chosen from among competing alternative and perhaps equally deserving programs. This competition among alternatives is crucial to testing the effectiveness and efficiency of proposed as well as current programs. The major components in PPBS are (Schultze, 1981, Letzukus, 1982):

1. **Specification and Analysis of Basic Program Objectives for Each Program.** Each program must have clearly delineated, measurable objectives that can be periodically analyzed for current congruence with overall organization goals.

2. **Formulation of Alternative Means to Reach the Desired Objectives.** In systems terms, equifinality means that a goal can be reached in many different ways. Thus, this part of the PPBS process entails a listing of every conceivable possible alternative way of meeting enumerated program objectives.

3. **Analysis of the Output of a Specific Program Based on the Original Objectives.** This means that each alternative program must be examined in terms of how outputs affect organizational objectives. Outputs may be such things as number of clients served, number of hot

meals delivered, number of counseling sessions during a month, or number of public education presentations, depending on what the alternative method of service delivery may be.

4. **Measurement of Total Program Costs,** not just for the year under analysis, but projecting several years into the future. For example, even though the initial or current costs of a project or program may be calculated to be low, that does not mean that future costs may be so. Therefore, projection of costs must include possible expansion of staff and/or space, inflation rates, increased costs, and so forth.

5. **Analysis of Alternatives,** with a focus on which will be the most effective in achieving the stated objectives *for the least cost.* This last step involves cost-benefits analysis as a basis for decision-making on programs that will be incorporated into a final organization budget.

6. **Preparation of a Functional Budget** that ties program costs to specific line item expenses.

PPBS is a budgeting system that relies heavily on central coordination; this is probably why it was tried in the federal government. But as originally formulated, it was not very workable in the nonprofit sector because it did not take into account the unique nature of nonprofit organizational relationships in which there is a clear delineation between budgeting and allocating. That is, the federal government can appropriate funds through tax levies to pay for its planned programs. Nonprofits cannot appropriate monies from outside sources. Other criticisms of PPBS are that it concentrates too much on ends rather than means; that it depends too much on economic and "scientific" rationality and has little recognition of the fact that budgeting is a political process that needs organizational consensus; and that it relies too much on the centralization of decisionmaking. Further, in the voluntary sector there is some autonomy of human service organizations from their allocation sources (United Way, 1975). Therefore, the allocation source may have little control over individual organization goals.

PPBS was formulated to be a more rational approach to budgeting than the incremental approach. In actuality, it lies somewhere between incremental budgeting and zero-base budgeting. There are three main differences between PPBS and ZBB. First of all, in PPBS there is no annual review of all ongoing programs; usually there is a review of all new programs and some selected ongoing ones. Secondly, there is no priority ranking for all programs and activities in PPBS as there is in ZBB. Thirdly, PPBS does not start each budget for ongoing programs with a base of zero. In other ways, they are very similar. That is, they try to tie programs to objectives, and use cost-benefits analysis to decide on alternative means.

This text will utilize a model developed by the United Way of America and called the Program-Planning and Budgeting Cycle. Program-Planning and Budgeting (PPB) is geared to the unique characteristics of the human service organization's budgeting process. In this model, adapted from the United Way, the place of budgeting may clearly be seen (See Figure 3-2). That is, it is an integral part of the planning process, in which programs are tied to organization goals and objectives,

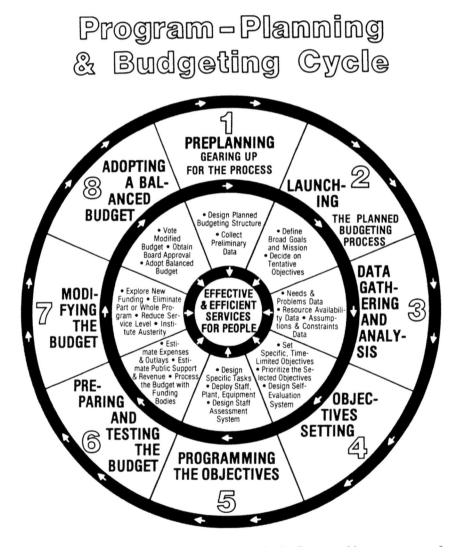

Figure 3-2: Program-Planning and Budgeting Cycle. Reprinted by permission of United Way of America, Inc.

and revenues and expenses are tied to specific programs. We shall discuss the planning aspects of the process here and leave budgeting specifics to the next chapter. The Program-Planning and Budgeting Cycle has the following components (United Way, 1975):

PLANNING

The first part of the PPB process entails the resolution of a number of issues for the organization that revolve around organizational structure and assessment. In this phase, the organization must make sure that it has a structure in place and the necessary data to enable it to carry out its planning and budgeting functions. This involves designing or using a planned budgeting structure, an analysis of organizational capability, and defining mission, goals, and objectives.

Designing Planned Budgeting Structure

Designing a budgeting structure is really part of designing a total financial management information system. This involves having an organizational structure with clear lines of authority and responsibility, one that is flexible enough to allow participatory planning, decision-making, and evaluation. At this early stage some crucial decisions have to be made about who will be responsible for budgeting. There are three main approaches to the budgeting process: the top-down approach, the bottom-up approach, and the goals down, plans up approach.

The Top-Down Approach

In the top-down approach, the development of the budget is done by the administrative staff and the organization's board. The budget is then presented to the rest of the human service staff as the plan for next year. In this approach, lower-level staff have no input into the budgeting process. One problem that may arise with this type of approach is that staff who have no input may feel less investment in working toward attaining the goals reflected in the budget. In many instances, they have no idea what is even in the budget or what items have been budgeted.

The Bottom-Up Approach

In the bottom-up approach, all units of the organization prepare their own plans, goals and budgets based on their knowledge of the capability of the unit and the needs of the organization. For example, program staff of each program may set goals and objectives in terms of number of units of service they plan to deliver in the forthcoming year and how much it may cost. These departmental budgets may then be grouped into a total agency budget to be submitted to the board and funding sources for approval. "Bottom-up planning is most often found in collegial organizations and smaller organizations" (Kotler & Andreason, 1997, p. 263).

Goals Down-Plans Up Approach

In this approach, an organization's goals and requirements are formulated by top management. Then each unit of the organization is responsible for developing plans to reach these goals (Kotler & Andreasen, 1997). The process usually begins with the issuance of general budget guidelines that have been formulated by top management, a budget committee or the funding source. The budget committee may consist of board members, administration, and directors of various programs or units. The guidelines may include organization goals, available resources, projected needs, and similar information. Once the information is received, the individuals who are responsible for achieving the desired goals formulate appropriate budgets for their programs or units. Individual budgets are then grouped together and sent up to top management and the budget committee. Negotiations take place, revisions are made, and the total budget package is eventually completed. As is true with the bottom-up approach, ultimate direction is still from the top, but there are some advantages to this more participatory method. For example, in the bottom-up approach, since the budget is constructed by employees who are intimately familiar with the workings in their departments, the budget figures that are derived will probably be more realistic and accurate. Also, if employees have an opportunity to present their views in an atmosphere in which their views are sincerely respected, this can enhance employee morale and job satisfaction.

Organizational Analysis

At this beginning stage of the process, the organization must collect some preliminary data for planning purposes. Types of data the organization board and staff are interested in here do not have to do with clients, but with the organization itself. The organization needs to step back figuratively and ask, where are we and where do we want to be going? What kind of image do we want our organization to have? What kinds of needs can the organization fill? This stage also involves gathering of data regarding available organization resources and current beneficiaries of organization programs. It also may involve some analysis as to the situation of the organization vis-a-vis other significant forces in its environment such as community needs, resources, and competing organizations.

Once the planning structure is in place and preliminary organizational analysis is completed, the organization can now move to the actual planning phase of the process.

Defining Broad Goals and Mission

As stated previously, defining mission and goals is what every new organization must do. After a period of time, many agencies tend to take these goal statements as enduring givens and begin to view them unquestioningly. However, agency administrators should never take for granted that there is an implicit consensus among staff regarding organization goals. Even in the same organization, there may be a wide divergence of opinion regarding the perceived and the preferred goals of an organization by staff and board members. Even if there is consensus to some extent, the actual operationalized goals may be very different than the stated goals. This is the phenomenon known as goal displacement, in which the organization moves into tangential areas in its push for homeostasis and a steady state. For example, an agency originally established as a family counseling center may move into nursing home care as a means of increasing revenue as there is more certainty of funding. Therefore, a periodic reassessment, perhaps every three to five years or so, is necessary for organizations (see Table 3-2).

How then does an organization define or re-evaluate its broad goals and mission? A good place to start is a board/staff brainstorming ses-

Table 3-2
TIME LINE FOR PLANNING/
BUDGETING PROCESS

Activity	Frequency of Activity
Planning	3–5 years
Programming	1–3 years
Budgeting:	
Budget Development	Yearly
Budgetary Control	Monthly/Quarterly

sion in which everyone is free to present ideas for discussion and re-view. The basic ground rule for a productive brainstorming session is that there be no censoring or negative/positive value attached to any ideas or statements. Censoring obviously inhibits creative thinking. Af-ter all the ideas are looked at and discussed, they may then be looked at for feasibility and matched with the needs data previously gathered. Organizational planners must ask: What is the need? What other group or organization is trying to deal with this problem? Have new problems arisen that our organization has the capability to address? Are these new goals congruent with our original mission? After a consensus has been reached, goals and mission must be voted on by the board for ap-proval. This is the most democratic, participatory approach to goal-set-ting in that the board has legal responsibility for the organization, but staff must feel that they have input into the goals set for the organiza-tion as they are necessarily involved in their implementation. This is in contrast to the top-down method in which the board of directors make these decisions and pass them along to the staff for implementation. Ac-tually, the board of the organization needs staff input, at least in terms of data, in order to make informed judgments regarding the direction of the organization.

Developing Tentative Objectives

Whereas *goals* are broad statements of desired future states, *objectives* are specific, measurable, time-limited statements that describe means to reach the goals.

Example: "The mission of this organization is to enhance the quality of life for minority youth and their families".

Goal 1: To encourage minority youth to finish school.

Objectives:

1. To provide 5 remedial counselors and tutors for minority youths in academic difficulty this year.

2. To provide 3 bilingual counselors to act as role models and give guidance to high school minority youth in one high school this year.

3. To train 10 peer counselors to help these youth with school and personal problems.

Goal 2: To facilitate the entry of minority youth into the world of work.

Objectives:

1. To develop one-day workshops for minority youths on job searching skills to be offered on ten Saturdays this year.

2. To develop a network of 20–30 employers who will serve as mentors to minority youth entering the business world.

Objectives formulated at this time are tentative because they need to be tested against the data gathering that the organization will do in the next step of the process, and perhaps revised based on the information obtained.

Gathering and Analyzing Data

At this stage, staff will be involved in the gathering and analysis of data that directly relate to the organization's programs. There are three types of data that the organization will need in order to make decisions regarding the direction that the organization is to take.

Needs and Problems Data

These data are important in helping the organization determine if the stated problem is really as severe as perceived by staff or persons in the community. Gathering these data essentially involves a needs assessment as to the extent, level, and severity of a particular problem. Data to be gathered are usually available from a variety of sources; the organization does not necessarily have to do a major survey. The local United Way may have its own community needs assessment study available. Community planning agencies, other human service allocation agencies, and counties or municipalities may have completed recent needs assessments for their own planning purposes. Other human service agencies may have completed a recent study. There may be a local college or university that has researchers interested in the problem at hand. There are a myriad of governmental data available through government offices or college and public libraries.

Resource Availability Data

The purpose of gathering these type of data is to give the organization an idea of the resources available to alleviate the problem. The organization is interested in what groups, organizations, or individuals are now or would be available for material or other types of support. In the preliminary evaluation of possible funding sources, the organization must also consider the positive and negative consequences of accepting resources from a particular organization. It must also consider whether sufficient community resources are already being mobilized to address the problem, perhaps lessening the likelihood that the organization will receive sanction and support for its activities in the area.

Assumptions and Constraints Data

Assumptions are beliefs that are used as the bases for problem formulation and program planning. They are not necessarily based on empirical evidence, but are usually the result of experience and informed hunches combined with the empirical data that the organization has collected. In this case, the assumptions are related to social, political, and economic activities or events that may affect the organization and its plans. For example, in targeting high school dropouts as a focus of intervention the organization will have examined trend data and other information. Based on its findings, the organization may assume that the trend will continue. In other cases, given a political climate in Washington, an organization may assume that present trends in funding of social programs will continue.

Constraints are external environmental conditions that may inhibit the organization in the accomplishment of its goals. Constraints may also be of a social, political, or economic nature. For example, social values regarding the targeted problem may so greatly interfere with the planned program as to make it almost impossible to carry out. This usually applies to social problems that are highly controversial and where there are wide divergence of views, for example, abortion, or sex education. If the targeted problem becomes highly politicized, there may be a dearth of available resources for the organization. This is not to say that a human service organization should avoid controversial social problems, but rather that it should be quite clear as to the constraints that may impact on its attempts to deal with certain problems.

Setting Objectives

Once organizational goals have been decided, needs and available resources ascertained, the planning group should now turn to its tentative objectives and reexamine them in the light of the new information obtained. Objectives should be examined for feasibility, that is, can the organization address this problem given the resources available to it? Can it gather enough community support to enable it to pursue its tentative objective(s)? Given that different members of the planning/budgeting team may prefer different approaches to the problem, some consensus must be reached toward prioritizing the most feasible objectives.

It was stated previously that objectives should be specific and measurable. After the final objectives have been agreed upon, objectives should then also be placed within some time frame. Time frames should be realistic and broken down into units of time, such as three to six month segments, for purposes of evaluation and feedback. An organization cannot do everything, therefore it must be able to prioritize its objectives so that the most important will be given top priority.

An important ingredient in the setting of objectives is that there be some sort of built-in monitoring or feedback mechanism to enable the organization to evaluate the efficiency and effectiveness of its efforts. There are a variety of evaluation methods; using financial data is one way to evaluate program efforts that will be discussed later in this book.

PROGRAMMING

In the programming phase of the planning/budgeting process, specific tasks and human and material resources are allocated to programs associated with the objectives. Thus specific tasks need to be defined, specific staff, equipment, and physical plant need to be assigned to the tasks, and an evaluation system should be designed.

Designing specific tasks essentially breaks objectives down into units of work. For example, an objective such as, "To provide temporary shelter and food to homeless persons" involves a multitude of tasks. Some such pertinent tasks would be selecting a site, checking city zoning laws, obtaining necessary city licenses, finding equipment, and so on. After listing all the tasks that need to be undertaken with a specific objective, staff, physical plant, equipment, and measurable outcomes should be listed. For example, the organization could devise a form similar to the one in Table 3-3 for planning purposes. This form lists the necessary tasks to be performed to meet a given objective, the staff required for the completion of the task, equipment needed, any physical plant requirements (e.g., install a kitchen, or acquire a building with a kitchen) and the anticipated cost of the equipment, plant, and staff. The last stage of the programming process involves some sort of evaluation system for staff performance of their duties.

Table 3-3
PROGRAM PLANNING CHART

Objective (List as complete sentence):

Tasks to reach objective	No./Type of Staff Required	Staff Cost	Equipment Required	Equipment Cost	Plant Required	Plant Cost	Total Cost
1.							
2.							
3. etc.							

BUDGETING

Now that the organization has defined its goals and objectives, ascertained community needs, and programmed objectives into meaningful, measurable programs and tasks, it is ready to prepare its budget. The actual budgeting process itself will be discussed fully in the next chapter, but first one must be acquainted with the types of budget documents that are the products of this process. While it is difficult to separate the budgeting process from the documents that go with it, this has been done here for ease of discussion. Different types of budget documents are used for a variety of reasons.

BUDGETARY DOCUMENTS

There are a variety of budgetary documents and formats that an organization may use. Choice of the appropriate documents is dependent on the type of process used by the organization, its own internal needs, and the requirements of funding sources. Often, a funding source mandates the documents or forms that must be submitted by those organizations receiving its funding. An organization should try to set up a budgeting system in such a way that its internal budget forms closely conform to those of its major funder; this facilitates the transfer of information from one set of forms to another. This may not always be possible, especially if the organization receives large sums from a variety of different sources, all with their own required budget formats. In this case, the organization should devise internal forms that are most convenient for its own internal operations. The most common budget formats are the line-item budget, the program budget, and the functional budget.

Line-Item Budgets

Line item budgets are simply lists by "object category" (for example payroll expense, supplies expense) of various components of the budget (see Table 3-4). As you can see from the budget of the Mythical Human Services Agency, Inc., all categories of revenue and expense are simply listed. One can see how much salaries and fringes, or supplies, cost the organization, but if the organization has more than one program it would be impossible to say how much of the total resources or of any resource category was allocated to any one program. Thus, they give incomplete information to the reader. This type of budget is the oldest and simplest, and may still be found in some small single program agencies or within a given program. From an organizational perspective, however, it is really an obsolete method of budgeting because the simplistic format does not give necessary information needed for decision-making and planning.

There are some advantages to the line item budget, however. Because this format allows the manager to readily see if any budget category is over- or under-expended, it allows a tight control over line-item categories. Thus the line-item format is useful for managerial fiscal control (Stretch, 1980).

Table 3-4
LINE ITEM BUDGET
Human Services Organization, Inc.
Line-Item Budget for Fiscal Year 2010

Line-Item Category	Budgeted Amount
Public Support and Revenue	
Contributions	$ 5,000
Allocations	100,000
Grants	150,000
Program Fees	20,000
Total Public Support and Revenue	$275,000
Expenses	
Salaries	$204,000
Employee Benefits	40,500
Occupancy	15,000
Supplies	6,000
Equipment	7,500
Travel	2,000
Total Expenses	$275,000

Program Budgets

A program budget lists revenues and expenses as broad categories by program only. This makes it impossible to know specific line-item costs associated with any program. That is, if only the total amount of expenses are listed for Program A, one cannot know how much was spent for salaries or supplies by Program A as opposed to Program B. This type of budget may often be seen in organization annual reports, newsletters, and brochures, although small agencies with only one or two programs may use it. It is a way of giving some information about the organization without divulging other information that the organization considers confidential (see Table 3-5 for an example of a program budget). You will notice that in the program budget there are two main categories óf program or service: program services and support services (usually called Administrative and General). The FASB's Statement of Financial Accounting Standards (SFAS) No. 117, *Financial Statements of Not-for-profit Organizations,* defines these categories in this way:

> *Program Services:* are activities that result in goods and services being distributed to beneficiaries, customers, or members that fulfill the purposes or mission for which the organization exists. *Support Services:* are all activities of a not-for-profit other than program services (SFAS-117, 1993, par. 27 and 28).

Support services may be further delineated into management and general activities such as business management, budgeting, record-

Table 3-5
PROGRAM BUDGET

Human Services Organization, Inc.
Program Budget for Fiscal Year 2010

Program Category	Budgeted Amount
Public Support and Revenue	
Contributions	$ 5,000
Allocations	100,000
Grants	150,000
Program Fees	20,000
Total Public Support and Revenue	$275,000
Expenses	
Counseling	$179,000
Family Life Education	26,000
Management and General	68,000
Fundraising	2,000
Total Expenses	$275,000

keeping, fund-raising activities, and membership development activities.

Functional Budgets

Functional budgets are also known as performance budgets and are used in PPBS and PPB. Early users of this type of budgeting were some federal departments in the 1930's. In this approach to budgeting, "objects of expenditure are viewed in relation to the programs they serve" (Swan, 1983, p. 23). As can be seen from the table below, the functional budget combines features of the line item budget with the program budget (see Table 3-6). On the left-hand column are listed the object categories. Across the top are the program categories. Thus the functional budget lists all categories of revenue and expense by program so that the reader can readily see how much is anticipated to be spent and received by each program as well as how much is to be spent by each category. The same program categories that are used in the program budget are also used in the functional budget.

One advantage of this format is that it does focus attention on costs per program, which the line-item approach does not. It also shows total costs for program and support services. The functional budget is the format required by most major funding sources as well as the *Standards*.

Table 3-6
FUNCTIONAL BUDGET

Human Services Organization, Inc.
Functional Budget for Fiscal Year 2010

	Counseling	Family Life Education	Mgt and General	Fund-raising	Totals
Public Support and Revenue					
Contributions	$ 2,500	$ 500	–	$ 2,000	$ 5,000
Allocations	60,500	14,500	$25,000	–	100,000
Grants	99,000	8,000	43,000	–	150,000
Program Fees	17,000	3,000	–	–	20,000
Total Public Support and Revenue	$179,000	$26,000	$68,000	$ 2,000	$275,000
Expenses					
Salaries	$136,000	$18,000	$50,000	–	$204,000
Employee Benefits	27,500	3,000	10,000	–	40,500
Occupancy	9,000	3,000	3,000	–	15,000
Supplies	2,000	2,000	1,000	$ 1,000	6,000
Equipment	3,500		4,000		7,500
Travel	1,000	–	–	1,000	2,000
Total Expenses	$179,000	$26,000	$68,000	$ 2,000	$275,000

Also, this format is very similar to one of the required financial statements of nonprofits, the *Statement of Functional Expenses*. The difference between the two is that the functional budget shows projected expenditures while the Statement of Functional Expenses shows actual expenditures.

This chapter presented the role of planning in the budgeting process. The next chapter will discuss the actual mechanics of assembling the various portions of the operating, or master, budget.

REFERENCES

Abels, P. & Murphy, M.J. (1981). *Human Services Administration: A Normative Systems Approach.* Englewood Cliffs, NJ: Prentice-Hall, Inc.

Financial Accounting Standards Board (1993). Statement of Financial Accounting *Standard (SFAS) No. 117: Financial Statements of Not-for-profit Organizations.* Stamford, CT: Author.

Kotler, P. & Andreason, A.R. (1997). *Strategic Marketing for Nonprofit Organizations.* Englewood Cliffs, NJ: Prentice-Hall, Inc.

Kugajevsky, V. (1981). Zero-base budgeting, pp. 177–186 in M.L. Gruber (Ed.), *Management Systems in the Human Services.* Philadelphia: Temple University Press.

Letzukus, W.C. (1982). Zero-base budgeting and planning-programming budgeting: what are the conceptual differences? Pp. 17–25 in R.J. Vargo & P.A. Dierks, *Readings and Cases in Governmental and Nonprofit Accounting.* Houston: Dame Publications.

Miringoff, M.L. (1980). *Management in Human Service Organizations.* New York: Macmillan.

Pyhrr, P. A. (1973). *Zero-Base Budgeting.* New York: John Wiley.

Schultze, C.L. (1981). What program budgeting is, pp. 23–32 in M.L. Gruber (Ed.), *Management Systems in the Human Services.* Philadelphia: Temple University Press.

Stretch, J.J. (1980). What human services managers need to know about basic budgeting strategies. *Administration in Social Work,* 4(1):87–98.

Swan, W.K (1983). Theoretical debates applicable to budgeting, pp. 3–59 in J. Rabin & T.D. Lynch (Eds.). *Handbook on Budgeting and Financial Management.* New York: Marcel Dekker.

United Way of America (1975). *Budgeting: A Guide for United Ways and Not-for-profit Human Services Organizations.* Alexandria, VA: Author.

Wildavsky, A. (1982). A budget for all seasons? Why the traditional budget lasts, pp. 4–12 in R.J. Vargo & P.A. Dierks, *Readings and Cases in Governmental and Nonprofit Accounting.* Houston: Dame Publications.

INTERNET RESOURCES

United Way of America. http://www.uwoa.org

Management Assistance Program for Nonprofits. http://mapfornonprofits.org

Chapter Four

BUDGETING

After reading this chapter you should be able to:

1. Understand the components of an agency budget;
2. Know factors in forecasting expenses and revenues;
3. Understand ways of allocating costs;
4. Present a proposed budget to a board or funding source.

INTRODUCTION

The crucial role of organizational planning was discussed in the last chapter. The end result of the planning process includes a budget that delineates organizational goals and objectives in financial terms. "Budget allocations have crucial, if not overriding significance for the implementation of strategies and plans" (Bryson, 1995, p. 170). If agency staff and board take advantage of the opportunity offered by the budgeting cycle, they will see that incorporating periodic organizational reviews into this process will help keep their organization at the forefront in the nonprofit community. Thus the budgeting process and the resulting budget documents can serve a number of useful functions for an agency. Some of these functions include clarification, coordination, communication, and control (Powell, 1980; Stretch, 1979).

FUNCTIONS OF THE BUDGET

Clarification

The budget can aid in clarification of goals. When a new agency is formed, its board of directors writes up a charter that states its mission and goals. However, the human service agency is a dynamic, open system—its mission and goals may change over time. A periodic re-evaluation is healthy for the agency. If the budget is used as part of a larger planning process in which the agency periodically reassesses its direction, clarification of underlying assumptions about the mission and goals of the agency can be useful to board, staff, clients, and the community at large.

Coordination

The budget can aid in coordination of activities. In the process of planning, programming, and preparing the budget, overlapping or competing activities of various departments may be highlighted and corrective actions taken. In programming for the delivery of planned services, the process may point to areas where reorganization of units may need to take place, or where clarification of authority and responsibility of different departments is needed. In addition, because of the typically tight budgets of most human service agencies, coordination of units and departments is needed in order to use agency resources most efficiently. The budgeting process therefore facilitates examination of alternative means of increasing communication.

Communication

The budget can aid in communication of agency objectives. The budget is a reflection of organizational goals, objectives, and priorities stated in monetary terms and thus communicates to staff and funders alike the planned direction of the agency within a specified period of time. The goals of the organization as reflected in the budget can also be communicated to the community at large. This is usually done through media such as annual reports and brochures that may use simple charts to illustrate how the organization has allocated and utilized its funds.

Control

The budget can aid in control. Control involves feedback mechanisms to ensure that the organization is proceeding with the completion of its stated goals and objectives. Goal implementation can be monitored in numerous ways, and budgeting is a very effective, measurable means of doing this. Control may also involve the setting up of monitoring systems to ensure that the agency is fulfilling its fiscal and stewardship responsibilities. This aspect of budgeting will be discussed more fully in the chapter on internal control.

There are two major aspects of budgeting with which we are concerned: budgetary processes and budgetary documents. A budget process and the documents generated by it are many times dictated by outside funding sources, as was discussed in the preceding chapter. As a process, budgeting is very much a political activity, both internally and externally.

Budget Processes

In the broadest sense, the direction and re-direction of resources is inherently political. More specifically, many human service organizations receive some funding from either federal or state agencies. This means that they are to some extent dependent on political decisions far removed from their community as to the nature, level, and extent of future funding that they may receive. Decisions made in Congress and state capitals impact greatly on human service organizations.

Many nonprofits are also dependent on the United Way or other federated allocation agencies such as Catholic Charities, or the Jewish Federation for funds. The decision-making that goes on at the community level of these funding agencies involves community politics and the values, needs, and priorities set by the local funding source. Politics and trade-offs may be involved in the negotiating that goes on between the community or federated funding source and each organization during budget hearings. And finally, there are internal politics that influence budget making because of the differing views, goals, values, and needs of individual board and staff members.

Budget Documents

There are essentially two types of organizational budgets: the operating (or master) budget and the capital budget. An organization may also prepare other types of budgets during the year, such as a fundraising budget and a grant proposal budget. The operating budget covers the agency's planned operations for usually a one-year period, sometimes more if it is part of a long-range plan. It is known as the operating budget because it specifies, in fiscal terms, plans for operations. The operating budget is made up of a number of other budgets (or schedules) including:

- a service volume/activity budget
- an expense budget
- a salary and wages expense budget
- a public support and revenue budget
- a cash flow budget
- budgeted financial statements.

The capital budget, on the other hand, is a plan for the future acquisition of major capital assets such as land, buildings, and large equipment. In this chapter, the focus will be on the operating or master budget. Budgets for grant proposals and fundraising will be discussed in those respective chapters. The capital budget will not be discussed here.

PREPARING THE BUDGET

Preparing the operating (master) budget involves a number of steps that basically entail the preparation of the separate budgets mentioned above. The steps to preparing the budget include: 1) developing a budget calendar; 2) forecasting service volume; 3) developing expense budgets; 4) estimating public support and revenue; 5) estimating cash flow; 6) modifying and adopting a balanced budget; 7) preparing budgeted financial statements (NIMH, 1983; Hartman, 1996).

Developing a Budget Calendar

After the planning and programming phases have been completed, the organizational planning team is ready to move to the budgeting phase. The planning team must now work with the budget committee to make sure that the budget reflects the organization's purposes. However, this phase is very time-sensitive as the organization has deadlines it must meet in submission of its budget requests to its various funding sources. Therefore, a budget calendar with deadlines, tasks, and responsible parties is often helpful in this regard (see Table 4-1 for an example of a budget calendar).

As can be seen in Table 4-1, a budget calendar delineates major tasks that must be completed by designated deadlines. The calendar may also list person(s) or departments responsible for the planning tasks. Such a calendar is extremely useful in ensuring that budget assignments are completed in a timely manner and should be distributed to all persons involved in the budget process.

Forecasting Service Volume

The first step in preparing the operating budget involves forecasting service volume, that is numbers of clients to be seen or units of service

Table 4-1
SAMPLE BUDGET CALENDAR
Human Services Organization, Inc.
Budget Calendar

Task	Date Due	Responsibility
Prepare draft budgets	May 1	Program Directors
Review requests	June 1	Executive Director
Prepare budget	June 15	Accountant, Exec. Dir.
Review budget	July 1	Board Budget Committee
Modify budget	August 1	Accountant, Exec. Dir.
Submit budget to funding source	September 1	Executive Director

to be delivered. For example, how many clients are desired or estimated to be seen by the agency's counseling program? Or how many units of service are to be delivered by the counseling program? In developing the forecast of service units to be delivered or numbers of clients to be served, a number of factors have to be taken into account. Some of these factors and their attendant issues are:

Past Levels of Service

How many units of service have been delivered, or clients served, within the past 2–5 years? What is the average number?

Trends in Service Levels

How have service levels changed in the past 2–5 years? Has there been an increase/decrease in levels of service? Has the agency had to add waiting lists or have demand for services declined?

Demographic Trends

How has the community served by the agency changed? Are neighborhoods "graying," or are seniors moving away? Are there new immigrant or ethnic groups with specific service needs moving into the community? What new social problems have come to public awareness?

Public Policies That Mandate Type or Content of Services

Has new legislation enabled response to service needs the organization is equipped to meet? If so, how best can the agency provide access to its services? What funding is available to pay for these increased services? Conversely, has funding dried up for a long-standing service offered by our agency? If so, how will the organization be able to provide the same level of service as previously?

Seasonal Patterns of Service Usage

Is there a pattern to service usage? Do more clients access services in the warmer months, at certain times of the year or month or even day? If so, these seasonal fluctuations can affect staff scheduling and even cash flow.

Public Attitudes

How do our consumers and the community view our services at large? If our services or the clients we serve are controversial or viewed negatively, will we have difficulty receiving continued funding for our programs?

Changes in Funding Patterns

What sorts of changes have occurred in funding for our programs? Are third-party payers (for example, Medicaid or managed care companies) paying less for the same services?

From information such as the above, one can try to extrapolate the coming year's volume of service. For example, if we see a trend of a 10% increase in service units provided in the last three to five years, we could assume a continuation of this trend (see Table 4-2 below for an example of a service volume forecast).

As can be seen from Table 4-2, in this organization projected volume is based on units of service for each month and totaled for the quarter. If a program has more than one type of unit of service, service volume charts should be developed for each one. However, it should be remembered that forecasts are just that—one's best professional estimates of what will happen. We cannot anticipate all possible future conditions

Table 4-2
PROJECTED SERVICE VOLUME/ACTIVITY
Human Services Organization, Inc.
Projected Units of Service for Program A for 1st Quarter

	July	Aug	Sept	Quarter Total
	Quarter			
Unit of Service	No. of Units	No. of Units	No. of Units	No. of Units
Hour of Therapy	250	255	260	765

and we often have no control over unforeseen circumstances that may arise.

In trying to forecast service volume for a new service that has not been previously provided, the agency can:

- set a goal of service volume based on what its resources are,
- ascertain the staff/client ratio indicated for the type of service to be provided,
- determine the likelihood that the number of service units targeted are feasible for the agency and can be delivered if funded, and
- take into account need for the service based on projections from community needs assessments, if available.

Developing Expense Budgets

After service volume has been estimated, the agency must next estimate the cost of providing each service by developing an expense budget and a salary expense budget. The salary budget lists all personnel salaries, fringe benefits, and taxes associated with paying staff. The expense budget lists all other non-salary expenses expected to be incurred in the operations of the agency and its various programs.

The Expense Budget

The expense budget reflects how money is to be allocated within the organization and its various units by focusing on operating, administrative, and other costs. There are somewhat different approaches to developing expense budgets depending on whether the budget is for a new or ongoing program. Some factors that need to be considered for an ongoing program are:

Past Usage

Some analysis of past usage of expense items, for example supplies, may indicate not only trends in use but fluctuations due to client volume. Is the organization using more of some types of items and less of another? Often agencies have no control system to monitor usage until an item is in low supply or consumed. But periodic inventory and perusal of supply expenditures will help in ascertaining usage trends (see Chapter Eight on "Internal Control").

Prevailing Prices

Prices for supplies and equipment can be ascertained from suppliers' catalogs. Nonprofits do not usually pay sales taxes on the items they purchase. In addition, a regular supplier often offers discounted prices to nonprofits.

Need for Items

The need for new or additional equipment or supplies should have been determined during the organizational planning and programming phases. At this point, a dollar amount needs to be attached to each item on the list of needed additional supplies or equipment.

Availability of Items

At times, due to obsolescence or material shortages, some expense items commonly used by the organization become difficult to obtain or even too expensive to obtain. As part of the planning and budgeting phases, search for such expense items from other sources needs to occur. A periodic review of prices and comparison shopping needs to take place because the agency may find a comparable item at a lower price or with better credit terms.

Age of Equipment

Age of equipment is related to usage and availability. Some factors often considered with equipment costs include repair costs, maintenance costs, and replacement costs. As equipment ages, it is often cheaper to replace it than to continue to pay maintenance and repair costs. Therefore, maintenance costs, including maintenance contracts and repair costs should be compared to the cost of new equipment.

Type of Expense

In budgeting, the expenses to be incurred should be identified and analyzed as to how they will vary according to an anticipated level of service. There are three main categories of expenses that need to examined in preparing the expense budget: *variable expenses, fixed expenses, and mixed expenses.*

Variable Expenses: Variable expenses are those that vary in direct relation to the volume of service. That is, the more services that are provided or the more clients that are seen, the more this expense will rise. For example, the cost of gasoline used in an agency van, or by case-

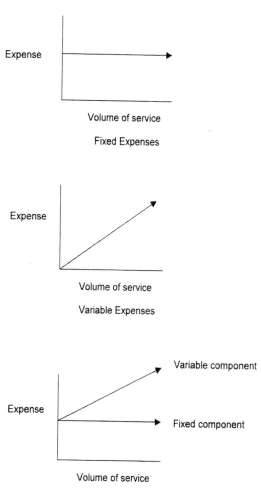

Figure 4-1: Types of Expenses

workers for home visits, varies in direct relation to the number of miles driven to provide agency services (see Figure 4-1).

Fixed Expenses: Fixed expenses, on the other hand, remain constant no matter how much volume of service is provided. For example, leasing of a building, vans, autos and some other equipment will be the same whether the organization sees 20 clients or 200 clients.

Semivariable or Mixed Expense: Semivariable or mixed expenses are those that have both a fixed and variable component. For example, there is a basic (fixed) monthly charge for utility services such as telephone, gas, and electric. If more than a certain amount is used, additional (variable) charges are assessed to the consumer.

Understanding the nature of an expense and its relationship to service volume is important in developing the expense budget. Past records of expenses and service levels will help the organization determine to what extent an expense may vary. If the agency is planning a new program for which it has no data, it must look to related programs or rely on the advice of its accountant for this determination. Another aspect of decision-making regarding costs involves deciding how to allocate expenses among the organization's various programs.

Unit Costs

There are a number of different techniques that have been developed to calculate the costs of human services programs. These costing methods differ in three main ways: 1) in addressing the question of who incurs the cost; 2) in addressing the object of the cost analysis; and 3) in the methodology used to calculate the costs (Gross, 1980). In terms of who incurs the cost, it may be the client, it may be a third party such as a federal or state organization or an insurance plan, or it may be a human service organization which tries to recoup its costs through public donations and allocations from community allocation agencies.

The object of the cost analysis may be the client, such as numbers of clients served, or it may be some other unit of measurement such as hours of service delivered, or number of meals served and so forth. Moreover, the methodology used to calculate the costs may vary tremendously, but tends to be related to the unit of analysis chosen.

The most common type of costing technique is related to costs incurred by the organization in delivering its services. Two common methodological approaches to ascertaining costs incurred by the organization are: unit costing and break-even analysis. Break-even analysis will be discussed in Chapter Seven.

The focus of unit costing is the cost of providing one unit of service (however defined). Defining a unit of service is based on the types of service offered by the organization, for example, if an organization offered counseling services, public education workshops, home help services and hot meals, then its units of service might be defined as one hour of counseling, one hour of public education, one hour of home help, and one hot meal.

"Five types of units of service have been conceptualized and defined:

(1) a *time unit,* such as one hour of counseling equals one unit, or one child-care day equals one unit;

(2) an *episodic unit,* such as one referral equals one unit, or one one-way trip equals one unit;

(3) a *material unit,* such as one article of clothing equals one unit, or one food basket equals one unit;

(4) an *output or service process completion unit,* such as one client completing the full 10-week training program equals one unit

(5) an *outcome unit,* such as one client demonstrating an improvement of at least 2 points on a 10-point depression scale equals one unit, or one client remaining drug free for at least one year equals one unit" (Bowers & Bowers, 1976; Kettner et al, 1990, p. 126).

The cost of a unit of service is found by dividing the total amount spent by a cost center or program by the number of units of service provided. To find total program costs, one must look at the Statement of Functional Expenses for the last year. Then one must also obtain the program count from program records. For example, in the example of the program in Table 4-2, if the cost of delivering therapy in the first quarter was $45,874 and 765 units of service were provided during that quarter, then the unit cost would be approximately $60 (see Table 4-3).

If an organization knows its unit costs, its projected volume can then be revised to show these costs in a table such as the in Table 4-4. As can be seen in this Table, units of service vary month to month. The organization can multiply its unit cost by the number of units of service for each month in order to obtain its projected service volume/activity budget. In this case, its unit of service was an hour of therapy and its cost per unit was $60 which can be multiplied by each monthly projected service unit.

Table 4-3
UNIT COSTING

	Formula	Source of data
Unit Cost =	$\dfrac{\text{Total program costs}}{\text{Number of units of service}}$	Statement of Functional Expenses Program Count
Unit Cost =	$\dfrac{\$45{,}874}{765}$	
Unit Cost =	$60 (rounded)	

Table 4-4
SERVICE VOLUME/ACTIVITY BUDGET
Human Services Organization, Inc.
Service Volume/Activity Budget for Program A
First Quarter: July-Sept (with prior month)

| | | | Quarter | | | Quarter |
		June	July	Aug	Sept	Total
Unit of Service	Rate per Unit	Units of Service	Units of Service	Units of Service	Units of Service	Units of Service
Hour of Therapy	$60	240	250	255	260	765

There are somewhat different factors to consider in developing an expense budget for a new program for an agency. In this instance the agency may have to:

Contact Similar Agencies

Other organizations running similar type programs tend to have similar costs. Another agency may be helpful in giving information about particular type costs and what its experience has been with certain costs.

Contact Suppliers

Suppliers can be helpful in giving information about costs of supplies and equipment. Remember that the cost of many items may be negotiable and that nonprofits often are able to receive substantial discounts. It is always useful to develop a relationship with a good supplier in order to obtain the best pricing. Another place to find low prices is with consortiums of nonprofits because buying in bulk reduces prices.

Add Costs Associated with Licensing, Insurance, and Attorney's Fees

New programs often have start-up costs that continuing programs may not have. Some of these start-up costs entail outlays to investigate zoning, licensing, and other regulations that may affect a program. Attorney's fees for filing various legal documents may also accrue. Insurance costs and outlays for down payments on rental, leasing, or purchase of land, equipment, supplies must also be included.

Program Expenses vs. Administrative Expenses

Nonprofits must set up some type of system to allocate costs between program services and support services. This is not a problem in a small, one program organization because all the expenses it incurs are related to that one program. It becomes much more of a problem to allocate costs when there are a number of different programs in an organization. Since so many nonprofits receive federal monies in the form of grants, contracts, or third-party payments, it is important to look at the federal guidelines regarding allocation of these types of costs. The most important guideline in this regard is U.S. Office of Management and Budget (OMB) Circular A-122, *Cost Principles for Non-Profit Organizations* (1995).

OMB Circular A-122 identifies two types of costs, direct costs and indirect costs. Direct costs are roughly equivalent to program costs, that is, they can "be identified specifically with a particular final cost objective, i.e., a particular award, project, service or other direct activity of an organization" (OMB, 1995, B 1). *Indirect costs* are roughly equivalent to support program costs. They are "those that have been incurred for common or joint objectives and cannot be readily identified with a particular final cost objective" (OMB, 1995, C 1). Indirect costs are classified within two broad categories: "Facilities" and "Administration." The facilities category includes depreciation, operations, and maintenance expenses. The administration category includes administrative and general expenses such as personnel in the executive director's office, accounting and personnel functions, and other support services.

OMB A-122 suggests three basic types of methods for allocating indirect costs: the simplified allocation method, the multiple allocation base method, and the direct allocation method:

The Simplified Allocation Method: This method assumes that all of the organization's programs benefit from its indirect costs to approximately the same degree. If this appears to be so, the indirect costs are allocated by:

1. Dividing all costs into either direct or indirect;
2. Dividing all of the indirect costs by some equitable distribution base.

For example, suppose an agency has a total of $400,000 in costs encompassing four programs. Eighty percent (80%) of its costs are direct (i.e., program costs) and 20% are indirect (i.e., administration and general).

$400,000 x 80% = $320,000 Direct Costs
$400,000 x 20% = $ 80,000 Indirect Costs
$80,000 divided by 4 programs = $20,000 to each program

The Multiple Allocation Base Method: This method is somewhat more complex and is based on the assumption that indirect costs benefit, or are used more, by one program than another. In this method costs are allocated by:

1. Dividing costs into direct and indirect;
2. Grouping indirect costs into "cost pools"; The cost pools are:
   A. Depreciation and use allowances, including the portion of the costs of the organization's buildings and equipment;
   B. Interest on debt of buildings, equipment, or capital improvements;
   C. Operation and maintenance expenses;
   D. General administrative and general expenses for overall administration.
3. Allocating the cost pools to the various agency programs based on actual conditions, that is how funds are to be spent by each program.

For example, an organization has pooled its operation and maintenance expenses for such items as janitorial services, repairs, security, property insurance, leasing of space, and so forth. This cost pool amounts to $100,000. The agency uses the square footage allocation basis for its measurement of this cost. Total square footage for the facility is 12,000 square feet. Program A uses 2,000 square feet (17%), Program B uses 9,000 square feet (75%), and administrative offices use 1,000 square feet (8%).

$100,000 x 17% = $17,000 allocated to Program A for Operations and Maintenance Expense
$100,000 x 75% = $75,000 allocated to Program B
$100,000 x 8% = $ 8,000 allocated to Administration and General for Operations and Maintenance Expense

The Direct Allocation Method: In this method all indirect costs consist of general administration and general expenses only. This method is the simplest for small organizations, but requires that the organization have a good idea of actual costs by program. This means that the agency must accurately measure the indirect costs that accrue to each program in some way. This may be appropriate for those organizations that consider all costs as direct costs except administration and general expenses and fundraising. In this instance, the agency may allocate its indirect costs by:

1. Listing all joint costs such as depreciation, operation and maintenance of facilities, telephone, utilities and so forth;
2. Dividing these costs among the organization's various programs according to their respective cost to each program.

For example, suppose an organization had $5,000 in telephone costs. Program A has much higher telephone use (80%) because it provides information and referral. Program B has very limited telephone use (10%) because it does community center activities. Administrative services also use about 10% of the phone service.

$5,000 x 80% = $4,000 telephone expense allocated to
    Program A
$5,000 x 10% = $ 500 telephone expense allocated to
    Program B
$5,000 x 10% = $ 500 telephone expense to Administration
    and General.

Once an allocation approach is chosen, there are two other steps that an organization can take to allocate expenses (National Health Council et al, 1988):

Record Expenses by Function: At the point of original entry into the journal, expense transactions should be coded not just as to object category, but to program category whenever possible. When an expense benefits more than one program, the expense can be determined in one of the ways mentioned above, that is, space used, time spent, or square footage.

Set Up Responsibility/Cost Centers: A responsibility/cost center is a program, department, or unit of an organization that is responsible for its own budget and expenses. This type of center thus has to keep track of its own expenses. A system such as this, common in the business world, makes managers much more cognizant and careful of the expenses they incur. Each responsibility/cost center will have to tie its goals to the budget it develops, be able to justify its expenses, and use variance budgeting to monitor its progress. Variance budgeting will be discussed in Chapter Eight, "Internal Control."

There is no one right way to allocate costs. The method used must be consistent and based on logic and reason or documentable evidence

Table 4-5
EXPENSE BUDGET

Human Services Organization, Inc.
Expense Budget for Fiscal Year 2010

	Program Services			Support Services		Total
	Prog. A	Prog. B	Prog. C	Mgt & Gen	Fund-raising	
Equipment Lease						
Insurance						
Postage & Printing						
Rent						
Supplies						
Telephone						
Utilities						
Etc						
Total						

that a program has benefited from the specific cost item. See Table 4-5 for an example of an expense budget.

As can be seen in Table 4-5, this organization has allocated its expenses between program services and support services. This type of budget is also known as a functional expense budget and is very similar to one of the financial statements required of the nonprofit human service organization–The Statement of Functional Expenses. The difference between the two is that the budget is a projection of anticipated expenses while the Statement of Functional Expenses is a statement of actual expenditures.

The Salary Expense Budget

The other type of expense budget is the salary expense budget. Salary expenses tend to be the largest cost in the human service organization since providing human services is a labor intensive activity. To estimate salary expense, one must be able to determine personnel needs. It is helpful to use a guide such as that in Table 3-3 (Chapter Three) in planning personnel needs and costs. Estimating salary expense is based on a number of factors such as:

Projected Service Volume

Projected service volume affects staffing needs in many ways. In some cases, there are required staff/client ratios that must be maintained, for example, many states have licensing standards stipulating ratios of staff needed by age of child in day care facilities. In other cases, increasing the number of clients simply means that more professional and support staff will be needed.

Program Staff Needs and Workload Trends

Staff needs may also be related to staffing patterns and workload trends. For example, what hours of the day or days of the week are staff needed most? What is the trend in use of overtime and compensatory time? What are the licensing requirements for numbers of staff that must be on hand?

Prevailing Wage Rates

Prevailing salaries for professional and clerical staff in an area should be surveyed. A number of factors affect salaries; some of them include economic conditions, the labor pool available, cost of living in an area, and the competition for staff in an area. Additional factors may include any legal requirements, for example, minimum wage laws, laws covering benefits, and social security as well as guidelines established by national organizations or local funding sources.

Fringe Benefits

Benefit packages (fringes) and inflation rates should be added into the final salary figures. Fringe benefits in nonprofits are often calculated as a percentage of salary. So, for example, one organization might find that its fringes represent 15% of salary, while in another the fringe rate may be 25%. The difference in fringe rates is due to the different types of benefits offered to employees and their respective costs to employers.

Allocating salary expense when staff have duties in more than one program can be approached by the following mechanisms:

Use Time Reporting: Personnel costs usually make up the largest proportion of costs in a human service organization. In large agencies, as an example of the principle of differentiation, job categories tend to be much more rigid and workers tend to fill one job or program function only. In small agencies, on the other hand, workloads tend to be much more flexible and workers must fill in wherever help is needed.

In these cases, it is even more important for time/function sheets to be used (see Table 4-6). However, the method of reporting chosen by the organization should not be burdensome to workers and create perceived additional, unnecessary paperwork. A daily time form could be used at periodic intervals to survey amount of work performed in various functions. This type of random sampling can give the organization a fair idea of the amount of time spent by employees whose jobs span more than one programmatic area.

Some key points in setting up a time report system:

* Randomly select representative employees. That is, not all employees should have to fill out the forms every time period. Choose different employees who are representative of essential positions. For example, rather than all child welfare workers having to time report, only a few from different offices or units would be sufficient.
* Train these employees, not just in filling out the form, but also in the importance of the form. If they do not understand the reasons for the form, they will view it as busywork.
* Require that reports be completed on a periodic basis, for example, one week a month per quarter.
* Make sure the reports are reviewed and signed by the appropriate supervisor. The supervisor should check and verify with the employee that the time reported for tasks listed is an accurate reflection of what the employee actually did that week.
* In designing the report form, ease and simplicity should be the

Table 4-6
SAMPLE TIME REPORT FORM
Human Services Organization, Inc.
Weekly Time Report Form

Employee Name _____ Date _____

Department/Unit/Program _____

Time Start	Time End	Task Performed	Program

Employee Signature _____

Supervisor Signature _____

Table 4-7
SALARY EXPENSE BUDGET
Human Services Organization, Inc.
Salary Expense Budget for Fiscal Year 2010

	Program Services			Support Services		Total
	Prog. A	Prog. B	Prog. C	Mgt & Gen	Fund-raising	
Salaries:						
Director						
Asst. Director						
Program Director						
Social Workers						
Aides						
Secretarial						
Subtotal Salaries						
Payroll Taxes						
Fringe Benefit						
Total						

key. Remember to include items such as task performed, hours spent on task, and program related to task.

- Finally, develop a summary report that can be used in preparing the Statement of Functional Expenses as well as the budget.

Reviewing the time sheet information can be an aid in projecting trends. This information can be used in the Salary Expense Budget. Administrative and General personnel expenses must also be allocated, especially in small organizations where an administrator may also provide direct services in one or more programs. See Table 4-7 for an example of a Salary Expense Budget.

Estimating Public Support and Revenue

Revenue

Revenue is income earned from the provision of goods and/or services. A revenue budget is "a summary statement of revenue plans for a given period expressed in quantitative terms" (Gaertner, 1982, p. 28). In for-profit organizations, the revenue budget is usually prepared first. In many nonprofit human service agencies, the revenue budget may be the beginning point on which other budget components may depend. However, as Powell (1980) has stated, there is a critical difference in the budgeting of the two types of organizations. That is, in for-profit enterprises, it is important to develop the revenue budget first in order to be able to allocate revenues. In nonprofit organizations, the level of service should be determined first, then the expenditures associated with a given level of service should be ascertained, and finally, policy decisions have to be made as to the financing of these services.

Targeting service level and costs associated with the providing of service helps the agency calculate its need for public support through allocations and contributions as well as set revenue levels. The revenue budget is usually prepared annually, though it may be broken down into quarterly or monthly periods for comparison.

In budgeting for revenues, timing of revenue inflows is an important factor to consider. There may be three types of revenue inflow patterns in any one agency (this includes public support as well as revenue): regular, seasonal, and random (Gaertner, 1982).

Regular Pattern of Revenue Inflows

This type of revenue is usually from the on-going activities of a program such as counseling, crisis intervention, or those other services offered by the organization. By examining current patterns in fees-for-services, the agency may feel comfortable in projecting future trends.

Seasonal Patterns of Revenue

Seasonal revenue usually comes from activities that occur during certain times of the year such as an annual campaign or other annual fundraising events. Or the organization may have a program that only occurs during one season, as for example, a summer camp program.

Random Revenue

Random revenue may come occasionally as public support without any pattern, for example, unsolicited donations, or special bequests. It is unexpected monies that the organization did not plan for in its operating budget.

Revenue inflows may also be *fixed* or *variable*. *Fixed* revenue is revenue that comes to the agency at a predetermined rate, such as a flat-fee contract or grant. In this instance, no matter how many clients are provided goods or services the amount of revenue will not change during the fiscal period. *Variable* revenue, on the other hand, does vary with the amount of goods or services delivered. For example, the more fee-paying clients or more items sold by the thrift shop, the more revenue will increase.

The basis of the projected revenue budget is usually past revenues earned. The human service administrator and appropriate staff may review past trends and take into account current environmental conditions (changes in demography of client population, changes in public policies, funding policies, economic conditions, and so forth) to formulate a revenue projection.

Some additional information that an organization might need to gather in order to estimate revenues includes the following:

- The numbers of clients currently being served, average number of visits per client, and average user fees paid. The budgeting team would presumably have already gathered this information when it was projecting service volume and unit costs.
- Data from the past 3–5 years on revenues from client services. These are available from the organization's financial statements and/or actual budget.
- Plans for change in the number of clients served. These would have been clarified in the planning that preceded the final budgeting process.
- Any planned increase in user fees and the date on which the change will take place.
- An estimate of potential users of service not now being served. This may be estimated from any community needs assessments that may have been recently conducted;
- Past revenues from any auxiliary services, for example, gift shop;
- Plans for changes in any auxiliary services.

Public Support

Public support is that income received in the form of grants and contracts from governmental sources, and contributions from the general public in the form of donations, bequests, endowments, in-kind goods and services. Information needed for estimating public support includes such items as:

- Statistics of income from public support broken down by source and showing changes and trends by percentages
- Current budget requests to all sources
- An estimate of priority of agency services by funding sources
- Data regarding trends in contributions broken down by year and shown as a percentage of fundraising costs
- Any grant proposals or fundraising projects currently in the works with projected dollar outcomes

There are other, more sophisticated, techniques now available for human service organizations that use already developed computer programs and spreadsheets for projecting trends. The acquisition and use of such programs will be discussed more fully in the chapter on financial information systems. See Table 4-8 for a Revenue and Public Support Budget.

As can be seen from this table, the main categories of the Revenue and Public Support budget are sources of revenue, sources of public

Table 4-8
REVENUE AND PUBLIC SUPPORT BUDGET
Human Services Organization, Inc.
Revenue and Public Support Budget for Fiscal Year 2010

	Program Services			Support Services		Total
	Prog. A	Prog. B	Prog. C	Mgt & Gen	Fund-raising	
Revenue						
Fees for Service						
Contracts						
Public Support						
Allocations						
Contributions						
Government Grants						
Other						
Total						

support, and government grants. Some organizations list all governmental support separately, even contracts. The allocation of monies from revenues and public support does not entail the same complexity as allocating expenses. One reason for this is that the distribution of administrative costs from contracts, grants, and allocations that an organizations receives is often predetermined by the funding source(s). The only discretionary money a nonprofit has is from revenues earned, that is, fees-for-services, or fundraising.

Estimating Cash Flow

The agency must anticipate its cash flow using a cash budget. The cash budget "summarizes planned cash receipts and disbursements" based on budgeted support, revenues, and expenses (Anthony and Herzlinger, 1980, p. 326). The cash budget is largely influenced by the seasonality of operations, that is month-to-month variations in either service levels or inflows of revenue, or both. The cash flow equation is simply:

$$CB_b + CR - CD = CB_e$$

Beginning cash balance + cash receipts − cash disbursements = ending cash balance.

Basically, a cash budget has the following components:

1. The beginning cash balance, which would have been carried over from the previous fiscal period;
2. Cash received during the month, which is added to this initial balance;
3. Cash payments made by the organization during the month, which are subtracted from total cash on hand.

These calculations result in an ending cash balance for the month (a simplified cash flow budget can be seen in Table 4-9).

As can be seen from the cash flow budget for this organization, the cash balance at the beginning of the quarter was $10,000. The organization received cash of $8,000 in the month of July, its total cash balance then became $18,000. It also spent $7,300 during that same month, leaving it with an ending cash balance of $10,700 ($18,000 - 7,300). This ending cash balance of $10,700 becomes the beginning cash balance for the next month, August, and so on.

Table 4-9
CASH FLOW BUDGET
Human Services Organization, Inc.
Cash Flow Budget for Three Months Ended June 30, 2005

	April	May	June
Cash Balance, Beginning	$10,000	$10,7000	$11,700
Cash Receipts:			
Client Fees	3,000	2,800	2,500
Contributions	5,000	5,500	5,300
Total Cash Receipts	8,000	8,300	7,800
Cash Disbursements:			
Operating Expenses	3,200	3,200	3,200
Salaries	4,100	4,100	4,100
Total Disbursements	7,300	7,300	
7,300			
Cash Balance, Ending	$10,700	$11,700	$12,000

PREPARING BUDGETED FINANCIAL STATEMENTS

Preparing the budgeted or pro forma financial statements is usually the last step in the budget forms process, although not all nonprofits do this step. The preparation of financial statements will be discussed in the chapter on financial reporting and analysis.

MODIFYING AND ADOPTING A BALANCED BUDGET

Before a budget is finalized it must be submitted for approval to the organization's board, then to one or more funding sources for approval, then back to the board for any modifications and final approval. The approach taken by an organization to balancing its budget depends on its overall planning approach and long-term goals. For example, if administrators and the board believe that the organization should take a proactive approach to planning and budgeting, they will aggressively seek alternative funding for programs they think are important in meeting community needs. On the other hand, if an organization takes a reactive approach, the budget committee will cut expenses to match revenues and feel fortunate in having balanced the budget. A moderate approach would take a proactive stance with new developing programs and a reactive one with declining ones (Ramanathan, 1982).

In any case, any shortfalls in support and revenue entail the revision of the original proposed budget. This involves compromise and negotiation with program directors, funding sources, and other interested parties. The final budget is not cast in stone, as subsequent events may require that the budget be modified or revised more than once during the fiscal year.

One way an organization can cope with the uncertainty of funding levels by allocation sources is to use a flexible budget. In this method, department heads are required to prepare alternative budgets that are with high, low, and some medium range amounts. For example, the program may estimate expenses based on 110% of last years costs, 90% of last year's costs, and 100% of last year's costs (see Table 4-10 below).

Another way to approach estimating is based on projected revenue, that is, if revenue is expected to be 115% of last year, then expenses are projected based on the same percentage. Or if one used service volume, 110% of service volume of last year will equal a 10% increase in expenses.

The operating budget is an expression of an organization's goals expressed in monetary terms. It outlines organizational objectives and approaches for achieving them. It aids in planning, in setting measures of performance, and in control of organization activities. We

Table 4-10
FLEXIBLE BUDGET
Human Services Organization, Inc.
Flexible Expense Budget Fiscal Year Ended June 30, 200x

	Service Activity Level (Cases)		
	3,000	4,000	5,000
Salaries:			
Caseworkers	$330,000	$440,000	$550,000
Supervisors	52,000	66,000	80,000
Subtotal Salaries	382,000	506,000	630,000
Fringes (15%)	60,800	74,400	93,000
Subtotal Salaries and Fringes	442,800	580,400	723,000
Other Expenses:			
Supplies	36,000	48,000	60,000
Misc. Fixed	80,000	80,000	80,000
Subtotal Other Expenses	116,000	128,000	140,000
Total Expenses	$558,800	$708,400	$863,000

have presented the ideal approach to the budget process, one that harnesses its potential usefulness to the organization while being cognizant of the reality that budgeting is just an incremental activity in some organizations. It is to the advantage of the organization that staff and board take the time to utilize the budget process to maximize effectiveness and efficiency in the organization.

Reading 4-1: Preparing, Presenting and Defending the Budget*

The following excerpt, while written some years ago, is one of the best the author has ever seen in explicating the real life issues and politics involved in presenting a budget. It has as much currency now as when it was written.

THE LOCAL BUDGET PROCESS IN PERSPECTIVE

Perhaps the most important point about the budget process is that it is a long-term management responsibility, not an isolated task to be completed once a year. Successful preparation of a local budget, resulting in approval of adequate funds to accomplish annual program goals, is a complex undertaking. Several observations are in order:

- Committing program goals to paper and tying them to specific amounts of money during the budget preparation phase are exercises in economic skill.
- Physical presentation of the budget before the budget authority is an exercise in salesmanship.
- Daily administration of your program and the budget that makes it possible is an exercise in management skill.

These observations illustrate that 'presentation' of a budget is not an action that takes place once a year when you appear before the budget authority. Rather, the presentation is reflected in every action you take in managing the . . . program and in every relationship you establish in the community. There is no magic formula for the successful preparation, presentation, or administration of a budget. It is only when fiscal responsibility is an integral part of an effective program that you will be consistently as successful as possible in your sit-

---

* Excerpted from: Basic Skills in Creative Financing, Student Manual. EMI Professional Development Series, Federal Emergency Management Agency, National Emergency Training Center, Emergency Management Institute, Emmitsburg, Maryland, 1983, pp. 211–220.

uation. Your personal credibility and the credibility of your program—coupled with sound working relationships with others in the community—are the keys to the budget process. And these must be established over time.

The Importance of Credibility

A budget hearing is an exercise in salesmanship. You appear before a group of individuals to 'sell' a product—maintenance of a sound program. The budget authority also hears other program managers and must determine how to allocate specific sums of money in the face of complex and often contradictory claims.

A beautifully prepared 'dog and pony show' with charts, graphs, and visuals may overwhelm the average budget authority and result in an adopted budget. But if you appear before the group the next year and nothing except another 'dog and pony show', chances are you will not only face rejection but also lose credibility, seriously hampering all future activities. Even if the budget authority is not perceptive enough to detect the illusion, other program managers competing for local dollars may be happy to point it out. They may also exercise time-honored methods developed by the bureaucracy to hamper every future move you make.

You must be certain your program is sound and shows annual progress. It must be accepted by others competing for the local budget dollar. . . . Once [your organization's] capabilities have been established, the techniques of budget presentation can be applied productively and effectively. But you should not assume that techniques are the reasons the budget is adopted. Techniques receive the most attention because the act of presentation is both visible and dramatic and results in specific actions others can see and evaluate. A smooth, effective, informative budget presentation tends to overshadow the fact that it is the result of days, weeks, months, even years of steady, competent activity within [your program].

. . . During various steps in the process, you identified real local problems and needs. You mobilized every community resource in support of [this problem]. You sought and applied to outside sources to meet needs not covered by local resources. In conducting these activities, you also talked to many people in the community and told them about your program goals and objectives.

If you have worked through some of these steps before your budget presentation, you may find that your credibility—and that of your program—is already on the rise. [Effective budgeting] is grounded in sound management techniques and approaches. Actions in the process are visible and effective. Results, and their impact on the local situation, can hardly go unnoticed. So, while creative financing is not the only effort you need to build credibility, it is a management tool you can use to improve your program. As your program improves, so will its credibility—and so will yours. As an effective leader and catalyst with a solid record of success, you are in a better position to deal with your local budget authority.

The Importance of Relationships

As you prepare to present the budget, you must also address your relationships with other . . . agencies competing for local dollars. Through awareness of their budget requests, you should point out elements of your proposal that make their objectives more attainable or that enable reductions in overall expenditures through cooperative use of resources.

Results of efforts to do everything possible with local resources can be used to show how . . . services interrelate. You can also describe and document how reductions in overlaps and gaps in services (due to creative strategies) will reduce expenditures in many areas. If you have obtained funds from outside sources, you can demonstrate how this will cut local costs.

. . . As various community programs and services begin to coordinate, cooperation is encouraged. Cooperation, rather than competition, also becomes feasible as roles and functions are clearly defined and overlap and waste reduced.

With this perspective on the local budget process, you can see the significant role overall management activities and successes play in gaining the community dollars you request. . . .

PREPARING THE BUDGET

Budget authorities usually deal simultaneously with requests from many programs. Although it may seem perfectly obvious to you that funds you are requesting are necessary and will be well spent in [your program], you must convince budget officials (who have limited funds) that your program is more deserving than others.

Regardless of the form your budget takes or the philosophy it reflects, it must be the result of thorough research and planning. If you are not thorough in your preparation, it will be evident during your presentation and defense.

One way you can demonstrate the thoroughness with which you have prepared your budget is to include a set of clear, concise statements relating to each specific budget line item. This information might include:

- Resources available to offset the cost of the activity (expense minus outside resources equals requested appropriation);
- The relationship of this expenditure to accomplishment of long-range goals of the program;
- The relative priority of this activity in terms of the overall budget;
- Procedures developed to ensure accurate monitoring of the activity, which demonstrates that the most efficient, economical means of accomplishing the program objectives have been selected;
- Support for overall goals of the community (for example, requested communications equipment can be used by other agencies; economies realized through resource management make funds available for other departments); and
- The impact on program objectives if line item allocations are modified (either increased or decreased).

In researching and documenting your funding needs, the following information can be helpful. Some documents may serve as supporting appendices to your budget.

- Estimates for specific expenditures from reputable sources . . .
- Resources available by type, origin, and relationship to the program. . . . (Resources gained at no cost form a valuable body of information. Their acquisition is testimony to your ability to reduce budget expenditures through maximum use of resources.)
- Past budget history of your agency.
- Documents establishing that your program will be receiving support from outside sources.
- Any data prepared by outside sources that show the supportive nature of your operations in relation to other local . . . [public or private agencies].

Next, you will have to select a presentation strategy suitable for your situation and abilities. Completing the following suggested 'homework' can help you develop an effective presentation strategy.

- Review all available data on the general budget and on budgets of agencies and programs with which you are interdependent. Identify components of those budgets that will be enhanced by adoption of your budget. Also identify components that make it possible for you to reduce your budget requests, should theirs be adopted.
- Become fully familiar with required local budget forms.
  - –Do you have enough of them?
  - –Do they clearly show various program elements and activities?
  - –Are you certain you are filling them out in accordance with the expectations of the budget authority? (Work closely with the fiscal officer responsible for preparing and reviewing the forms.)
- Determine time frames you must meet in the budget preparation process. Even the best budget faces problems if it comes in late or out of sequence.
- Determine the date, time, and place of your budget hearing. Plan to be there! Be sensitive to such factors as time of day. If you must face the budget authority at the end of a long session, members may be restless and abrupt. Insistence on adhering to a long, detailed presentation may result in an unreasonable (but very human) termination of your presentation and an arbitrary setting of the amount they will approve.
- Review the political and economic climate on the national, state, and local levels. Identify factors that support your program and budget request. Pinpoint factors that may cause criticism of any budget elements and address them, preferably in advance of the budget hearing.
- Identify individuals who advise the budget authority on fiscal matters, especially those dealing with [your type of program].
- Know your audience, both allies and enemies. Review your relationship with members of the budget authority, fiscal office, and other departments and agencies. If you have maintained steady, positive contact with them throughout the year, they should be familiar with your program and conditioned toward acceptance.
- Consider the interests and needs of the budget authorities and how your budget takes those interests and needs into consideration.
- Develop a portfolio of photographs, charts, graphs, and other visuals to illustrate major points.

Finally, in choosing a strategy (or set of strategies), consider the following points:

- What are the advantages and disadvantages inherent in particular strategies?
- What characteristics do individuals on the budget authority possess that would make particular strategies effective or ineffective?
- How would use of particular strategies be viewed by the news media, other officials, and the taxpaying public?

In considering various strategies, bear in mind that they are techniques rather than components of a sound, well-developed, and properly administered . . . program. Techniques have enough validity to be effective under certain circumstances, so be prepared to use any that may improve your presentation. However, their use should be in support of, rather than as a replacement for, day-to-day application of sound management techniques.

Adequate preparation before your presentation is critical to the success of your presentation strategy. If your homework has been thorough, you should be prepared to deal with any issue. Ask yourself the following questions to ensure that you have been as thorough as possible:

- Do I know the history of past budgets—how much was requested and how much granted?
- Am I aware of the total budget picture? What underlying principles will dictate the budget authority's attitudes?
- Do I know the fiscal officer? Have I used the procedures he or she requires for budget document preparation?
- Have I identified all conditions applying to my budget and unique to my program (i.e., federal matching requirements, grants management regulations, personnel pay scales)?
- Have I prepared a brief written statement of support for each line item in my budget?
- Have I included documentation from outside sources attesting to the accuracy of my program assumptions . . . ?
- Am I personally familiar with every item in my budget, and can I personally support each proposed expenditure clearly and effectively?
- Do I have documentation on past budget projections and on program attainments to support those projections?
- Have I identified and included all sources of revenue beyond local dollars?

- Have I clearly identified outside sources of revenue and established their impact on reducing my request to the local budget authority?
- Can I clearly identify and explain portions of my budget over which I have limited control (i.e., mandated services, ongoing commitments, recurring expenses)?
- Can I relate possible cutbacks to specific effects on individual program elements?
- Am I aware of conditions facing the budget authority in relation to my budget (i.e., taxpayer attitudes toward my program, degree of acceptance by other [agencies], misconceptions on the part of individuals serving on the budget authority)?
- Am I familiar with all other program budgets and at least aware of their relationship to the total budget being considered by the budget authority?
- Have I demonstrated internal controls established to assure the budget authority that I am personally concerned with maintaining accountability?

A final suggestion for presentations is to organize your material so that the main message–the point with the most impact–is given as the opening statement. Isolate the most positive point you want to stress, the most startling statistic, the best result your program has achieved, and turn it into the 'lead' sentence of your presentation. When you begin, you can be fairly sure of having the full attention of the budget authority. Use these valuable moments to make the most important announcements of your presentation so you can be sure it will get across. You may also be able to hold the authority's attention longer if you have a good, strong opening.

PRESENTING AND DEFENDING THE BUDGET

As you have seen, points that will allow you to defend your budget are built into the document as it is prepared. When you go before the budget authority, you should be so well prepared that you have nothing to think about but last-minute details and communicating effectively. The following points can aid you in giving your presentation smoothly and professionally.

- Be flexible. Remain alert to on-the-scene conditions that may alter the manner in which you should deliver your budget presentation. Everyone attempts to be professional about such activities, but human factors cannot be discounted. If you happen to follow a department that has been engaged in a heated argument with the budget authority, members may carry over their feelings. Be aware of this and adapt to it.

- Key your brief, explanatory remarks to applicable line items, so the budget authority can clearly see the relationship between money requested and goals you expect to accomplish.

- Have present any individuals who can lend professional support to your budget proposal, but resist the temptation to parade a string of 'character witnesses' before the budget authority. The budget authority is busy and probably eager to complete the process. If others can contribute concrete testimony, bring them. If not, put their words on paper and offer an appendix.

- Be alert to questions and comments of budget authority members. If they show interest in an area you did not intend to cover fully, switch directions and address their interests. Unresolved issues are normally decided in favor of the action that costs the least. If the members 'feel' there are areas not fully addressed, they may reduce the appropriation just to 'play it safe.'

- Emphasize program successes. Show how previous expenditures have . . . enabled your program to respond effectively to local [problems].

- Point out how your services complement those of other agencies.

- Demonstrate how various aspects of your budget are interrelated, and how lack of funding in one area might jeopardize services in another area.

- Illustrations, examples, charts, graphs, and other visuals should be used only when you are certain they support specific points. Every moment spent displaying visuals not of direct interest is one more moment the viewers can devote to thinking about other matters.

REFERENCES

Anthony, R. N. & Herzlinger, R. E. (1980). *Management Control in Nonprofit Organizations*. Homewood, IL: Richard D. Irwin.

Bowers, G. E. & Bowers, M. R. (1976). *The Elusive Unit of Service*. U.S. Department of Health, Education, and Welfare, Office of the Secretary, Office of Intergovernmental Systems. Project Share. Human Services Monograph Series, No. 1.

Bryson, J. M. (1995). *Strategic Planning for Public and Nonprofit Organizations* (Rev. Ed.). San Francisco: Jossey-Bass Publishers.

Federal Emergency Management Agency (1983), National Emergency Training Center, Emergency Management Institute, *Basic Skills in Creative Financing, Student Manual.* EMI Professional Development Series, Emmitsburg, Maryland, pp. 211–220.

Gaertner, J. (1982). Revenue budgets, pp. 28–34 in Tracey D. Connor & Christopher Callahan (Eds.). *Financial Management for Nonprofit Organizations.* New York: AMACOM.

Gross, A.M. (1980). Appropriate cost reporting: an indispensable link to accountability. *Administration in Social Work,* 4(3):31–41.

Hartman, S. W. (1996). Gaining control of revenues with nonprofit budgeting, pp. 8–34 in Jae K. Shim, Joel G. Siegel & Abraham J. Simon. *Handbook of Budgeting for Nonprofit Organizations.* Englewood Cliffs, New Jersey: Prentice Hall.

Kettner, P. M., Moroney, R. M., & Martin, L. L. (1990). *Designing and Managing Programs: An Effectiveness-Based Approach.* Newbury Park, CA: Sage Publications.

National Health Council, Inc., National Assembly of National Voluntary Health and Social Welfare Organizations, Inc., & United Way of America (1988). *Standards of Accounting and Financial Reporting for Voluntary Health and Welfare Organizations* (3rd. Ed.). New York: author.

National Institute of Mental Health (1983). *Accounting and budgeting Systems for Mental Health Organizations.* Mental Health Service System Reports, Series FN No. 6, by J.E. Sorensen, G.B. Hanbery & A.R. Kucic. Washington, D.C.: U.S. Government Printing Office.

Office of Management and Budget, OMB Circular A-122, *Cost Principles for Non-Profit Organizations* (1995)

Powell, R. M. (1980). *Budgetary Control Procedures for Institutions.* Notre Dame: University of Notre Dame Press.

Ramanathan, K. V. (1982). *Management Control in Nonprofit Organizations.* New York: John Wiley & Sons.

Stretch, J. (1979). Seven key managerial functions of sound fiscal budgeting. *Administration in Social Work,* 3:441–452.

INTERNET RESOURCES

What you need to know about nonprofit charitable organizations: http://www.nonprofits.about.com/

Nonprofit Financial Center: http://www.nfconline.org

SmarterOrg: Online courses in nonprofit budgeting and project management: www.smarterorg.com/budgeting_description.htm

Chapter Five

MARKETING AND FUNDRAISING

After reading this chapter you should be able to:

1. Understand concepts of marketing as applied to nonprofits;
2. Discuss the advantages and disadvantages of various fundraising techniques;
3. Plan and design fundraising strategies;
4. Understand the financial and tax implications of contributions for nonprofit organizations.

INTRODUCTION

In 1997, there were 1,188,000 nonprofit organizations in the United States (Independent Sector, 2001). Their total revenues in 1997 were $664.8 billion. Of this amount, 19.9% was private contributions raised by these organizations through their fundraising efforts. Raising funds to ensure survival of the nonprofit, maintaining its on-going programs, and developing new ones are crucial organizational activities. In systems terms, funds are resource inputs that are used in the process (throughput) stage of the marketing subsystem of the organization; they are used so that services may be provided. In the systems view, there are other resources used in the fundraising process such as staff, volunteer time and materials, and donors. These resources are used in the planning and solicitation processes in an attempt to secure more resources for the organization (see Figure 5-1).

Fundraising is the acquisition of assets, either in the form of money or in-kind goods or services, for the organization by means of solicitation. The acquiring of funds in this way is the result of asking individuals, groups, or organizations for resources without always giving a tangible product or service in return. However, if nonprofit organizations wish to acquire external funds by means of fundraising, then they must be aware of any restrictions placed on fundraising by their funding sources. In addition, they must be aware of any state and local laws regulating fundraising by nonprofits. Many states require registration of organizations that raise a certain dollar amount by means of fundraising,

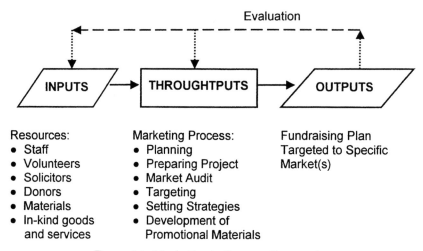

Figure 5-1: Marketing in Systems Perspective

for example, over $25,000. Also, many states require registration of professional fundraisers hired by an organization. Each state has registration forms that have been standardized to make it easier for organizations that wish to fundraise in more than one state. This standardized form is known as the *Unified Registration Statement* and is accepted in all but a few states.

Since human service agencies are dependent to a large extent on outside organizations and individuals for funding, the level of funding for a specific program is usually a decision made by external bodies such as contracting or grant-making agencies. This means that unanticipated additional income in the form of grants or contributions may reduce the level of support from a given funder rather than being extra support that is available to be used at the board's discretion. In addition, many allocation sources do not want a nonprofit's fundraising to interfere with their own, so an organization may be restricted by a funding source to fundraising during certain periods of the year only. For example, if an organization is receiving funds from an allocation body such as a United Way, the organization may not be able to schedule an event during the United Way's campaign. An allocation agency may also have guidelines that specify that certain methods of obtaining operating funds may not be used, since this would mean that certain groups of contributors would be approached twice. These factors must be kept in mind in planning any type of fundraising activity for a nonprofit.

In the past, fundraising, in terms of grantwriting, was thought to be a staff function, while fundraising, in terms of solicitation of contributions, was thought to be an administrative (director and board of directors) and volunteer function. While human service workers in large organizations may not be very involved with fundraising in their organizations, they should be familiar with aspects of it because they will be expected to take on fundraising tasks as they assume increasing administrative responsibility. On the other hand, everyone who works in a small human service organization will be involved in fundraising in some way as part of the job.

In this chapter, the concept of marketing as applied to human service organizations will be discussed, as will various types of fundraising. Also covered are strategies and approaches to these fundraising activities.

First, let us define two key terms: *contributions* and *in-kind goods or services*.

Contributions

Contributions are sums of money or in-kind goods or services donated by individuals or groups to support the work of a nonprofit organization. Usually the nonprofit does not provide a specific service or product to obtain them. The contributions may be solicited as part of a regular, organized campaign, or by special events that are planned as a one-time occasion for a specific purpose or goal.

In-kind Goods or Services

In-kind goods or services are nonmonetary contributions given to further the goals of a nonprofit. They are termed "in-kind" because they are in lieu of cash. They may be any kind of donation that they organization can use, from groceries to office supplies, or that can be converted by the organization into cash, such as cars, houses, stocks or bonds.

In this chapter fundraising as a means of raising additional funds for a nonprofit will be explored. To be specifically delineated is the art of fundraising from contributions using well-known principles of marketing. A major reason that fundraising is highlighted here is that many agencies are too dependent on limited sources and thus are at the mercy of the vagaries of the economy, trendy social issues, and shifting political coalitions. Human service organizations need to look to marketing principles as a means of increasing their funding opportunities, as well as a way of increasing their client populations and the effectiveness of service delivery to those populations. Finally, in this chapter we will discuss implications of contributions to the nonprofit organization and ways that certain types of contributions have to be recorded and reported.

THE ROLE OF MARKETING IN FUNDRAISING

Marketing may be defined as "the analysis, planning, implementation, and control of carefully formulated programs designed to bring about voluntary exchanges of values with target markets for the purpose of achieving organizational objectives" (Kotler, 1982, p. 5). What does this mean? Actually, marketing involves activities common to all human service organizations. For example, all agencies need to analyze the needs of their client populations, they need to plan services, and to be able to implement them. Also, marketing involves carefully formulated programs, again a characteristic of well-run, effective human service organizations. Marketing "utilizes market segmentation, consumer research, concept development, communications, facilitation, incentives and the exchange theory to maximize target group response . . . [it] can be used to bring products, services, organizations, persons, places, or social causes to the attention of a market" (Kotler, 1982, p. 495).

Most central to marketing is the concept of exchange, that is, the reciprocal transfer of something of value. The importance of the principle of exchange must be underscored. The basic idea of exchange is that there is some type of benefit that accrues to both parties in the process. Before an exchange can take place, the organization must try to learn as much as possible about the individuals or groups with whom they want to exchange. These individuals or groups are called 'targets' or 'publics', and the more a target is understood, the easier will be the process of exchange. Of course, the same applies to the clients that we serve, the more we know about them the easier is the process of helping.

Through the process of exchange, the organization obtains the resources it needs by giving something in return. Just as with the services that it offers, what the organization offers in return for contributions has tangible and intangible components. Tangible aspects include tax deductions, or a seat on an important committee or board; intangible aspects include a feeling of being socially useful, of fulfilling religious commandments to help the needy, of contributing to causes that one believes in, and so forth. This exchange process is obviously very different in the nonprofit area than it is in the for-profit market, where the process has much more tangible aspects. Even in the for-profit sector, though, subconscious motivation plays a part. Marketing researchers have spent enormous sums of money trying to understand why people purchase the products that they do. Marketing also involves selecting target markets and concentrating on those market segments that potentially will have the highest possible response to the organization's campaign.

Finally, the purpose of marketing is to achieve the organization's goals and objectives. In business, the goal is profit. In the human services, the goal is community service or socially useful service. But it is important for human service organizations to remember that effective planning and marketing requires that the organization develop specific goals and objectives that can be measured or quantified. In conjunction with planning, it must also be remembered that marketing is user-oriented. That is, it takes into account the needs, wants, desires, and special characteristics of the client, rather than designing services or campaigns that are inappropriate to the client or target population.

Components of Marketing

Marketing uses what is called the "marketing mix" to design an appropriate marketing strategy. The social marketing mix is made up of five components, often called the five P's: publics, product, price, promotion, and place (Kotler & Andreasen, 1991, Lauffer, 1997). An organization that wants to develop an effective fundraising campaign must find the right "mix" of these elements for its organization. The components of the mix will be examined here.

Publics: are those persons, groups, and organizations that are in interaction with the nonprofit. These include input publics, those that supply resources to the organization; internal and intermediary publics, those that transform the resources into products or services to be marketed; and consuming publics, those that consume or use the services or products, including clients, the general community, and other interested parties.

Product: refers to the main products or services offered by an organization. Obviously, the services offered by the nonprofit are, or should be, styled and packaged in a way that reflects quality. One of the intangible aspects of an organization's product is the reputation it builds in its community. This reputation is of extreme importance in fundraising: the mention of a nonprofit's name should generate a positive response by the public. Product may also refer to what is offered to potential donors in return for their contributions. For example, a marketing product developed for a campaign may be an expensive dinner to which tickets must be purchased, art items sold at a fundraising auction, used items sold at a garage sale, craft items sold at a bazaar and so forth.

Price: refers to the price that the publics are willing to pay (Lauffer, 1997). This includes fees for services charged by the organization. This setting of fees in nonprofits differs from for-profits because the price is not always based on an amount that can cover costs, rather user fees typically only pay a fraction of an organization's overhead. The support garnered from funding sources and service fees is matched against operating costs. The organization must then determine the break-even point or the gap between revenue and expenses. This gap, the excess of expenses over revenue, is usually the amount the organization must target to be raised through its fundraising activities. Price may also refer to the amounts charged for fundraising products. That is, a dinner may be donated by a restaurant, but contributors are charged $50 each for it. They pay this price because they know that the money will go to the nonprofit organization, not because they think the dinner is worth $50.

Promotion: involves communication by the organization to its many constituencies to stimulate increased utilization of services or increased contributions. Promotion is often thought of as marketing, but as can be seen here is only one aspect of marketing. We often call this promotion "outreach" in the human services. Many times it involves public education to increase public awareness about a particular social problem, or to encourage public utilization of new programs as, for example, child abuse hot-lines, or respite care for caregivers of Alzheimer's patients. Communication is critical in developing or shaping an organization's image and reputation. Some tools of promotion include advertising, personal selling (the one-on-one contact involved in soliciting large contributions), and publicity. All of these promotional tools need to be utilized in the marketing campaign.

Place: refers to the channels through which an organization distributes its products or services. Distribution or place also refers to transportation, referral arrangements, the organization's physical plant, and so forth. Since most human service agencies are in direct contact with their clients, distribution may not be an important issue in delivery of services. From a marketing point of view, distribution is critical in the link from the organization to the larger public from which it is soliciting funds. That is, what is the best way for a organization to reach the largest number of its target market in order to deliver its fundraising appeal?

All of these components make up the marketing mix of an organization. They can be controlled to some extent internally by organization staff and board, but there are external factors such as government regulation, competition, and social focus which may be constraints on the organization's mix at any point in time (Vanderleest, 1985).

THE MARKETING PROCESS APPLIED TO NONPROFIT ORGANIZATIONS

No matter what type of fundraising program adopted by the organization, marketing principles can be applied. An organized approach may involve a total marketing process. The marketing process usually consists of the following components (Rubright & MacDonald, 1981; Kotler & Andreasen, 1991): the initial planning stage, the market audit, setting of marketing goals and objectives, setting strategies, implementing strategies, and evaluating.

Initial Planning Stage

The initial planning stage involves setting up a fundraising committee of board members, some staff, and interested volunteers. This committee will be responsible for the design and implementation of the fundraising project. An essential component for membership is the enthusiastic commitment of the participants, as this enthusiasm and commitment will help keep them going through endless meetings, a thousand tedious details, and occasional setbacks and fatigue.

One of the first tasks of the committee will be to set up a schedule of marketing planning tasks to be completed with tentative dates for completion. One example of such a schedule or checklist can be seen in Table 5-2. After marketing strategies have been selected, another timetable should be developed to keep the project on track and on time.

Another important task of the planning committee is to investigate and be familiar with the state and local laws relating to fundraising activities as well as the rules and guidelines of major funding sources. For example, a large number of states have laws governing fundraising activities in order to protect the public from unscrupulous and fraudulent fundraising schemes. Local municipalities may also have laws regulating fundraising activities and persons who engage in them. Organization staff may have to obtain a permit or a license, may have to check

Table 5-1
NONPROFIT FUNDRAISING CHECKLIST

Task	Target Date	Date Completed	Comments
Fundraising committee established			
Organizational goals clarified			
Organizational need determined			
Feasibility study completed			
Market audit completed			
Marketing objectives developed			
Target markets selected			
Marketing strategies chosen			
Fundraising approaches selected			
Budget developed			
Promotional materials developed			
Evaluation mechanism established			

zoning ordinances and so forth. An organization attorney or board member may be helpful in this regard.

The Market Audit

A market audit evaluates the organization's markets, services, marketing programs, and overall marketing effectiveness. The audit usually consists of three parts:

- an evaluation of the *marketing environment* of the organization—its markets, publics (clients, customers, competitors) and macroenvironment. This attempts to answer such questions as: what type of clients and as donors are we attracting? What organizations are potential competitors for donors? What are the constraints and opportunities in our environment? Macroenvironmental questions may have to do with demographic trends and their impact on the organization (Espy, 1993). For example, the aging of the baby boom generation has implications for many organizations in terms of services needed, availability of volunteers, interest and ability to contribute money and in-kind goods and services, and so forth.

The organization needs to research what is known about giving in the United States. For example, recent studies have shown that 70.1% of American households contributed to nonprofits in 1998 and the average annual household contribution was $1,075 (Independent Sector, 2001). Most of the contributions went to religious organizations (60.1%), while 9% went to human services, 6.5% to health, and 4.9% to youth development.

- an evaluation of the *marketing system* of the organization–its objectives, programs, and implementation. This is the hardest aspect for many small nonprofits, for staff are often unaware that they actually have such a thing as a marketing system within their organization. While it is often unstated, unplanned, and certainly not written anywhere, it exists nevertheless. The object here is to be aware of, and articulate, what this system is.
- an evaluation of the major areas of *marketing activity* in the organization–its publics, products and services, pricing, place, and promotion. Some of the things the organization may be concerned with here include perceptions of the organization by its publics, especially prospective donors, and motivations for giving by current and prospective donors (Espy, 1993). In addition, the organization may want to look at its effectiveness in attracting potential and actual clients due to factors such as product or service, price, place, promotion or lack thereof. The audit thus can be the basis for more effective planning by the organization. Some types of fundraising activity an agency may be involved in include: annual campaigns, capital campaigns, deferred giving programs, endowment programs, and special events.

Types of Fundraising Programs

Annual Giving Programs or Campaigns: seek funds from donors who will give repeatedly over time. An annual giving program should be the cornerstone of an organization's fundraising plan. This type of program seeks to build a pool of contributors who will regularly give to support organization activities. The funds received from this type of activity can be used for new or on-going programs of the organization. A comparison of some of the costs and benefits of this and other fundraising programs may be seen in Table 5-1. An annual giving program should be the cornerstone of any nonprofit's fundraising efforts. The

Table 5-2
COMPARISON OF FUNDRAISING PROGRAMS*

Type of Program	Staff Time/ Effort	Cost	Productiv- ity
Annual Giving Program	High	Variable	High
Capital Program	High	Low	High
Deferred Giving Program	Low	Minimal	High
Endowment Program	Low	Low	High
Special Events	High	Variable	Variable

*Extrapolated from Freyd, W. (1980). "Methods of Successful Fund Raising," pp. 4–19 to 4–28 in Connors, T.D. (Ed.). The Nonprofit Organization Handbook. New York: MacGraw Hill.

staff time involved may be high, depending on the size of the agency and the extent of its volunteer pool. But the payback in terms of agency visibility as well as dollars raised can be very high.

Capital Programs: usually seek larger gifts, in installments over several years for capital projects such as renovating or buying existing buildings, or constructing new ones. The purpose of this type of fundraising effort is to have contributors committed to the long-range capital improvement of the organization's facilities. The staff time and effort involved in a capital campaign may be high, although other costs may be low. It may also involve the time of volunteers such as attorneys, mortgage brokers, and others with the expertise needed for the campaign.

Deferred Giving Programs: seek monies that are bequeathed to the organization from an estate or trust. In this form of giving, a contributor plans to leave money in a will or trust fund for the organization. It is called deferred giving because it will take place at a future time. To design a suitable program of this type requires the expertise of a financial planner, attorney, and accountant, therefore staff involvement may be low. This type of program takes consistent effort over a period of time, but can reap long-term rewards for the organization.

Endowment Programs: seek funds whose principal is to be invested, with the money earned from interest to be used for organization projects or programs. This type of money is restricted as the principal, or original amount given, cannot be spent. The money earned from the principal may also be restricted by the donor. Endowment programs may involve little staff time, except those of top administrators, but can yield high returns to the organization. Endowments are more fully discussed in Chapter Nine, Investments.

Special Events: use a variety of means to seek contributions from those who would not normally give to one's organization. The distinguishing characteristic of an event is that it is usually a one-time occurrence for the organization, it is not necessarily an activity that occurs regularly or even yearly. The staff time and effort needed for a special event may be high and may not be of much benefit to the organization unless those involved have the know-how to do it well.

In this chapter, the focus will be mainly on annual campaigns and special events, although the marketing principles discussed apply to all types of fundraising programs. Annual campaigns and special events are the most common types of fundraisers for human service agencies. They are also less complicated to plan and implement than are deferred giving programs or endowment programs.

Setting Marketing Goals and Objectives

It is crucial for an organization to set marketing goals in writing after going through brainstorming and planning sessions with staff and board members. Goals are broad statements of future desired states; objectives are specific, measurable, and time limited statements of how a goal is to be reached. There is a difference between organization goals and marketing goals. For example, an organizational goal might be:

- to provide foster care services to children under ten years of age.

Some *organizational objectives* to reach this goal may be:

- to locate and screen thirty new foster families during this calendar year;
- to train and certify thirty new foster families during this calendar year.

A *marketing goal* might be:

- to increase the number of referrals from child welfare agencies.

Some *marketing objectives* to reach these goals may be:

- to prepare materials regarding the organization to present to child welfare agencies within three months;
- to obtain new contracts with child welfare agencies (both state and local) by the end of the year;
- to increase the positive image of the organization as a child care provider this year by use of media.

After specific marketing goals and objectives have been agreed upon, the next step is selection of the specific target market that the organization wishes to reach.

Targeting

Targeting involves the "identification of individuals, groups, or people with special characteristics and with whom the organization wants to initiate and manage exchanges" (Rubright & MacDonald, 1981, p. 10). Individuals and groups that are usually targeted for fundraising include families of clients, former clients, other organizations, corporations, and certain groups of contributors. Targeting is a selective process; high priority groups who are possible givers are targeted first.

Once a group is targeted, the next stage involves what is called "market segmentation", breaking up the target market into more homogeneous groups that have a common interest in a particular cause, who have similar demographic profiles, who live in a particular geographic location, or some other common characteristic (Lauffer, 1997). For example, if your organization serves children with learning disabilities, then one target market segment might be parents or other relatives of such children. By segmenting the target market, the organization is better able to develop an appeal that will be appropriate for the audience chosen. Thus every segment is viewed as a separate audience. Then potential donors are ranked according to the likelihood that they will be responsive to your campaign.

Again, the organization must be aware of what is already known about different target markets. For example, some studies have found that men and women respond differently to different types of marketing approaches by nonprofits. Men have been found to respond more favorably to utilitarian (ego-gratification or help-self) appeals and females to altruistic (relationship or help-others) appeals (Brunel & Nelson, 2000).

Setting Strategies

Deciding on marketing strategies involves the delineation of tasks needed to be completed in order to reach your target markets and thus fulfill your marketing objectives. Four general marketing strategies that may be applied to fundraising are:

- **market penetration:** increasing fundraising efforts in the area and to the population currently targeted;
- **market development:** targeting fundraising programs to new markets;
- **product development:** improving present fundraising strategies;
- **diversification:** developing an entirely new campaign.

In deciding on marketing strategies, an organization must also keep in mind its 5 p's: publics, products, place, promotion, and price. Once the nonprofit has decided on one or more general marketing strategies, it must then examine some of the traditional approaches to fundraising, whether for a campaign or special event:

Collections: seek small sums from large numbers of people, most commonly in the form of setting canisters out, passing the basket, or going door-to-door with the help of volunteers. This approach may be used as a special event, although it is an annual fundraising approach for some small organizations. This method is very unsophisticated, can be very time-consuming, and may not generate much money for the organization. It is unsophisticated because it uses a "blanket" approach and does not target a market from which it could gain the maximum return for the amount of time invested (see Table 5-3 for a comparison of fundraising approaches).

Phone Solicitation: is a variant of collection in person. In this approach, individuals are often "cold called" either through random digit dialing or through the targeting of certain telephone exchanges. Occasionally, an organization will send notices out to members or prospective donors informing them that they will be called during a specific period of time. Often colleges, universities, large federated allocation

Table 5-3
COMPARISON OF FUNDRAISING APPROACHES*

Approach	Staff Time/Effort	Cost	Productivity
Direct Mail	High	High	Variable
Collections	Low–staff; High–volunteers	Low	Low
Merchandise Sales	Medium	Variable	Low
Merchandise Sales by Mail	Low	High	Variable
Advertising	Medium (but complex)	High	High
Internet Fundraising	Medium	Medium	Unknown

*Extrapolated from Freyd, W. (1980), "Methods of Successful Fund Raising," pp. 4–19 to 4–28 in T.D. Connors (Ed.). The Nonprofit Organization Handbook, New York: MacGraw Hill, Inc.

agencies do this. The calls need not be just for money. Occasionally calls are used to solicit in-kind contributions of clothing, household items, large appliances, autos, and similar items in this way.

Direct Mail: seeks gifts through the mail from large groups of donors who could not effectively be reached by other means. This approach is usually used for annual, capital, or endowment campaigns, rarely for a special event. Part of the secret of a successful mail campaign is to have a good mailing list. The development of such a list can be compiled by using present and former clients and contributors, targeting certain residential sections of the city, or even buying one or more lists from companies that specialize in direct mailing. A list of prospective contributors most useful to a specific organization may take a while to develop. Costs are very high in direct mailings; even with a bulk-rate permit or nonprofit permit, a large part of the cost may be for postage and printing. But if a good list can be developed, there is potential for a good return.

Merchandise Sales: seek sums through the selling of a product. Bazaars, flea markets, and bake sales are some examples of this approach. The investment in staff and volunteer time may be somewhat high, although cost may be negligible. If the organization can use donated items to sell, or goods made by volunteers, then the cost of such an effort will be low. But if the organization has to buy goods to sell, the cost may be too high for the amount of return involved. This approach is also relatively unsophisticated because it does not usually target a market segment, rather it seeks sales from any passerby. This approach is usually part of a special event, although some organizations regularly schedule them as an annual fundraiser.

Merchandise Sales by Mail: combines features of mail solicitation with offering a small product as an incentive to the potential donor. These are often unsolicited items, that is, the donor did not order them. They are sent to persons on mailing lists that may have been bought by an organization, and also include any persons who may have donated in the past. There is an interesting psychological element to this approach. That is, even if the item was not ordered by the donor, people often feel guilty using something they did not pay for. Thus instead of sending the item back, which for many people is a bother, they send a check.

Advertising: seeks to reach a great many people quickly with a message. It is most effectively used in crisis situations, for example, if an organization were soliciting funds to be used for the victims of a disaster such as a fire, flood, or earthquake. This approach may be used either for an annual campaign or special event. Some organizations use ads all year long as part of an annual campaign to solicit donations of big ticket items such as cars. A good advertising campaign takes the expertise of a professional who knows how to write good copy. The cost of advertising can be high, therefore this approach may be out of reach for most small human service agencies. However, all agencies should make use of the free public service announcements that are available through local media to keep their programs in the public eye and increase positive image and name recognition.

In addition to these traditional approaches to fundraising, there are new approaches being tried. One of the newest is by use of the internet.

Internet Fundraising: uses the internet to solicit funds, sell merchandise, or even to hold auctions for nonprofits. A number of websites have been set up by companies (both for-profit and nonprofit) who act as middlemen for nonprofits. They provide the website, they also may post photos of merchandise, and provide other services as well, including the processing of credit card payments. Some large nonprofits have begun using the internet in this way themselves. This is a new and relatively uncharted area, so at this point it is not clear how charitable nonprofits will be regulated regarding this type of fundraising, how widespread is the use, or what real costs are entailed (See the listing of online fundraising resources for nonprofits at the end of this chapter).

The type of fundraising strategy attempted by a particular organization depends on a number of factors, such as available funds for start-up, expertise of staff and board, commitment of staff, board, and volunteers, time availability of staff, and results of any feasibility study that may have been done. Actually, an organization should use a variety of approaches aimed at different target markets, and marketing should be an on-going activity in every organization. Nonprofits should also be aware that any successful fundraising strategy may take a few initial lean years, with each year bringing more expertise, more name-recognition in the community, and hopefully, a bigger response to organization efforts.

In addition to choosing one or more of these strategies, the fundraising committee must draw up a schedule of crucial tasks, including a time-line for completion and persons responsible for each phase of the project. A Gantt chart is a useful way to do this planning (See Table 5-4). Record keeping is important for funding sources, tax agencies, credit-rating bureaus, and the general public. A list of needed records must be compiled and stored in a secure place. Adherence to record

Table 5-4
SAMPLE GANTT CHART

Tasks Event	Person(s) Responsible	12	11	10	9	8	7	6	5	4	3	2	1
Obtain space	Joe	■											
Obtain permit	Joan	■											
Solicit donated items	Pete, Sylvia, Jo	■											
Tag and mark items	Fred, Ida, Don		■	■	■	■	■	■					
Contact media	Joe and Sue					■	■	■	■				
Schedule volunteers	Joan					■		■		■		■	■
Meet with volunteers	Sue									■		■	■
Put up signs	Tom and Sylvia										■	■	■
etc.												■	■

keeping guidelines should be assured by the organization's book-keeper, accountant, or board treasurer.

Budgeting

Unfortunately, most funding sources do not dispense money for fundraising. Yet fundraising costs money. As the old saying goes, "It takes money to make money". Thus money for fundraising must come from unrestricted revenue, not public support. And since fundraising can be expensive, it must be budgeted for. The cost of a fundraising event will depend on a number of factors such as type of fundraising strategies chosen, expertise of staff, support of volunteers, image and name-recognition of organization, public attitudes toward the services offered by the organization, size of the organization, and so forth. Initial costs of starting an annual campaign may be very high, depending on approach, but over time the costs should go down. A nonprofit should always try to keep its fundraising costs as low as possible, however, since this is one area in which human services agencies may be publicly criticized if these costs are too high in proportion to costs of service delivery.

Some of the components of a fundraising budget may include the following, although all the items may not be applicable to all programs (Pendleton, 1981):

- preliminary feasibility study
- salaries, including time of administrators, program directors, line staff and supervisors, secretaries (this time must be apportioned between fundraising expenses and program expenses)
- office expenses, including rent (this must also be apportioned)
- postage, printing, photography or other art work
- cost of mailing list
- travel and lodging
- meals
- professional fees
- cost of materials or items for resale
- any other miscellaneous costs (see Table 5-5 below).

All of these and any other related costs must be subtracted from the projected amount of monies obtained through fundraising efforts, something organization planners sometimes forget to do. When developing the fundraising budget, it is also important to show in-kind contributions as well. Without considering the total costs of fundraising, the organization may be very disappointed when the final results of their efforts gain little.

Table 5-5
SAMPLE FUNDRAISING BUDGET
HUMAN SERVICES ORGANIZATION, INC.
PROJECTED BUDGET FOR ANNUAL FUNDRAISER: DINNER AND AUCTION

Expense Item	Cash	In-kind Contributions
Secretarial (10% time)	$1,200	–
Volunteer time	–	$ 5,000
Office expense (including rent; 10%)	$3,000	–
Cost of items for sale	–	$10,000
Materials for signs	$ 75	–
Newspaper ad	–	$ 100
Food for volunteers	$ 100	–
Food for sale	–	$ 5,000
Total	$4,375	$20,100

Total cost of fundraiser	$24,475
Less in-kind contributions	$20,100
Cash outlay	$ 4,375
Fundraising goal (proceeds)	$15,000
Total cash needed to be raised	$19,375

Implementing Strategies

If the organization has planned well, and has structures and mechanisms in place for deploying its resources of staff and volunteers to the fundraising effort, then implementation is nothing more than following the steps laid out. One key to any such effort is having a well-organized coordinator to oversee the day-to-day fundraising operation. Larger organizations have a development person in charge of such activities, but small nonprofits cannot afford such a person. Usually an administrator or volunteer becomes responsible then for this coordination. One important aspect of any fundraiser is communication, especially communication to those publics the organization is trying to reach. This involves development of promotional materials.

Development of Promotional Materials

Since many small human service agencies cannot afford to pay professionals to develop these materials, they often must do it themselves. Other agencies usually have volunteers or board contacts who can provide this service at minimal or no cost. Another place where help may be obtained at a somewhat lower cost is the art departments of colleges and universities. Art students may be hired to help, or faculty members may volunteer their services. If an organization is developing a website or wishes to fundraise via the internet, then it must seek the services of computer programmers or others with expertise in these areas. There are a number of sites on the world wide web that offer services to nonprofits, some of these for free. Whatever the means, the important thing to remember is that the marketing materials that are developed should be the product of a planning process to reach appropriate targets.

Evaluation, Feedback, Modification

Finally, the marketing process should involve evaluation, feedback, and internal adjustment in order to modify or revise any part of the marketing plan that does not seem to be working effectively. Fundraising is not an end in itself, it is a means to an end—the provision of services to those in need.

The organization needs to evaluate the success of its fundraising efforts by more than the criterion of reaching a stated dollar amount. The organization must also evaluate the cost/efficiency of reaching its goals.

So, for example, the organization may have reached its goal of raising $25,000, but at what cost? Was the time spent by volunteers and staff in terms of person-hours worth the effort? How much did it cost the organization to raise that $25,000? One study of returns on fundraising showed that charities related to religious causes achieve higher rates of return than other categories of nonprofits (Sargent & Kahler, 1999). Interestingly, animal protection receives the next highest rate of return on money spent for marketing, even higher than children, mental health or the physically disabled. The organization's fundraising committee needs to ask, what could have been done differently to make the outcome more productive?

Another aspect of success is the good will created by volunteers and staff involved in a fundraising effort. If there are negative comments in the community or press, if there are complaints, then the organization has failed, no matter how much money was raised. For agencies with little experience in marketing and fundraising, it is a learning experience that involves trial and error. Once the organization has developed some expertise, it will find that these events become easier to manage although one must always be alert to unforeseen occurrences.

IMPLICATIONS OF FUNDRAISING FOR NONPROFITS

There are implications of fundraising for nonprofits that must be kept in mind, both in the planning phase as well as the end or acquisition phase. For example, even though nonprofit human service organizations are tax-exempt, they are subject to corporate taxes on what is called unrelated business income. They are also required to report their contributions in specific ways as well as reporting the contribution time of certain of their volunteers. Finally, nonprofits must consider how fundraising costs will be allocated and reported on their books, to the IRS, and to the general public through annual reports, posting of their 990's, and other means.

Unrelated Business Income Tax

Even though nonprofits are exempt from federal income tax they are still required to file annually with the IRS. Further, there is a federal tax known as the Tax on Unrelated Business Income of Exempt Organizations (commonly called UBIT) that a nonprofit should be aware of. Nonprofits are exempt from taxes on income from normal activities carried out in furtherance of their mission. But if a nonprofit engages in a trade or business not substantively related to its mission (the reason for its exemption), then it may be subject to a tax. Internal Revenue Publication 598 (U.S. Department of the Treasury,1998) states:

> Unrelated business income is the income from a trade or business that is regularly carried on by an exempt organization and that is not substantively related to the performance by the organization of its exempt purpose or function, except that the organization uses the profits derived from this activity.

For most nonprofits that engage in periodic or annual fundraisers, the UBIT is not a problem (Hines, 1998). The annual or periodic activity, if not regularly carried on, does not come under this definition. But even fundraising activities carried out on an ongoing basis, if they contribute substantively to the main mission of the organization, may also be exempt. For example, a sheltered workshop whose goal is rehabilitation of handicapped persons or a halfway house workshop whose goal is rehabilitation or job training, both of which receive revenue from items made by these persons, are exempt from unrelated business income tax (U.S. Department of the Treasury, 1998). On the other hand, the rental of parking spaces in its parking lot on weekdays by a church may be questioned as an on-going activity not substantively related to the church's mission.

Accounting for Contributions

In 1993 the Financial Accounting Standards Board (FASB) issued Standards of Financial Accounting Statement (SFAS) 116, *Accounting for Contributions Received and Contributions Made.* This had a tremendous impact on nonprofits, not so much because it tried to bring uniformity in the way that contributions were treated, but because of the scope of what was included under the rubric of "contributions".

SFAS-116 defines a contribution as " . . . an unconditional transfer of cash or other assets to an entity. . . . Other assets include securities, land, buildings, use of facilities or utilities, materials and supplies, intangible assets, services, and unconditional promises to give those items in the future" (1993, par. 5).

SFAS-116 further states that contributions received by a nonprofit have to be recognized as revenue or gains in the period received. These contributions have to be measured or recorded at their fair market value. They also have to be reported as either restricted support or unrestricted support, depending on the stipulations of the donor.

In addition to the material kinds of contributions that nonprofits are familiar with, they are now also required to report the activities of certain types of volunteers as contributions. Contributions of volunteer time are an important aspect of nonprofit operations. It has been reported that a large number of Americans volunteer, in fact 55.5% of the adult population of the United States volunteered some time to nonprofits in 1998 (Independent Sector, 2001). Those 34–44 years of age had the highest rates of volunteering, 67.3%, for an average of 3.7 hours per week. Eleven percent (11.4%) of the volunteering was for human service organizations. The total value of the adult volunteer time for all nonprofits in 1998 was estimated at $225.9 billion dollars (at a rate of $14.30 per hour).

SFAS-116 has these criteria for deciding whether a volunteer service should be recognized as a contribution:

1. The services create or enhance nonfinancial assets, for example, volunteers build a new facility or make major improvements to existing facilities; or
2. The services meet all three of the following criteria:
    a. Require specialized skills,
    b. Are provided by persons possessing those skills, and
    c. Would typically have to be purchased if not provided by volunteers.

So for example, if a volunteer who was a professional computer technician installed a new computer system for an organization, this would meet all three of the criteria listed above. If all three of these criteria are met, the organization may have to list the volunteer services as income or public support in its financial statements. However, it may also allocate the value of the services as expenses to program or support as well in much the same way it does for program staff. And if the amount of the donated services are not significant, an organization may not need to report them at all (FASB, 1993). In making such a determination, nonprofits may wish to consult with their CPA, as is true with the issue of allocation of costs as described below.

Allocating and Reporting Fundraising Costs

In the past, there has been much question as to how nonprofits reported and allocated fundraising costs. Some felt that nonprofits used "creative accounting" to hide fundraising costs and thus make it appear that they spent less on fundraising and more on program activities (Williams & Teutsch, 1983). Nonprofits, on the other hand, claimed that often what they did was not just fundraising, but fundraising activities that also might include programmatic elements such as public education or outreach.

In 1998, the American Institute of Certified Public Accountants (AICPA) issued Statement of Position 98-2, *Accounting for Costs of Activities of Not-for-profit Organizations and State and Local Government Entities That Include Fund Raising*. This statement applies to all nonprofits and establishes financial accounting standards for costs of joint activities as well as how they should be disclosed. *Joint activities* are activities that are "part of the fund-raising function and ha[ve] elements of one or more other functions, such as program, management and general, membership development, or any other functional category used by the entity" (AICPA, 1993, p. 84). *Joint costs,* then, are costs that may include both fundraising and program components.

How do we decide whether an activity is a "joint activity"? SOP 98-2 has three criteria for joint activities, all of which have to be met. If not all three are met, the activity cost must be allocated to fundraising only. The criteria are:

1. **Purpose:** Does the joint activity accomplish program or management and general functions? To accomplish a program function, it must call for "specific action by the audience that will help accomplish the entity's mission" (par. 9). Asking an audience just to make a contribution does not meet this criteria, the action must involve activities that are related to the organization's mission. For example, it is not enough for a health organization, in conjunction with a fundraising activity, to inform an audience about the dangers of smoking. It must also call for some action, such as asking the audience to stop smoking or to participate in a "No Smoking Day".

To accomplish program and management and general functions, other factors, in addition to a call for action, are to be considered, including whether compensation or fees for performing the activity are based on contributions raised. If this is the case, then all costs associated with the activity would be considered fundraising. Another factor to be considered is whether any similar program activities or management and general activities have been conducted on the same scale using the same medium (for example, a mailing) without a fundraising appeal. If so, then joint costs can be allocated.

2. **Audience:** Does the audience (or recipients of a mailing, or similar target) contain prior donors only or those likely to contribute to the organization? If so, then the activity is a fundraising activity, not a joint activity. To meet the audience criteria, the audience must be chosen because it needs to engage in the specific action called for, it has the ability to take the specific action, or the audience has reasonable potential for use of the management and general component. For example, there are adults or teenagers in the target group who need to stop smoking, they have the ability to stop smoking, or they are potential clients of the health agency's stop smoking workshop.

3. **Content:** Does the purported joint activity support both fundraising and program, or management and general, functions? The content criterion will be met if the joint activity calls for action by the audience that helps to accomplish the organization's mission or if the joint activity fulfills one or more of the organization's management and general responsibilities.

If all of the criteria are met, a nonprofit that allocates joint costs should disclose them in the notes to their financial statements. The disclosure should include types of joint activities for which costs were incurred, a statement that costs were allocated, and the total amount allocated as well as the portion allocated to each functional expense category (AICPA, 1998, par. 18). SOP 98-2 also addresses the issue of means of allocating costs, these were discussed in Chapter Four, Budgeting.

ETHICAL ISSUES FOR ORGANIZATIONS THAT ENGAGE IN FUNDRAISING ACTIVITIES

Because of the potential for unethical behavior on the part of some individuals and organizations purporting to be engaging in charitable fundraising, the public has a right to be wary of solicitations and other fundraising approaches. There are two organizations that were formed as a service to individuals and companies wishing to know something more about organizations approaching them for funds. These organizations are the National Information Charities Bureau (NICB) and the Philanthropic Advisory Service (PAS) of the Council of Better Business Bureaus (CBBB). Both of these organizations have developed standards for organizations soliciting funds. See Reading 5-1 for excerpts from standards of PAS applied to all 501(c)(3) organizations. In addition, some professional fundraising groups have developed a donor's bill of rights. Excerpts of that can be found in Reading 5-2. Nonprofits should be familiar with these standards and consider whether they want to incorporate basic principles of ethical fundraising into their bylaws or charters.

Fundraising is an important and vital activity in nonprofit human service organizations. While some agencies have developed sophisticated fundraising approaches, others are at a loss as to the most rudimentary steps. Marketing and fundraising know-how are essential survival skills for nonprofits, many of which tend to depend too heavily on too few resources. While managing a marketing or fundraising event has become more complicated, it can be rewarding to nonprofits, not just in terms of additional resources, but also in terms of building and expanding community goodwill, volunteer support, and other positive consequences.

Reading 5-1: CBBB Standards for Charitable Solicitations*

Public Accountability

1. Soliciting organizations shall provide on request an annual report.
2. Soliciting organizations shall provide on request complete financial statements.
3. Soliciting organizations' financial statements shall present adequate information to serve as a basis for informed decisions.
4. Organizations receiving a substantial portion of their income through the fundraising activities of controlled or affiliated entities shall provide on request an accounting of all income received by and fundraising costs incurred by such entities.

Use of Funds

1. A reasonable percentage of total income from all sources shall be applied to programs and activities directly related to the purposes for which the organization exists.
2. A reasonable percentage of public contributions shall be applied to the programs and activities described in the solicitations, in accordance with donor expectations.
3. Fund raising costs shall be reasonable.
4. Total fund raising and administrative costs shall be reasonable.

* Council of Better Business Bureaus, 1982. http://www.bbb.org/about/charstandard.html

5. Soliciting organizations shall substantiate on request their application of funds, in accordance with donor expectations, to the programs and activities described in solicitations.
6. Soliciting organizations shall establish and exercise adequate controls over disbursements.

Solicitations and Informational Materials

1. Solicitations and informational materials, distributed by any means, shall be accurate, truthful and not misleading, both in whole and in part.
2. Soliciting organizations shall substantiate on request that solicitations and informational materials, distributed by any means, are accurate, truthful and not misleading, in whole and in part.
3. Solicitations shall include a clear description of the programs and activities for which funds are requested.
4. Direct contact solicitations, including personal and telephone appeals, shall identify a) the solicitor and his/her relationship to the benefiting organization, b) the benefiting organization or cause and c) the programs and activities for which funds are requested.
5. Solicitations in conjunction with the sale of goods, services or admissions shall identify at the point of solicitation a) the benefiting organization, b) a source from which written information is available and c) the actual or anticipated portion of the sales or admission price to benefit the charitable organization or cause.

Fund Raising Practices

1. Soliciting organizations shall establish and exercise controls over fund raising activities conducted for their benefit by staff, volunteers, consultants, contractors, and controlled or affiliated entities, including commitment to writing of all fund raising contracts and agreements.
2. Soliciting organizations shall establish and exercise adequate controls over contributions.
3. Soliciting organizations shall honor donor requests for confidentiality and shall not publicize the identity of donors without prior written permission.
4. Fund raising shall be conducted without excessive pressure.

Governance

1. Soliciting organizations shall have an adequate governing structure.

2. Soliciting organizations shall have an active governing body.
3. Soliciting organizations shall have an independent governing body.

Reading 5-2: A Donor's Bill of Rights*

Philanthropy is based on voluntary action for the common good. It is a tradition of giving and sharing that is primary to the quality of life. To assure that philanthropy merits the respect and trust of the general public, and that donors and prospective donors can have full confidence in the not-for-profit organizations and causes they are asked to support, we declare that all donors have these rights:

1. To be informed of the organization's mission, of the way the organization intends to use donated resources, and of its capacity to use donations effectively for their intended purposes.
2. To be informed of the identity of those serving on the organization's governing board, and to expect the board to exercise prudent judgment in its stewardship responsibilities.
3. To have access to the organization's most recent financial statements.
4. To be assured their gifts will be used for the purposes for which they were given.
5. To receive appropriate acknowledgment and recognition.
6. To be assured that information about their donations is handled with respect and with confidentiality to the extent provided by law.
7. To expect that all relationships with individuals representing organizations of interest to the donor will be professional in nature.
8. To be informed whether those seeking donations are volunteers of the organization or hired solicitors.
9. To have the opportunity for their names to be deleted from mailing lists that an organization may intend to share.
10. To feel free to ask questions when making a donation and to receive prompt, truthful, and forthright answers.

REFERENCES

---

* Developed by the American Association of Fund Raising Counsel, Association for Healthcare Philanthropy, Council for Advancement and Support of Education and National Association of Fund Raising Executives. http://www.afpnet.org.

American Institute of Certified Public Accountants, Inc., *Accounting Standards Executive Committee (1998). Statement of Position 98-2: Accounting for Costs of Activities of Not-for-profit Organizations and State and Local Governmental Entities that Include Fund Raising.* New York, New York.

Brunel, F.F. & Nelson, M.R. (2000). Explaining gendered responses to "help-self" and "help-others" charity ad appeals: The mediating role of world-views. *Journal of Advertising,* 29(3):16–28.

Council of Better Business Bureaus, Philanthropic Advisory Service (1982). CBBB *Standards for Charitable Solicitations.* New York. http://www.bbb.org/about/charstandard.html

Espy, S. (1993). *Marketing Strategies for Nonprofit Organizations.* Chicago, Lyceum Books, Inc.

Financial Accounting Standards Board (1993). Financial Accounting Standard (SFAS) 116, *Accounting for Contributions Received and Contributions Made.* Stamford, CT.

Hines, J. R. Jr. (1998). *Nonprofit business activity and the unrelated business income tax.* National Bureau of Economic Research (NBER) Working Paper No. W6820.

Independent Sector (2001). *The New Nonprofit Almanac in Brief: Facts and Figures on the Independent Sector 2001.* Washington, D.C.: Author.

Kotler, P. (1982). *Marketing for Nonprofit Organizations.* Englewood Cliffs, NJ: Prentice-Hall, Inc.

Kotler, P. & Andreasen, A. R. (1991). *Strategic Marketing for Nonprofit Organizations* (4th ed.). Englewood Cliffs, NJ: Prentice-Hall, Inc.

Lauffer, A. (1997). *Grants, etc.* (2nd ed.). Thousand Oaks, CA: Sage Publications.

Pendleton, N. (1981). *Fundraising.* Englewood Cliffs, NJ: Prentice-Hall, Inc.

Rubright, R. & MacDonald, D. (1981). *Marketing Health and Human Services.* Rockville, Md: Aspen Systems.

Sargeant, A. & Kahler, J. (1999). Returns on fundraising expenditures in the voluntary sector. *Nonprofit Management and Leadership,* 10(1):5–19.

U.S. Department of the Treasury. Internal Revenue Service (1998). Publication 598: *Tax on Unrelated Business Income of Exempt Organizations.* Washington, D.C.: U.S. Superintendent of Documents. http://www.irs.ustreas.gov/prod/forms_pubs/pubs/p598toc.htm

Vanderleest, H.W. (1985). Needed: a clear understanding of the marketing process. *Nonprofit World,* 3(6):20–22.

Williams, L. & Teutsch, C. (1983). Suite charity. *Dallas Times Herald.* October 16.

INTERNET RESOURCES

Association of Fundraising Professionals. http://www.afpnet.org

Capin, Gregory B. & Tannenbaum, Joel (1998). How to report a joint activity. *Journal of Accountancy,* Online Issues, August 1998. http://www.aicpa.org/pubs/jofa/aug98/capin.htm.

Council of Better Business Bureaus. http://www.bbb.org

Chronicle of Philanthropy. http://www.philanthropy.com

Elementary E-Philanthropy. http://www.genie.org/hottopic_pages/
     e_philanthropy.htm
Internet Nonprofit Center. http://www.nonprofits.org/npofaq

Chapter Six

GRANTWRITING AND GRANTS MANAGEMENT

After reading this chapter you should be able to:

1. Understand the grantwriting process;
2. Know where to look for potential funding sources of grants;
3. Write a grant;
4. Know where to go for additional information;
5. Be familiar with federal grants management guidelines.

INTRODUCTION

A grant is an allocation of funds from a governmental agency, a private foundation, or sometimes a federated funding source, to a human service organization for a specific program or project. Grants differ tremendously in terms of amounts, eligibility requirements, purposes, and regulations. Some are open to any nonprofit organization; some are restricted to specific purposes or types of organizations. For example, some funding sources only fund certain types of activities such as health, welfare, education, alcohol, drug rehabilitation, and so forth. Other sources only fund organizations in particular geographic areas, such as their home state, or their own county. Each federal department with grant monies available obviously only funds in its area of interest, but within that area of interest the appropriate grantees may be narrowly defined.

The availability of grants also varies with the economic and political climate, so that in the "social reform" era of the 1960's and early 1970's there was ample grant money available from the federal government, while in the 1980's this source of funds became more constricted. As a result, there was increased competition for fewer funds. More and more nonprofits began to look to private and corporate foundations for grants and, as a result, the foundations were flooded with applications. In the early 21st century, there are grant monies available, especially from federal and state governments. In fact, governments are the major funders for many large nonprofits by means of grants as well as contracts (Boris, 2000).

To obtain a grant, a nonprofit needs to submit a proposal to the funding source outlining exactly what it intends to do with the money, for what period of time, and agree to abide by the evaluation and reporting guidelines of the grantor. While an organization may receive funds from its local United Way and/or other federated funding source for continuous on-going support, most grants are not given for this purpose. Grants are usually given for a limited period of time; so one of the factors an organization must consider when it looks to granting agencies for funds as seed money for new projects or programs is how it will continue the program or services after the grant money is no longer available.

In grantwriting, there are two main concerns of the grantwriter: (1) Where do I find information on funding sources? (2) How do I write the grant proposal? The purpose of this chapter is to acquaint you with the nature of the grantwriting process, which involves a number of different activities culminating in the submission of a grant proposal. The main focus will be the planning necessary in developing a project and the searching for, and screening of, funding sources. A brief discussion of the actual mechanics of writing a grant proposal will follow. There is a wealth of information on grantwriting and sources of grants on the world wide web; these may be found at the end of the chapter. Lastly, grants management will be discussed. That is, what it is that the organization needs to do once it receives a grant? In the following discussion, "the organization or agency" refers to those designated individuals in the organization responsible for the grantwriting effort, as well as administrators and staff who are ultimately responsible for the grant project.

THE GRANTWRITING PROCESS

Grantwriting is a process that involves much more than sitting down and writing a proposal. It is a planning process with colleagues within the organization as well as outside of it. It is also a political activity in the sense that the grantwriter must be able to garner community support, as well as use the available help from the funding source to write a better proposal. There are two main ways that an organization may become involved in writing a grant proposal for funding:

- In response to an RFP (request for proposal) circulated by a governmental organization or private funding source;
- In response to a specific community need or problem, in which case the organization initiates the grant proposal and contact with a funding source.

In the former case, organization staff have a specific funding source in mind and are thus spared the tedious search for an appropriate donor. The grantwriter(s) may then proceed to the actual mechanics of writing the grant. In the latter case, staff must expend time and energy to find a suitable funder for the organization's project. In the grantwriting process to be described below, the assumption is that the organization looking for funds is not responding to an RFP and thus has to search for a funding source.

While the grantwriting process may be viewed in different ways, there are some basic steps in the process that may include the following (Lauffer,1997; Lindholm, et al,1982; FEMA, 1983): 1) Assign grantwriting responsibility; 2) plan program/project; 3) search for appropriate funding source(s); 4) evaluate and select appropriate funding source(s); 5) initiate contact with funding source(s); 6) write and submit grant (see Figure 6-1).

Assign Responsibility

Someone has to be responsible for the grantwriting effort, the coordination of information and resources, the contacting of potential funders, and the shepherding of the actual grant. Often one individual is the actual grantwriter and calls on others within the organization as well as outside of it for help as needed. In other cases, a grantwriting committee is established and the various tasks divided up among the committee members.

In either case, someone has to have the responsibility as well as the authority to make decisions regarding the grant, the funding source, and the proposed project. Often this person is the one who will eventually implement the proposal if the grant is funded, since the writer is the most knowledgeable about the project. If only one individual is responsible for writing the grant, s/he should receive assurances that additional help will be forthcoming, as needed, and that organization resources will be available to complete the grant proposal in a timely manner. Once these matters are settled, the actual planning can begin.

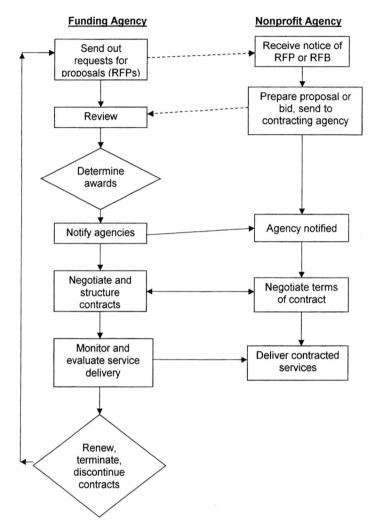

Figure 6-1: The Grantwriting Process

Plan Program/Project

Define Your Problems or Needs

The organization may be aware, from a variety of sources, of certain needs or problems in the community that are not being met by other community agencies. These needs or problems may have come to its attention because of the types of clients it is already serving, because of input from other agencies or groups in the community or because the organization has done a systematic assessment of needs. Due to the nature of the problems and the mission of the agency, it may feel uniquely qualified to deliver services to meet these needs or problems. The services that need to be delivered may be necessary adjuncts to services that the organization already provides. For example, if the organization treats troubled youth, then a logical offshoot program might be a family counseling program, or a teen pregnancy program. If it provides meals to homeless persons, then other logical adjunct services could be job counseling, or housing placement. Or the organization may desire to branch out into a new area of service because it knows the needs are there and it has the staff with expertise to provide the service.

In defining the need or problem area for a grant proposal, the organization must be able to explicate the needs or problems in the community. In other words, it must be able to document the needs or problems (see Witkin & Altschuld, 1995). There are a number of different ways to do this. The organization may want conduct a needs assessment in the community, or if it does not have the time, money, or expertise to carry on such a study it could try to collect data from secondary sources such as a United Way, a University, a city planning department, or a community group. Other sources of information include college or community libraries that contain current census data, key informants in the community, and staffs of elected officials.

The documentation should be able to illustrate who is affected by the problem, that is, what segments of the population, what age groups, ethnic groups, and how many in the community are affected. The documentation should also describe the ways in which the target population is affected by the problem or need, and what will happen if intervention does not take place. Sometimes it is very difficult to state definitively all the ways that people are affected by a problem, especially since some problems are not manifest for years. In these cases, the proposal writer could extrapolate from what is known now about the affects of some problems and project how these would impact on the population in the community or the community itself in the future.

Develop Goals, Objectives, and Strategies to Meet Needs and/or Solve Problems

After an examination of the existing human service needs in the community, the organization can then move on to developing goals, objectives, and strategies to meet these needs or problems. The writing of goals and objectives was discussed previously in another chapter. Remember that goals are broad statements of desired future states, while objectives are specific, measurable, time-limited means to reach goals.

Strategies are specific actions to reach objectives. In the case of most human service agencies, objectives involve choosing the most appropriate level or method of intervention to reach the target population with the stated problem.

Once objectives are formulated they should be prioritized, first by how congruent they are with the current short- and long-range goals of the organization; second, on the basis of a number of different variables, including costs, the existing resources of the organization, its capabilities, staff available or needed to be hired, and what is known about the most effective ways of ameliorating certain human conditions. Other factors include the priorities of the potential funding source(s), if known at this time, and the projected effect on current clients and programs.

After objectives have been prioritized, organization staff can start developing strategies to meet each objective. A program plan can be developed that includes tasks involved, a timetable, a budget, staff and material resources needed, duties and responsibilities of staff, and some measures to evaluate the effectiveness of the program. Use of a program planning chart or Gantt chart is useful in clarifying the implementation steps of the proposed project and reflects in-depth thought on the part of staff.

Describe the Strengths and Capabilities of the Organization

After defining needs, goals, and objectives, the organization must look to its capabilities in meeting the stated needs for which grant money is desired. Information that can be used in describing the capabilities and achievements of the organization are annual reports, brochures, and other materials that have, in all probability, already been prepared for other purposes. In addition, some summary of the qualifications of existing program staff to manage the proposed project or activity should be prepared. Up-to-date resumes of staff should always be kept on hand, or be readily available for this purpose.

In addition to staff qualifications, other information needed to describe the strengths of the organizations relates to current programs and clients served, and how the proposed project fits or deviates from current organizational goals and activities. Physical plant and other resources of the organization should be described, as well as organization location and accessibility to the target population and other community resources.

Based on the data available, the organization has started building its case for grant funds, but the organization should be honest with itself and the funding source in answering these questions: Do these problems or needs lend themselves to funding as a solution, or is the real purpose of this grant proposal just a scheme to keep the organization afloat? Are there really no alternative means to dealing with the stated need or problem besides the implementation of a new service or program? If the organization is not willing to ask these questions, be assured that the funding source will.

Now that you know what it is your organization wants to do, it is now time to find an appropriate funder for your project if you have not already done so by replying to a request for proposal (RFP).

Search for Appropriate Funding Source

One of the most important aspects of obtaining grants is knowing where to look for sources that award grants. It is not enough just to have a good idea, or know the techniques of writing. If you cannot communicate your idea to the people who are interested in funding the type of problem your organization is trying to address, then you are wasting your time. This is why it is necessary to spend some time on the crucial step of matching your organization priorities with those of an appropriate funding source. It is not wise to use the "shot-gun" approach by submitting proposals to every foundation and government organization whose address is available. Rather, you should take some time to research whether this funding source is most appropriate for your agency.

Where then, does one look to find out where the money is? There are three main sources of grant funds: governments (federal, state, and local), foundations, and corporations. The first place to go for information on most of these sources is your local public or university library. Many libraries have a section devoted to information on grants, in fact there are federal regional depositories as well as regional depositories of the Foundation Center all over the country (see internet resources for website). If your library does not have such a center, ask the librarian for some of the publications discussed below as well or go online to search for such resources. The internet is a useful and convenient spot to find information.

Governmental Funding Sources

For information on federal government grants, the two best sources are the *Catalog of Federal Domestic Assistance* and the *Federal Register*. These are published by the Federal Government and available from the

Superintendent of Documents, many local libraries, as well as the internet (see internet sources at the end of chapter).

The Catalog of Federal Domestic Assistance: The Catalog of Federal Domestic Assistance identifies over one thousand assistance programs administered by 51 Federal government agencies. It is the basic reference source for information about Federal government programs, since it is a compilation of programs administered by various Federal departments and agencies all in one place. It is a useful tool in identifying programs which may be of interest to the grant writer. The Catalog is published annually, usually in June, and an Update with the latest information on monies available after the passage of the Federal budget is published, usually in December.

The Federal Register: The Federal Register is published daily, Monday through Friday, throughout the year. It publishes legal notices issued by federal agencies, thus, it is the place to look for requests for proposals (RFP's). The requests for proposals published in the Federal Register contain the general guidelines and other information pertinent to the proposal. The RFP's also contain contact persons names and numbers for more information in each state. Since the Register is published every day, it has more up-to-date information than the Catalog, but the Catalog is a good place to start to get a general overview. Certain times of the year seem to be best for using the Register. For example, after the annual federal budget is passed, there are likely to be RFP's issued by the Department of Health and Human Services, and other agencies. When major legislation relating to human services is passed throughout the year, there will be a good possibility that RFP's will be issued when monies are available.

State and Local Funding Sources: There may not be information on state and local governmental funding readily available in some states. The grantwriter must call relevant agencies, for example, Departments of Human Services, Social Services, Youth Services, Drug and Alcohol Abuse, and so forth, and ask to be put on a mailing list to receive announcements of RFP's when that department issues them. In addition, all states have home pages on the world wide web where various departments can be searched. They all use the same format: www.[name of state].us

At the county and city level, again, calling is useful, but so is being up-to-date on the politics in the local area. Being in contact with city planning and council staff may be useful. In some areas, a proposal has to be presented before the city council or county commissioners. The grantwriter has to explore the specifics of the local area.

Foundation Funding Sources

For information on foundations, there are national and state foundation directories available, even county foundation directories available in some cases. Some of the best sources for national and state information are the Foundation Directory and the Annual Register of Grant Support.

The Foundation Directory: The Foundation Directory is one of the best sources for getting information on foundations interested in your subject area. It provides information on the nation's largest foundations that make grants, those that have assets over $1 million and that give at least $100,000 in grants annually. The Directory is arranged by state and alphabetically by foundation name within each state. It lists much useful information about each foundation, including types of grants, interest areas, and so forth. The Directory is published by the Foundation Center, which also publishes other resource materials for grant seekers (see web address at end of chapter).

Annual Register of Grant Support: The Annual Register of Grant Support includes information of grant programs of governmental agencies, public and private foundations, as well as other types of special interest organizations. The Annual Register lists thousands of entries in its latest edition.

There are a number of other resources available to the grantwriter, but the ones mentioned here are the best places to start looking. There are many sources available on the internet. Just type in a keyword such as "grants" or "grantwriting" to do a search and a wealth of information can be found. Also, if one is interested in more detailed information about a particular foundation, about 500 foundations publish annual reports that the prospective grantee can obtain upon request.

Corporate Funding Sources

Corporations should be the last resort for the grantwriter, as they give much less to social programs than either government or foundations. New tax laws make it less attractive than it used to be for corporations to do this, although they have never been major funders in the social service area. Those corporations wanting to donate to nonprofits often use the corporate foundation as the vehicle to accomplish this end. However, corporations should not be totally ruled out, as some of the large corporations in a community may be willing to donate monies or in-kind goods and services if your organization can present a good case and the project is one that interests the funder (see list of internet resources at end of chapter). Corporations often like to develop goodwill in communities where they have their corporate headquarters or other major investments, so they may become involved in major community projects to create a positive image.

There are two main ways that a corporation may donate money to a nonprofit organization: indirectly, through a corporate foundation set up for this purpose; or directly, through a corporate committee set up to screen such requests.

Approaching the corporate foundation is done the same as approaching any other foundation, as will be discussed below. Approaching the corporation directly involves finding and contacting the person in charge of community relations activities for the corporation. Once this person is identified, the contact involves doing some of the same kind of screening as for any other funding source. That is, the nonprofit needs to ask a number of pertinent questions as explained below. Once likely candidates for funding are located, they must be evaluated for appropriateness.

Evaluate and Select Appropriate Funding Sources

As the grantwriter searches through directories of assistance for possible funding sources, some criteria should be kept in mind for evaluating and selecting possible sources for further inquiry. This will help eliminate those resources that are not appropriate for the organization. A screening list such as that shown in Table 6-1 may be helpful. Some of the questions to be asked in matching an organization with appropriate funding sources are:

Does this Source Fund in Your Agency's Geographical Area?

What are the geographical boundaries of the funding, e.g., local, regional, national? This is one of the first things to be ascertained in screening a funding source. If the potential funding source is not interested in funding in your geographical area, you are wasting your time and this source should be eliminated from further consideration.

Table 6-1
SCREENING FUNDING SOURCES

Criteria	Yes	No	Unknown– Need more information
1. Does this source fund in my agency's geographical area?			
2. Does this source fund programs similar to those of my agency?			
3. Does this source have enough resources to fund the project?			
4. Is the potential dollar amount adequate?			
5. Does my agency meet the minimal eligibility requirements?			
6. Is the grant duration sufficient for the project?			

Does This Source Want to Fund the Types of Programs/Activities That are Similar to Those of Your Agency?

What kinds of programs/activities have recently received funding from this source? Look to see what types of projects or programs the funding source has targeted for its funding. Most funding organizations list their funding priorities. Are these activities in any way related to the types of activities your agency has in mind? If so, continue to scan for more information.

Does the Source Have Enough Resources to Fund This Project?

In looking at the resources of the funder, one of the most important questions is whether or not it has enough to fund your project. Usually the assets of most foundations are listed in the foundation directories, so one needs to look for information such as: how much money has the funder given recently? You might also try to ascertain the dollar amount that the organization has reserved for grants for the coming year.

Is the Potential Dollar Amount What the Agency is Seeking?

What is the average size grant? Determining the average size awarded in the past gives a clue as to the amount of grant that is likely to be funded in the coming year. Finding this information helps give clues as to the appropriateness of the funder for your agency's proposal.

That is, if the average size grant is much smaller than your organization is looking for, chances are slim that you will get the amount you want from this source.

Does My Organization Meet the Minimal Eligibility Requirements?

Given that this funding source funds in your geographical area, is interested in your stated problem or need, and has grant monies available in the amounts you are requesting, try to gauge whether your organization meets the eligibility requirements of the funder. Even though your agency may be nonprofit established for charitable purposes, it may still not meet the requirements of the funder who may specify a certain type of organization that it is seeking to fund, for example, one that serves a specific population or group – the disabled, women, minorities, children, and so forth.

Is the Duration of the Grant of Sufficient Length?

Try to determine the duration of the grant and whether it is long enough to complete the organization's new program, or at least demonstrate its effectiveness. Try to ascertain whether renewals of the grant will be considered. If not, then additional funding for ongoing operations must be explored.

After these basic criteria have been used to screen potential funding sources, some may be selected at this point for gathering further information. Usually the directory lists a contact person as well as whether or not s/he will accept queries by phone.

Initiate Contact with Funding Sources

After the potential funding sources have been narrowed down to those that appear most likely to fit the organization in terms of goals, amounts provided, interests, and so forth, someone from the organization needs to call, write, or email the contact person at the funding organization who is listed on the RFP or grant directory. The most likely person to do this is the executive director of the nonprofit, who may be involved in the grantwriting effort.

The director or staff person should try to obtain as much information as possible regarding the application process, including forms, procedures for submission of the proposal, guidelines for the proposal, criteria for review of the proposal, frequency of review committee meetings, funding dates, and so forth. The grantwriter should try to ascertain whether the organization's proposed activity fall within the interests of the funding organization, and whether funder staff are willing to provide any technical assistance or feedback regarding the grant proposal. If the grantwriter has ascertained that the organization's project falls within the purview of the funder, s/he should then ask for application instructions and materials from the sources selected.

If the organization grantwriter has followed all the steps listed here, s/he is now ready to write the grant proposal.

WRITING THE GRANT PROPOSAL

Many funding sources have specific guidelines for the grant proposals they will accept for review. This is certainly true for government grants. Also, there are regional clearinghouses of grantmakers who use a common application form to make it easier for grant seekers to write the grant (see resources at end). If the organization has done its homework and planning properly, this step is basically following guidelines of the funding source in writing and submitting the grant proposal. If the guidelines are not followed, especially for governmental grants, the proposal will be rejected before it is even read.

In discussing the mechanics of putting together a proposal, there are certain aspects of the writing that are assumed here, namely that the writer is able to write clearly, concisely, using correct English grammar and style, that the plan has been well conceived and can be explained simply in a logical fashion. Given these factors and the adherence to the specific requirements of the funding source, the grantwriter will be on the right track to getting in the competition for the scarce resources needed by the human service organization to fulfill its social mission.

Federal or State sources of support usually require that an application form with specific instructions be completed. Most federal sources use the Standard Form (SF) 424 application package (see resources at end). Requirements for the narrative portion of SF 424 correspond to the standard proposal elements discussed below. In completing SF 424 or any other special application package from a public source, be sure to follow instructions exactly. Remember that failure to follow application instructions is one of the major reasons that review committees reject proposals.

Foundations and other private sources may not provide a specific application form or package. The may provide general instructions about application requirements and procedures, often they only require a letter outlining your project. The standard elements described in Reading 6-1 can be used to structure the narrative portion of the letter. This will help ensure that the proposal material is organized in a coherent manner. The proposed budget should be a separate attachment.

In submitting a proposal to a corporation, personal contact, organizational credibility, and the ability to "sell" your project are equally important. A solid base of personal contact and interaction may have to be initiated before you reach the stage of putting anything in writing. Sometimes, nonprofit executives or board officers may be able to obtain a corporate contribution though negotiation alone.

GRANTS MANAGEMENT

After the grant is submitted and accepted, the management of the grant itself begins. This responsibility not only entails implementing the project or program as funded, but in addition, maintaining program and fiscal records to demonstrate accountability to the funding sources. This is not usually a problem with foundation grants, in which the organization may only have to submit a final or end-of-year report. But organizations receiving grants from the federal government are required to follow the guidelines of OMB (Office of Management and Budget) Circular A-110: *Grants and Agreements with Institutions of Higher Education, Hospitals, and Other Non-Profit Organizations* (1999) and Circular A-122: *Cost Principles for Non-Profit Organizations* (1998). Even an organization that has received federal funds indirectly, through an award at the state level, must comply with the requirements of OMB A-110. OMB Circular A-122 was discussed in Chapter Four, "Budgeting". Here we will be concerned with OMB Circular A-110 because of its particular relevance for managing the grant. Those aspects of grants management covered by A-110 include: financial and program management, property standards, procurement standards, reports and records, termination, and closeout procedures (see Reading 6-2 for excerpts).

Once an award has been granted, the agency must set up a system to monitor and maintain the grant. This includes designating an agency person for the day-to-day monitoring as well as reporting functions; setting up of accounts to be used for the grant, setting up and/or procuring grants management software (see Chapter Fourteen); setting up a schedule of reporting deadlines; and devising or procuring data collection forms that can be used to capture the data needed for monitoring and reporting of grant activities.

For example, agencies should compare budgeted amounts with actual expenditures for each award on a regular basis. If an agency does not use the accrual method of accounting, it must develop accrual data for its reports. If an agency receives advances on funds, rather than on a reimbursement basis, it must maintain the funds in interest bearing accounts unless it receives less than $120,000 per year. Any interest received over $250.00 has to be returned to the federal government.

Contributions may be accepted as the agency's part of cost sharing or matching. These contributions may be cash, or in-kind contributions such as volunteer services or donated supplies, equipment, buildings or land. If contributions are to be used for cost sharing, the agency must keep records that reflect the market value of the goods or services received. All income earned during the grant period as a result of the grant funding may be retained by the grant recipient and may be either added to funds already committed by the Federal awarding agency or used to finance the non-Federal share of the program. Close-out procedures and reporting schedules should be strictly adhered to.

Grants are often major sources of funding for nonprofit organizations that can help them achieve their short- and long-term goals of improving the lives of citizens in their communities. Proper implementation of grant-funded programs and efficient management of grants can help assure that the organization will continue to receive grant monies.

Reading 6-1: Writing the Grant Proposal*

The Basic Components of a Proposal

There are eight basic components to creating a solid proposal package: (1) the proposal summary; (2) introduction of organization; (3) the problem statement (or needs assessment); (4) project objectives; (5) project methods or design; (6) project evaluation; (7) future funding; and (8) the project budget. The following will provide an overview of these components.

The Proposal Summary: Outline of Project Goals

The proposal summary outlines the proposed project and should appear at the beginning of the proposal. It could be in the form of a cover

---

* Excerpted from: Catalog of Federal Domestic Assistance (2000), *Developing and Wring Grant Proposals, Part Two: Writing the Grant Proposal.* http://www.cfda.gov/public/cat-writing.htm.

letter or a separate page, but should definitely be brief—no longer than two or three paragraphs. The summary would be most useful if it were prepared after the proposal has been developed in order to encompass all the key summary points necessary to communicate the objectives of the project.

Introduction: Presenting a Credible Applicant or Organization

The applicant should gather data about its organization from all available sources. Most proposals require a description of an applicant's organization to describe its past and present operations. Some features to consider are:

- A brief biography of board members and key staff members.
- The organization's goals, philosophy, track record with other grantor's, and any success stories.
- The data should be relevant to the goals of the Federal grantor agency and should establish the applicant's credibility.

The Problem Statement: Stating the Purpose at Hand

The problem statement (or needs assessment) is a key element of a proposal that makes a clear, concise, and well-supported statement of the problem to be addressed. The best way to collect information about the problem is to conduct and document both a formal and informal needs assessment for a program in the target or service area. The information provided should be both factual and directly related to the problem addressed by the proposal. Areas to document are:

- The purpose for developing the proposal.
- The beneficiaries—who are they and how will they benefit.
- The social and economic costs to be affected
- The nature of the problem (provide as much hard evidence as possible).
- How the applicant organization came to realize the problem exists, and what is currently being done about the problem.
- The remaining alternatives available when funding has been exhausted. Explain what will happen to the project and the impending implications.
- Most importantly, the specific manner through which problems might be solved. Review the resources needed, considering how they will be used and to what end.

Project Objectives: Goals and Desired Outcomes

Program objectives refer to specific activities in a proposal. It is necessary to identify all objectives related to the goals to be reached, and the methods to be employed to achieve the stated objectives. Consider quantities or things measurable and refer to a problem statement and the outcome of proposed activities when developing a well-stated objective.

Program Methods and Program Design: A Plan of Action

The program design refers to how the project is expected to work and solve the stated problem. Sketch out the following:

- The activities to occur along with the related resources and staff needed to operate the project (inputs).
- A flow chart of the organizational features of the project. Describe how the parts interrelate, where personnel will be needed, and what they are expected to do. Identify the kinds of facilities, transportation, and support services required (throughputs).
- Explain what will be achieved through 1 and 2 above (outputs); i.e., plan for measurable results.
- Whenever possible, justify in the narrative the course of action taken. The most economical method should be used that does not compromise or sacrifice project quality.
- Highlight the innovative features of the proposal which could be considered distinct from other proposals under consideration.
- Whenever possible, use appendices to provide details, supplementary data, references, and information requiring in-depth analysis.

Evaluation: Product and Process Analysis

Most Federal agencies now require some form of program evaluation among grantees. The requirements of the proposed project should be explored carefully. Evaluations may be conducted by an internal staff member, an evaluation firm, or both. The applicant should state the amount of time needed to evaluate, how the feedback will be distributed among the proposed staff, and a schedule for review and comment for this type of communication. Evaluation designs may start at the beginning, middle or end of a project, but the applicant should specify a start-up time. It is practical to submit an evaluation design at the start of a project for two reasons:

- Convincing evaluations require the collection of appropriate data before and during program operations; and,
- If the program design cannot be prepared at the outset then a critical review of the program design may be advisable.

Future Funding: Long-Term Project Planning

Describe a plan for continuation beyond the grant period, and/or the availability of other resources necessary to implement the grant. Discuss maintenance and future program funding if program is for construction activity. Account for other needed expenditures if program includes purchase of equipment.

The Proposal Budget: Planning the Budget

A well-prepared budget justifies all expenses and is consistent with the proposal narrative. Some areas in need of an evaluation for consistency are: (1) the salaries in the proposal in relation to those of the applicant organization should be similar; (2) if new staff persons are being hired, additional space and equipment should be considered, as necessary; (3) if the budget calls for an equipment purchase, it should be the type allowed by the grantor agency; (4) if additional space is rented, the increase in insurance should be supported; (5) if an indirect cost rate applies to the proposal, the division between direct and indirect costs should not be in conflict, and the aggregate budget totals should refer directly to the approved formula; and (6) if matching costs are required, the contributions to the matching fund should be taken out of the budget unless otherwise specified in the application instructions.

Reading 6-2: Excerpts from OMB Circular A-110: *Grants and agreements with Institutions of Higher Education, Hospitals, and Other Non-Profit Organizations.*

SUBPART C:- Post-Award Requirements

Financial and Program Management (C.21–28):

___.21 Standards for financial management systems
    (a)Federal awarding agencies shall require recipients to relate all financial data to performance data and develop unit cost information whenever practical.
    (b)Recipients' financial management systems shall provide for the following:
        (1)Accurate, current and complete disclosure of the finan-

cial results of each federally-sponsored project or program . . .

(2) Records that identify adequately the source and application of funds for federally-sponsored activities.

(3) Effective control over and accountability for all funds, property, and other assets.

(4) Comparison of outlays with budget amounts for each award . . . .

____22. Payment

(k) Recipients shall maintain advances of Federal funds in interest bearing accounts, unless (1), (2) or (3) apply.

(1) The recipient receives less than $120,000 in Federal awards per year.

(2) The best reasonably available interest bearing account would not be expected to earn interest in excess of $250 per year on Federal cash balances.

(3) The depository would require an average or minimum balance so high that it would not be feasible within the expected Federal and non-Federal cash resources.

(l) Interest amounts up to $250 per year may be retained by the recipient for administrative expense.

____23. Cost sharing or matching. (a) All contributions, including cash and third party in-kind, shall be accepted as part of the recipient's cost sharing or matching . . .

____24. Program Income

(b). . . program income earned during the project period shall be retained by the recipient and, . . . shall be used in one or more of the ways listed in the following.

(1) Added to funds committed to the project by the Federal awarding agency and recipient and used to further eligible project or program objectives.

(2) Used to finance the non-Federal share of the project or program.

(3) Deducted from the total project or program allowable cost in determining the net allowable costs on which the Federal share of costs is based.

____25. Revision of budget and program plans. (b) Recipients are required to report deviations from budget and program plans . . .

____26. Non-Federal Audits

(a) Recipients that are . . . nonprofit organizations (including hospitals) shall be subject to the audit requirements contained in the Single Audit Act Amendments of 1996.. and revised OMB Circular A-133, *"Audits of States, Local Governments, and Non-Profit Organizations."*

____27. Allowable Costs. The allowability of costs incurred by non-profit organizations is determined in accordance with the provisions of OMB Circular A-122, "Cost Principles for Non-Profit Organizations."

Property Standards

____31. Insurance coverage. Recipients shall, at a minimum, provide the equivalent coverage for real property and equipment acquired with Federal funds as provided to property owned by the recipient.

____32. Real property. (a) Title to real property shall vest in the recipient subject to the condition that the recipient shall use the real property for the authorized purpose of the project . . . and shall not encumber the property without approval of the Federal awarding agency.

____34. Equipment.

(a)Title to equipment acquired by a recipient with Federal funds shall vest in the recipient, subject to conditions of this section.

(f)(1)Equipment records shall be maintained accurately . . .

(2)A physical inventory of equipment shall be taken and the results reconciled the equipment records at least once every two years.

(3)A control system shall be in effect to insure adequate safeguards to prevent loss, damage, or theft of the equipment.

Procurement Standards (a) All recipients shall establish written procurement procedures.

Reports and Records

____.51 Monitoring and reporting program performance.

(a)Recipients are responsible for managing and monitoring each project, program, . . . or activity supported by the award.

(b). . . performance reports shall not be required more frequently than quarterly, or less frequently than annually. Annual reports shall be due 90 calendar days after the grant year; quarterly or semi-annual reports shall be due 30 days after the reporting period.

(d)When required, performance reports shall generally contain . . . brief information on each of the following.

(1)A comparison of actual accomplishments with the goals and objectives established for the period . . .

(2)Reasons why established goals were not met, if appropriate.

(3)Other pertinent information including . . . analysis and explanation of cost overruns or high unit costs.

SUBPART D–After-the-Award Requirements

___.71 Closeout Procedures

(a)Recipients shall submit, within 90 calendar days after the date of completion of the award, all financial, performance, and other reports as required by the terms and conditions of the award.

(b)Unless the Federal awarding agency authorizes an extension, a recipient shall liquidate all obligations incurred under the award not later than 90 calendar days after the funding period or the date of completion . . .

(d)The recipient shall promptly refund any balances of unobligated cash that the Federal awarding agency has advanced or paid and that is not authorized to be retained by the recipient for used in other projects.

REFERENCES

Annual Register of Grant Support: A Directory of Funding Sources:2001. R.R.Bowker Publisher.

Boris, E.T. (2000). *Myths about the nonprofit sector.* A brief in the Series, "Charting Civil Society," by the Center on Nonprofits and Philanthropy at the Urban Institute. www.urgan.org/periodcl/cnp/cnp_4.htm

Catalog of Federal Domestic Assistance (2000). *Developing and Writing Grant Proposals.* http://www.cfda.gov/public/cat-writing.htm,

Federal Emergency Management Agency (1983). *Basic Skills in Creative Financing, Student Manual.* EMI Professional Development Series, , National Emergency Training Center, Emergency Management Institute, pp. 185–196.

Foundation Center (2001). *The Foundation Directory.* New York: author.

Lauffer, A. (1997). *Grants, Etc.* (2nd Edition). Thousand Oaks, CA: Sage Publications.

Lindholm, K., Marin, G., & Lopez, R.E. (1982). *Proposal Writing Stategies.* Monograph No. 9, Los Angeles: Spanish Speaking Mental Health Center, UCLA.

Office of Management and Budget (1999). OMB Circular A-110: *Grants and Agree-*

ments with Institutions of Higher Education, Hospitals, and Other Non-Profit Organizations. http://www.whitehouse.gov/omb/circulars/a110/a110.html

Office of Management and Budget (1998). Circular A-122: *Cost Principles for Non-Profit Organizations* http://www.whitehouse.gov/omb/circulars/a122/a122.html

Witkin, B. R. & Altshuld, J. W. (1995). *Planning and Conducting Needs Assessments.* Thousand Oaks, CA: Sage Publications.

INTERNET RESOURCES

Catalog of Federal Domestic Assistance. http://www.cfda.gov

Chronicle of Philanthropy. http://philanthropy.com

Committee to Encourage Corporate Philanthropy. http://www.corphilanthropy .org/

Corporate Giving Reference Desk. http://www.internet_prospector.org/corp-giv.html

Corporate Philanthropy Social Programs. http://www.fundsnetservices.com/soc01 .htm

The Council on Foundations. http://www.cof.org

Federal Register. http://www.gpo.gov/su_docs/aces/aces140.html

The Foundation Center Online. http://fdncenter.org

Foundation Directory Online. http://fonline.fdncenter.org

Office of Management and Budget. http://www.whitehouse.gov/omb

RFP Bulletin published by the Foundation Center. http://fdncenter.org/pnd/rfp/ index.jhtml

Standard Form 424: http://www.psc.gov/forms/SF/sf.html

Chapter Seven

PURCHASE OF SERVICE CONTRACTING, FEES FOR SERVICE, AND THIRD-PARTY PAYMENTS

After reading this chapter you should be able to:

1. Understand the basics of purchase of service contracting;
2. Be able to calculate costs for delivering a service;
3. Know the principles of a fair fee-for-service schedule;
4. Increase knowledge of third-party payment mechanisms.

INTRODUCTION

Increasingly, human service organizations have become dependent on additional types of resource inflows other than allocations, donations, and grants. Vendor contracts with governmental and other entities as well as third-party payments from Medicaid, Medicare, and managed care organizations (MCOs) are also major sources of revenue for many organizations. Fees-for-services are not a large part of the revenue source for most human service agencies. Most have some sort of fee schedule, but not all clients can pay the full cost of the services rendered. The difference between the full cost and what the client can or does pay is, in many instances, covered by purchase of service contracts or third-party payments.

In this chapter we will look briefly at issues for nonprofits and clients related to these types of payments. In addition, this chapter will provide an overview of the contracting process, mechanisms of third-party reimbursement, and approaches to fees-for-services systems. This chapter will also briefly present an introduction to break-even analysis.

PURCHASE OF SERVICE CONTRACTING

Purchase of service contracting (POSC) is a service delivery method often used by federal, state and local governments. It is pervasive in

147

human services. POSC may be defined as an agreement between a governmental entity and a private for-profit or nonprofit organization in which the organization will provide a specific level and quality of service in exchange for payment (Manchester & Bogart, 1988, Kamerman & Kahn, 1998). POSC is a form of privatization, though not the only one. Both contracting and privatization are ways that public agencies transfer responsibility for providing a good or service to the private sector.

Contrary to some popular views, contracting out in human services is not a new phenomenon; rather it has been with us since colonial times, though not to the same extent as present. For example, in colonial times, overseers of the poor on the local level contracted out to town residents willing to take in the poor for the lowest bid (Abramovitz, 1986). Human service organizations such as asylums, orphanages, hospitals, and other charitable institutions also received contracts from local and state authorities to provide services. It wasn't until the Great Depression that the federal government became involved in human service provision.

The 1960's saw the real growth of contracting. A 1967 amendment to the Social Security Act permitted public agencies to purchase social services for recipients of Aid to Families with Dependent Children (AFDC) from private agencies (Kamerman & Kahn, 1998). This was expanded further in 1975 with another amendment to the Social Security Act, Title XX. In 1979 it was estimated that fifty-five percent (55%) of all social services provided by states was done through the mechanism of contracting. An additional one billion dollars a year was awarded in contracts to private and voluntary human service agencies through Title XX (Martin & Kettner, 1994). In 1996, welfare reform expanded contracting still further by permitting *for-profit* agencies to be eligible vendors of publicly funded services to children and families in need.

Today all state and county social service agencies use contracting to some extent. The major contracted services include child welfare, adoption, community corrections, services for the homeless, and child-support collection. Contracted services also include those mandated by federal or state statute. The services of nonprofit organizations are often mandated to clients who are, in many instances, unwilling or unable to pay for those services. Some examples include court-mandated drug and alcohol counseling, child welfare visits, parenting classes for welfare mothers, counseling in halfway houses for persons released from prison, and so forth. In these cases, the client often pays nothing for the services rendered. It is often the "sending" organization, the court, child welfare department, or some other agency, that pays for the service through a contractual arrangement with the "receiving" organization.

THE CONTRACTING PROCESS

Kettner and Martin (1990) conceptualized two approaches to purchase of service contracting which they termed the "partnership model" and the "market model". They perceived the partnership model as using contracting as a way to enable governmental contracting agencies and contractors to join together as partners in collaboration to maximize the efforts of state or local human services systems. In this model, decisions regarding contractors tend to be based on history and tradition as well as maintenance of the human services system. Some administrative mechanisms used in the partnership model include requests for proposals, cost-reimbursement contracts, and multi-year contracts.

In the market model of contracting, governmental agencies encourage competition to increase productivity while at the same time driving down the price they pay for service delivery. In this model, decisions regarding contractors tend to be based on cost, productivity, and availability and capability of contractors. Administrative mechanisms associated with this model include invitations for bids, unit cost, fixed-fee, and incentive contracts, single year contracts, and the inclusion of for-profit organizations as eligible bidders.

In that the federal government has mandated ***performance-based contracting*** as the preferred mode for contracted services, it has adopted the market model. This was codified in public law and in policy via a letter sent to all heads of federal executive agencies and departments (USOFPP, 1991). The United States Office of Federal Procurement Policy (USOFPP) defines performance-based contracting as:

> " . . . structuring all aspects of an acquisition around the purpose of the work to be performed as opposed to either the manner by which the work is to be performed or broad and imprecise statements of work" (USOFPP, 1991, p.1).

There is a synergistic and interdependent relationship between the contracting agency and the agency receiving the contract (see Figure 7-1). A nonprofit may be on a list of approved contractors and re-

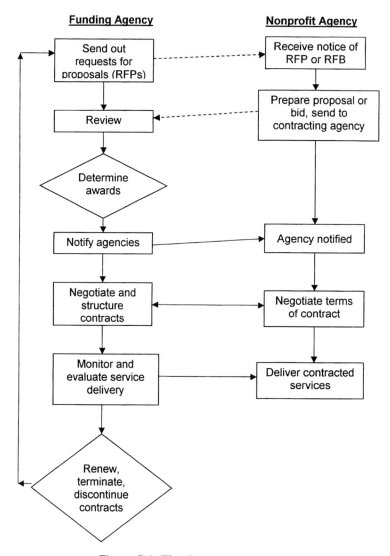

Figure 7-1: The Contracting Process

ceive notice of bids. Or a nonprofit may find the invitation for bids on a funding source's website or in a newspaper such as the *Commerce Business Daily*. Once the nonprofit receives notice of a request or invitation to bid, it prepares and submits a proposal or bid to the funding source.

The funding source reviews the bids or proposals and determines awards based on its stated criteria. It then notifies the organizations it has approved for an award and negotiates and structures the contracts with these agencies.

After receiving the contract, the nonprofit delivers the contracted service and the funding source monitors and evaluates the quality and quantity of the service delivery. At the end of the contract period the funding source must decide whether it will renew, terminate, or discontinue its present contracts or offer new ones. Some of this decision is based not only on the quality of the service delivery, but also on the availability of funds and the political climate.

TYPES OF CONTRACTS

In purchase of service contracting, the funding source is the purchaser of goods or services. As such, it defines what services will be delivered to the target population, decides who will deliver them, and how much it will pay for the services by the mechanism of a contract. Some common elements of the contracts include: "[1] Definition of the service to be provided, including components of quality standards; and [2] Rules defining the funding source's responsibility and method of payment for services provided" (Richardson, 1989, p. 163). There are many different types of contracts, some of the most common include:

Fixed-Price: As the name implies, vendors receive a set price for the specified services performed by a certain date. Performance based service contracting encourages the use of fixed-price contracts (USOFPP, 1998, p. 17).

Cost-plus reimbursement: This is payment based on a fixed price with an additional reimbursement for certain costs only. A cost-reimbursement contract may be used when the cost of the service cannot be estimated reliably in advance (Anthony & Govindarajan, 1995).

Unit Cost reimbursement: Payment for services is based on a computation of the unit cost of the service. Services easily and precisely defined are most appropriate for this type of reimbursement (Baumunk, 1989). You may recall that unit costs were discussed in Chapter Four.

ADVANTAGES AND DISADVANTAGES OF CONTRACTING

There are advantages and disadvantages to purchase of service contracting, both to the funding source as well as the human service agency. Advantages for funding sources in contracting out a service may mean avoidance of cash layout for start-up costs, avoidance of restrictive civil service regulations, flexible use of personnel, better service coordination and cost effectiveness, among other things. For human service agencies, purchase of service contracting may mean increased funding for a service in which an agency has demonstrated expertise, a more stable revenue inflow, maximum use of its professional staff, and the opportunity for a public-private partnership (Gibelman & Demone, 1989, Gurin & Friedman, 1989).

Disadvantages of purchase of service contracting for the funding source may include unreliability of contractors, difficulty in monitoring contracts, difficulty in ensuring that standards are met, and the loss of public control and accountability. For human service agencies, some disadvantages may be loss of autonomy through increased regulation and restrictive contracts, dependence on public agencies, instability of funding due to changes in public policy, cash flow problems due to delays in receiving reimbursement, and the tendency to displace agency goals in order to provide only publicly funded services or to address the priorities of public funders (Gibelman & Demone, 1989, p. 32; Kraft & Gibelman, 1997).

In spite of the disadvantages, purchase of service contracting is expected to remain a significant source of funding and control in the human services for some time to come. If contracting is to be used as a means of revenue for the human service organization, there are two key concepts that human service professionals must be familiar with: break-even analysis and cost-efficiency. Break-even analysis is discussed later in chapter. Cost-efficiency is discussed in Chapter Thirteen on financial analysis. For further information on purchase of service contracting, please also consult the website addresses at the end of this chapter.

FEES FOR SERVICES

In addition to contracts, grants, and allocations, another source of funding for nonprofit human service organizations is the charging of a fee for services rendered. Fees for services represent a very small part of the revenue of many nonprofit human services. This is because, as has been mentioned, many of the clients are mandated to obtain services and/or they cannot afford to pay for the services that are being provided. Thus, nonprofit human service organizations provide a socially beneficial role in providing crucial services for those unable to pay. This is the whole purpose of federated fundraising, that is, to generate funds for organizations that provide charitable services and to subsidize the cost of providing services to low-income and indigent clients. It is also one of the reasons that nonprofits are exempt from federal income tax.

There is very little current research on fees for services. One study found, that, despite the view of some that charging fees is therapeutic to clients, the decision by human service administrators to charge fees did not result from a perceived benefit to the client so much as from pressure from external sources such as funders (McMillan & Callicutt, 1981). Another common practice today, that of charging a "no-show" fee or the cost of the service to those who do not keep appointments, was found to significantly reduce the no-show rate at a community mental health center (Lesaca, 1995). It seems there is a dynamic tension between an organization's need to cover some of the cost of a service by charging a fee and a client's ability or willingness to pay for a service. In some instances, not having to pay for a service may attract or keep clients in treatment. One study found that eliminating fees, even very low fees, increased the retention rate of clients in a methadone maintenance program (Maddux, et al., 1994).

Yet, at the same time, our capitalistic system has fostered the notion that what is free or low-cost is not of the same quality or value as that which is more expensive. Our culture has developed marketing strategies based on attaching status to that which is costly. We even have a saying that reflects this notion, "You get what you pay for." Thus, some questions related to fees are: what fee, if any, should be charged for services? What system should be instituted for fee payment? An additional question, one related to equity, is, what is a fair price?

Setting Fees

There are basically two approaches to pricing as it relates to setting fees. The first approach is cost-oriented, that is, it is based on " . . . the cost of the input used to create the goods or services . . . " (Moore, 1995, p. 473). The second approach is market oriented, that is, it may be seen as a " . . . tool for eliciting a certain response from a potential consumer" (Moore, p. 473).

Human service organizations do not often compete with one another for clients, as do for-profit corporations, through the use of marketing. There are many reasons for this, including the fact that often clients have no choice of provider, or there may be only one provider in a community, and/or the inability to pay limits options (McCready, 1988). For some types of services, however, a nonprofit may compete with a for-profit. For example, nonprofits and for-profits may compete in home health services, nursing homes, wellness programs, mental health counseling, community corrections centers, and so forth. In these instances, a market-oriented approach to pricing may be necessary.

On the other hand, for many years, human service organizations have used only the crudest estimates as to the true cost of providing their services. So while they have desired to be cost oriented, they were more service oriented. The calculation of fees involves knowing more than unit costs; it also involves knowing break-even and marginal costs; these are discussed in this chapter. In addition, there is another aspect of charging for services that should be of concern to human service agencies. This has to do with fairness and equity as related to client's ability to pay. For-profits have to be concerned about making a profit and shareholder returns on investments. Nonprofits have to be concerned about providing a socially useful service in a cost-efficient manner.

"Fee-for-service schedules in social service agencies attempt to resolve the tension between consumers' expectation of paying fees for service, their ability to pay, the true cost of the service, and an agency's need to raise additional revenue" (Wernet et al., 1992). Other factors that may exacerbate this tension are "what clients are willing to pay, how much [they] can get the services for elsewhere, [client readiness to pay for hard vs. soft services], and funding source expectations. . ." (Prochaska & DiBari, 1985, p. 56).

Most human service organizations that charge a fee-for-services use a sliding fee scale to determine how much a client will pay. These fee scales take into account the gross or net income of the client and family size. Taking into account income and family size, the sliding fee scales use a formula that reduces the fee as the number of members in the client household increases (Wernet et al., 1992). National organizations may also take into account the differential cost of living in different parts of the country.

One of the problems in implementing a fee for service system in the nonprofit organization, besides the equity issue, is assuring that the fee schedule is implemented as intended. Some necessary components of developing a fair and equitable fee system include systems that require high worker involvement and discretion, written guidelines that provide sufficient information for making such decisions, and training to further inform the process. Most agencies do not systematically collect good information on client income, which makes it difficult for workers to assess a proper fee. In addition, in most nonprofits there is little pressure to obtain fee income as it is not usually a part of worker evaluations (Rubenstein et al., 1985; Prochaska and DiBari (1985).

Principles of Fee Setting

Nonprofits charge fees in an attempt to raise revenue, to offset the costs of providing services, to subsidize those unable to pay, and to create a sense of value for their services. As mentioned, most nonprofits use some form of sliding fee scales to help make the cost affordable for the client. Most sliding fee scales take into account factors such as family income and number in household in creating the fee scale. Given this, some principles gleaned from the literature to take into account in designing a payment schedule are summarized below:

- Inability to pay should not be a determining factor in service eligibility (NASW Code of Ethics, 1997, 1.13)
- A system of payment collection should be implemented and standardized using sound principles of internal control (see Chapter Eight)
- Social workers and other direct care providers should not be responsible for collecting fees without proper training and written guidelines
- Fee scales based on national accrediting guidelines should be adapted to regional cost-of-living indices
- Cost of services should be available to clients in printed form and explained to them by business office staff.

THIRD-PARTY PAYMENTS

Third-party payments from health insurance companies as well as federal or state governments are now common sources of revenue for many nonprofits. Human service organizations receive third-party payments for services such as counseling, substance abuse treatment, home health visits, and other social work services. "Third-party payers are agents of patients who contract with providers (the second party) to pay all or part of the bill [for] the patient (the first party), and have had an important affect on healthcare organizations over the last 70 years" (Nowicki, 1999, p. 49).

The two most common types of third-party payers are private insurance companies and public payers, including the federal government (Medicare and Medicaid) and state and local government. For example, if an organization provides services to senior citizens it will, in many instances, be reimbursed for these services through Medicare or Medicaid. If it provides services to low-income families or individuals it may receive reimbursement from Medicaid or local public assistance authorities. Middle-class clients may have health insurance that covers behavioral health care such as family counseling or drug and alcohol counseling. These and many other types of social services, including community care for the mentally ill, family support, and early intervention programs have been increasingly delivered under third-party contracts (Felty & Jones, 1998).

Medicare

Medicare is a benefit under Title XVIII of the Social Security Act Amendments of 1965 that covers persons aged 65 and over. Under Medicare, a number of health and social services are reimbursed. There are two parts to Medicare, Part A and Part B.

Part A: Is mandatory and encompasses certain hospital services that are funded by a payroll tax on employers and workers.

Part B: Is voluntary and includes services performed by physicians. Funding for Part B is through monthly premiums of participants and federal government general revenues.

Medicaid

Medicaid is a benefit under Title XIX of the Social Security Act Amendments of 1965. Medicaid differs from Medicare in that while Medicare is a universal benefit to anyone aged 65 and over, Medicaid is available to low-income individuals of any age who meet certain income requirements, as well as the medically indigent. Services provided under Medicaid include those similar to Medicare, including health and behavioral health care services. However, because Medicaid is a federal matching program with the states, and is administered by each state, the range of services available in each state is specified by a state Medicaid plan. Medicare, on the other hand, is fully funded by the federal government, with Medicare services available to those covered across the country.

Reimbursement rates under Medicaid and Medicare are usually capitated, that is, only a fixed rate will be paid for a service no matter what the actual cost to the provider.

Private Insurance/Managed Care

Private insurance plans are also known as managed care organizations (MCO's). "Managed care organizations are organizations that manage the cost of healthcare, the quality of health care, and the access to health care" (Nowicki, 1999, p. 52). Managed care has permeated the health and human services. Its aim is to control costs while maintaining a given level of quality of service (Wernet, 1999).

There are a number of issues related to managed care of concern to human service organizations. First of all, much of mental health care is controlled by the MCO's. They often determine who can deliver a service through a preferred provider network. They determine which providers belong to the network. Sometimes the networks are restricted to a certain number. In addition, they decide whether or not a client can receive treatment, and if so, for what number of treatment sessions. As they utilize a medical model, a client's problem must fit the diagnostic criteria of the American Psychiatric Association's *Diagnostic and Statistical Manual of Mental Disorders* (DSM-IV). Because one of the main purposes of an MCO is to control costs, they tend to discourage in-patient treatment and to limit certain other types of treatments.

One of the effects of managed care on human service organizations has to do with the recruitment and hiring of personnel. Increased costs to human service agencies result from having to hire staff who are eligible for third-party reimbursement by meeting certain licensing and other requirements established by the MCOs. Lack of sufficient trained staff, with appropriate credentials, may lead to competition among agencies for those personnel who meet licensing qualifications. Yet, at the same time, reimbursement may not be sufficient to meet such personnel and other costs. Further, there is often a long lag-time between submission of claims and payment to the provider.

Because MCO's and other third-party payers are often in a position to dictate reimbursement costs, nonprofits are at a disadvantage when they find themselves in the situation of having to contract for less than the real cost of a service. An important concept to understanding these issues is that of *breaking-even*. An organization must know how to calculate its *break-even point* if it desires to negotiate contracts, fees, and third-party reimbursement while maintaining financial soundness. The next section will hopefully illuminate some basic break-even concepts.

BREAK-EVEN ANALYSIS

Cost-volume-revenue "(CVR) analysis deals with how revenue and costs vary with a change in service level. It looks at the effects on revenues of changes in certain factors, such as variable costs, fixed costs, prices, service level, and mix of services" (Shim & Constas, 1997, p. 1). Break-even analysis is a part of CVR; it determines the **break-even point,** that is, *the point at which revenues match costs.* Nonprofits, of course, by their very nature are not in business to make a profit. But it is still important for an organization to be able to know its breakeven point for a variety of reasons:

- To better plan for service delivery
- To determine an appropriate level of service for grants and contracts
- To determine how changes in service levels affect revenues
- To plan fundraising functions in which contributions exceed costs
- To help in setting fees-for-service
- And, overall, to be able to target a level of revenues sufficient to fund agency services

Break-even Analysis

As one can see, there are a number of useful functions of break-even analysis for nonprofit organizations. In order to compute the break-even point, we must know some things about our agency costs, that is, its fixed and variable costs, the fees being charged for services, and the number of units of service (service volume) either provided or anticipated. Fixed, variable, and semivariable costs (here used synonymously with expenses) were discussed in Chapter Four.

As you may recall, fixed costs remain the same no matter how many clients are seen, as for example, rent. Variable costs vary with the number of clients seen, as is the case with supplies. Semivariable costs have both a fixed and a variable component, as with utilities. Fees are sometimes charged on a flat-fee basis, as may be the case with a hot meal; or fees may be charged on a sliding scale basis according to the client's ability to pay.

Knowing these variables, we may compute the break-even point for different purposes: 1) to find a break-even cost for a service; 2) to find the number of units of service needed to break even; or 3) to examine the changes in revenue and costs associated with a given level of service.

As an example, let us assume that a mythical agency, Human Services, Inc., has only one service, family counseling. As this is its only service, its unit of service is one hour of counseling. For the purposes of our discussion, we will assume that this organization is charging a flat-fee for a service. This service has no sliding fee scale, everyone is charged $50 per visit. The agency's total fixed costs are $6,000 per month. These fixed expenses include rent, insurance, the fixed portion of its utilities, and salaries. Its variable cost per unit of service is $35. This includes supplies, the variable portion of utilities, and a percentage of fee to the therapists.

In order to compute the break-even point we must know the **unit contribution margin.** The *unit contribution margin* is the excess of revenue over variable costs (Fess et al., 1993). For example, in the case of Human Services, Inc.:

Fee per unit of service	=	$50
Variable cost per unit of service	=	$35
Unit Contribution Margin	=	$15

The fee per unit of service of $50 less the variable cost per unit of service of $35 equals $15, which is the unit contribution margin.

Now the Executive Director of Human Services, Inc. wants to know how many units of service need to be delivered in order for the organization to break-even. To find the break-even point, the formula is:

$$\textbf{Break-Even Point} = \frac{\textbf{Fixed Costs}}{\textbf{Unit Contribution Margin}}$$

$$= \frac{\$6000}{\$15}$$

$$= \textbf{400 Units of Service}$$

We divided our fixed costs of $6,000 by our unit contribution margin of $15 to discover that our agency needs to deliver 400 units of service per month in order to break-even. Any units of service over 400 will result in an excess of revenue for the organization.

The proof of this can be seen by the following:

Revenue (400 units of service × $50)	=	$20,000

Variable costs (400 units of service × $35)   =   -$14,000
Fixed costs   =   -$ 6,000
Surplus (deficit)   =   0

As can be seen, given our fixed and variable costs as well as the fee charged, we can compute our break-even point fairly easily. We can see how many clients would need to be seen in order for the agency to break-even by the end of the month. We can also graph the break-even point as in Figure 7-2 below.

In Figure 7-2, the lines that intersect at the point of revenue and total expenses represent the break-even point in total revenue and units of service. The graph shows that the break-even point for the nonprofit at $50 per unit of service is 400 units of service. Every unit of service after that brings a surplus to the organization. Operating surplus will be earned when revenue levels are to the right of the break-even point. Operating losses will occur when revenue is to the left of the break-even point.

Now suppose that the organization has a maximum capacity of 600 units of service in its current office space. What would be the break-even price for a unit of service, in this case again, one hour of counseling?

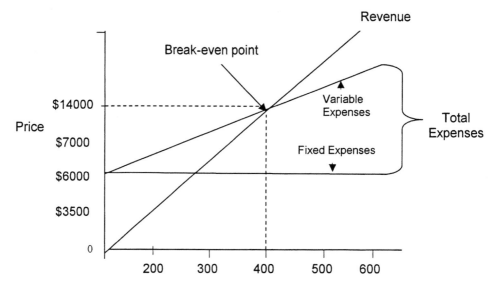

Units of Service Volume

In this instance, we can use the following formula:

$$\frac{\text{Price}}{\text{Cost}} = \frac{\text{Total Fixed Costs} + \text{Target Profit}}{\text{Unit Volume}} + \text{Unit} \quad \text{Variable}$$

$$\text{Price} = \frac{\$6,000 + \$0}{600 \text{ units of service}} + \$35$$

Our price or fee is equal to our fixed costs of $6,000 plus our target profit of zero (the break-even amount) divided by our volume of 600 units of service plus our unit variable cost of $35.

$$\text{Price} = 10 + \$35$$
$$\text{Price} = \$45$$

Thus, at 600 units of service, a charge of $45 per hour of counseling will result in break-even for the agency. Any fee over that will bring a surplus. We can see the proof of this below:

Revenue (600 units of service × $45)	=	$27,000
Variable Costs ($35 × 600)	=	-$21,000
Fixed Costs	=	-$ 6,000
Surplus (deficit)	=	0

The accuracy of cost-volume-revenue analysis depends on certain assumptions, which may or may not apply to individual nonprofits. These assumptions are:

1. That the relationship between revenue and costs is a linear one, that is, as service units increase, so will costs. This assumption may not hold true for large organizations that may be able to affect economies of scale in which case costs per unit may decrease (Lohman, 1976);
2. That fixed and variable costs can be ascertained with some certainty; and
3. That costs will remain constant during the specified period of time under consideration (Fess et al., 1993).

Also, this type of analysis is simple when it involves a small agency that only offers one type of service at a fixed price. It becomes more difficult, though not impossible, to ascertain break-even points when the agency has many services at different price points or one service on a sliding fee scale. In any case, this basic introduction to break-even concepts can be useful in program planning and budgeting for nonprofits.

This chapter has attempted to introduce the reader to some of the concepts and issues in some common sources of revenue for the non-profit, including contracts, fees-for-service, and third-party payments. Sources of additional information about these topics can be found in the reference list and the internet sources cited at that end of this chapter.

REFERENCES

Abramovitz, M. (1986). The privatization of the welfare state: A review. *Social Work,* 31(4): 257–265.

Anthony, R.N. & Govindarajan, V. (1995). *Management Control Systems.* Chicago: Richard D. Irwin, Inc.

Baumunk, E. (1989). Unit-cost contracting for health and social services, pp. 176–181 in H.W. Demone and M. Gibelman (Eds.). *Services for Sale: Purchasing Health and Human Services.* New Brunswick, NJ: Rutgers University Press.

Felty, D. W. & Jones, M. B. (1998). Human services at risk. *Social Service Review,* 72(2):192–208.

Fess, P.E., Warren, C.S., & Reeve, J.M. (1993). *Accounting Principles* (17th Edition). Cincinnati: South-Western Publishing Co.

Gibelman, M. & Demone, H.W., Jr. (1989). The Evolving Contract State, pp. 17–57 in H.W. Demone, & M. Gibelman (1989). *Services for Sale: Purchasing Health and Human Services.* New Brunswick, NJ: Rutgers University Press.

Gurin, A. & Friedman, B. (1989). The efficacy of contracting for service, pp. 310–324 in H.W. Demone and M. Gibelman (Eds.). *Services for Sale: Purchasing Health and Human Services.* New Brunswick, NJ: Rutgers University Press.

Kamerman, S.B. & Kahn, A.J. (1998). *Privatization, Contracting, and Reform of Child and Family Social Services.* Prepared for the Finance Project. http://www.finance project.org/private.htm

Kettner, P. M. & Martin, L. L. (1990). Purchase of service contracting: Two models. *Administration in Social Work,* 14(1):15–30.

Kraft, S. & Gibelman, M. (1998). Purchasing substance abuse services: Experience from the perspective of a voluntary, community-based agency, pp. 151–163 in M. Gibelman & H.W. Demone, Jr. (Eds.) *The Privatization of Human Services, Vol. 2: Case Studies in Purchase of Services.* New York: Springer Publishing Co.

Lesaca, T. (1995). Assessing the influence of a no-show fee on patient compliance at a CMCH. *Administration & Policy in Mental Health,* 22(6):629–631.

Lohman, R.A. (1976). Break-even analysis: tool for budget planning. *Social Work,* 21:300–307.

Maddux, J.F., Prihoda, T.J., Desmond, D.P. (1994). Treatment fees and retention on methadone maintenance. *Journal of Drug Issues,* 24(3):429–443.

Manchester, L. D. & Bogart, G. S. (1988). *Contracting and Volunteerism in Local Government: A Self-Help Guide.* Washington, D.C.: International City Management Association.

Martin, L. L. & Kettner, P. M. (1994). Purchase of service at 20: Are we using it well? *Public Welfare,* 52(3):14–22.

McCready, D. J. (1988). Ramsey pricing: A method for setting fees in social service organizations. *American Journal of Economics and Sociology,* 47(1):97–110.

McMillan, B. & Callicutt, J.W. (1981). Fees for counseling services: Why charge them? *Administration in Mental Health,* 9(2):100–122.

Moore, S. T. (1995). Pricing: A normative strategy in the delivery of human services. *Social Work,* 40(4):473–481.

National Association of Social Workers. (1999). *Code of Ethics.* Approved by the 1996 NASW Delegate Assembly and revised by the 1999 NASW Delegate Assembly. Washington, D.C.: author. http://www.naswdc.org

Nowicki, M. (1999). *The Financial Management of Hospitals and Healthcare Organizations.* Chicago: Health Administration Press.

Prochaska, J.M. & DiBari, P.M. (1985). Toward a fundamentally fair fee system: A case study. *Administration in Social Work,* 9(2): 49–58.

Richardson, D.A. (1989). Purchase of services, third-party payment, market conditions, and rate-setting. In H.W. Demone and M. Gibelman (Eds.). *Services for Sale.* New Brunswick: Rutgers University Press, pp. 162–175.

Rubenstein, H., Bloch, M. H., Wachter, A. R., & Vaughn, H. H. (1985). The implications for administrative practice of fee systems based on client's ability to pay: The results of a survey. *Administration in Social Work,* 9(2):37–48.

Shim, J. K. & Constas, M. (1997). Does your nonprofit break even? *CPA Journal. http://luca.com/cpajournal/1997/1297/features/1361297.htm.*

United States Office of Federal Procurement Policy (OFPP). (1991). *Policy Letter 91-2 To the Heads of Executive Agencies and Departments,* April 9.

United States Office of Federal Procurement Policy (OFPP), Office of Management and Budget (OMB), Executive Office of the President. (1998). *A Guide to Best Practices for Performance-Based Service Contracting* (Final Edition, October). *http://www.arnet.gov/Library/OFPP/BestPractices/PPBSC/BestPPBSC.html* Retrieved 3/25/02

Wernet, S. P. (Ed.) (1999). An introduction to managed care in human services. *Managed Care in Human Services.* Chicago: Lyceum Books, Inc.

Wernet, S. P., Hulseman, F. S., Merkel, L. A., McMahon, A., Clevenger, D., Coletta, A., & Leeds, V. (1992). The fee-for-service schedule: A new formula. *Families in Society: The Journal of Contemporary Human Services,* 73:109–115.

INTERNET RESOURCES

American Managed Behavioral Healthcare Association. http://www.ambha.org

Commerce Business Daily. http://cbd.cos.com

Digital Marketplace for the Government Contracting Industry. http://govcon.com

Managed Care Industry Research Center http://www.hcp.med.harvard.edu/Sloan/research.html

III. RESOURCE DISTRIBUTION AND CONTROL

Chapter Eight

INTERNAL CONTROL

After reading this chapter you should be able to:

1. Understand the concept of internal control;
2. Set up a system for controlling costs;
3. Develop variance budgets;
4. Set up a system for control of cash.

INTRODUCTION

Management control involves the "measurement and correction of performance in order to make sure that enterprise objectives and the plans devised to attain them are being accomplished" (Koontz et al., 1982, p. 463). No matter what aspect of the organization is under scrutiny, there are certain aspects of control that apply in every case. That is, control as a process involves three steps: "(1) establishing standards, (2) measuring performance against these standards, and (3) correcting variations from standards and plans" (Koontz et al, p. 464). While this may be clear from a management perspective, there was no clear consensus in the financial community about this concept. In 1987 the National Commission on Fraudulent Financial Reporting (known as the Treadway Commission after its chair) began work on a project to develop a common conceptual framework for the notion of internal control (Steinberg, 1993). In 1992, the Committee of Sponsoring Organizations of the Treadway Commission (COSO) published its report entitled, *Internal Control–Integrated Framework.* This report, called the *COSO Report,* defined internal control as "a process, effected by an entity's board of directors, management, and other personnel, designed to provide reasonable assurance regarding the achievement of objectives in the following categories:

- reliability of financial reporting.
- effectivemenss and efficiency of operations . . .
- compliance with applicable laws and regulations" (COSO, 1992, p. 9).

167

The COSO Report has had a major impact on financial reporting for all organizations because it, among other things, established a standard against which all organizations can measure their internal controls (Steinberg, 1993). This standard has been incorporated in both the private sector, as in the AICPA's Statement on Auditing Standards (SAS) No. 78, *Consideration of Internal Control in a Financial Statement Audit* (1996) as well as in the public sector, in OMB Circular A-133, *Audits of States, Local Governments, and Non-Profit Organizations* (1997). Because OMB A-133 requires the auditor to review the internal controls of an organization, it is important for nonprofits to have some familiarity with these standards. And just as importantly, it is important for nonprofits to incorporate concepts of internal control in order to enhance the efficiency and effectiveness of their operations.

In systems terms, control is a sort of sensing procedure that continually scans and checks internal organization processes as well as the environmental climate and brings feedback to the organization so that it may make whatever adjustments are necessary to achieve its goals and maintain homeostasis. The usual analogy given in discussing control is that of a thermostat and the way it regulates temperature to stay at a constant level.

There are many types of information that the organization uses in order to regulate its many service related and maintenance related activities. *Service related activities* involve direct service delivery, and thus service related information may include numbers of clients seen, number of units of service delivered, for example, hours of counseling, number of meals served, number of families referred for shelter, and so forth. *Maintenance related activities* are those tasks that need to be performed in order for the organization to survive or maintain itself. Maintenance related information may include such items as amount of money raised from fundraising efforts, amount of income was derived from investments, amount of in-kind goods and services donated to the organization, and so forth.

Once the organization has gathered and received this feedback, it must measure its findings with the goals, plans, policies, procedures, and budgets that it has formulated. It must then take the necessary steps to discover and correct the causes of the variations that it has discovered (See Figure 8-1 for a systems view of the control process). In the discussion that follows, the focus will be on control mechanisms that involve the financial management subsystem of the organization.

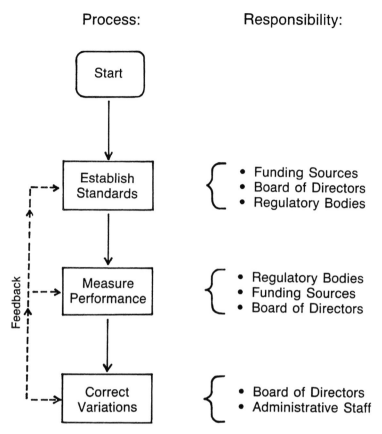

Figure 8-1: A Systems View of the Control Process

THE ORGANIZATIONAL CONTROL SYSTEM

An internal control system must be based on organizational goals and objectives. It should be part of the evaluation system built into the organization's financial information system. The COSO Report defined five interrelated components of internal control: control environment, risk assessment, control activities, information and communication, and monitoring. These components are intricately bound together in a continual process of ensuring adherence to organizational standards.

CONTROL ENVIRONMENT

The control environment is the organizational culture that creates the ambience of an organization; it is seen as the foundation for all the other components of control. It involves board, administration, staff, and others in the philosophy that guides operations. If administrators feel strongly that their stewardship function entails having strong internal controls in place, staff will know it.

Ethical precepts regarding stewardship were mentioned at the beginning of this text. The National Association of Social Workers, as well as other professional associations in the human services, has a Code of Ethics for those persons licensed, certified, or otherwise identified as professional social workers. Many parts of the Code address issues of direct pertinence to financial management. The issues excerpted in Reading 8-1 are seen as the most relevant.

RISK ASSESSMENT

Risk assessment involves analysis of, and planning for, risks that may hinder achievement of organizational goals. These include risks involving money, personnel, clients, and property. Some of the risks involving cash and personnel that have to do with internal controls are discussed here. Other risks involving personnel, clients, and property have to do with adequate screening and training of staff, protection of staff from violent clients, and adequate professional liability and property insurance.

CONTROL ACTIVITIES

Control activities involve policies and procedures set up to minimize risk and assure that organizational goals will be reached. In the following discussion, the focus will be on two main types of control in the human service organization: controlling costs and controlling cash and other assets. Controlling costs involves an understanding of how to figure and allocate costs. Control of cash and other assets involves the setting up of a system of checks and balances to minimize the potential of loss to the organization. Developing the kinds of control mechanisms described here will help the organization more effectively use the limited resources that it has.

Controlling Costs

Every human service organization operates in an environment in which it must compete with other valued entities and activities for scarce resources. For example, $150,000 that goes to one organization means that $150,000 will not be able to be used for a competing, but equally worthwhile, program because resources are finite. Thus the social programs that human service agencies use to promote the general welfare of a community and its citizens not only produce a social good, but have a cost as well.

Remember that when the organization prepares its operating budget, it estimates various costs related to its programs. But these are just estimates and plans of how funds will be allocated, rather than an actual list of expenditures that have taken place. In addition, the costs of certain organization activities are often hidden in the master budget because they are either part of a larger activity, or may be spread across programs. Thus, while budgets may serve as monetary reflections of organization goals and desired levels of programmatic activity expressed in dollars, they do not tell us the "true" costs of providing programs and serving clients.

To be able to control costs, the organization must first be able to isolate and identify costs. It must also be able to allocate costs by program or service unit. Finally, it must be able to report variances from budgets on a regular basis. One of the first steps in devising a system for controlling costs is the setting up of a chart of accounts.

The Chart of Accounts

A chart of accounts may be defined as "a system for identifying and classifying various account titles and accounting transactions by:

(1) The type of account or nature of transaction (what is it?), and
(2) The function of the accounting transaction (for what purpose did the transaction take place?); and, may incorporate a coding scheme composed of numerals and/or letters of the alphabet" (United Way, 1974, p. 34). Table 8-1 illustrates the chart of accounts system developed by the United Way of America.

A chart of accounts is an integral part, indeed, it is at the core of an accounting system in an organization. The purpose of the chart of accounts is to enable users to use identify and classify organization activities easily, quickly, and in a uniform manner. Some of the other purposes of a chart of accounts are:

1. To facilitate the recording of financial transactions in a methodical, organized way;
2. To facilitate the posting of data with a minimum of effort; and

Table 8-1
UWAACS, UNITED WAY OF AMERICA CODING SYSTEM
In the UWAAC System, the core accounting codes are designated as follows:
Core Accounting Codes

Fund Codes:	Balance Sheet Accounts
1: Current Unrestricted	1000-1999: Assets
2. Current Restricted	2000-2999: Liabilities
3. Land, Bldg. And Equipment	3000-3999: Fund Balances
4. Endowment	4000-4999: Public Support
5. Custodian	5000-5999: Fees & Grants from Govt.
6. Add if Necessary (AIN)	6000-6999: Other Revenue
7. AIN	7000-7999: Employee Compensation
8. Loan	8000-8999: Other Expenses
9. Annuity	9000–9999: Other Expenses

The first column on the left is reserved for fund codes, numbers one through nine. For example, 1 is reserved for the current unrestricted fund, 2 for the current restricted fund, and so forth.

The set of numbers on the right are reserved for balance sheet accounts, with codes numbered 1000 to 9999. So in this case, codes 1000 to 1999 are for asset accounts such as cash, 2000 to 2999 are for liability accounts such as mortgage payable, and so forth.

If an organization had an account coded as follows: 1-1999, this would mean that monies received were to go to the current unrestricted fund, in an asset account.

3. To facilitate the gathering and reporting of financial information to interested outsiders.

While a chart of accounts does not necessarily require a coding system, it does facilitate accounting operations, especially if the organization wants to computerize its operations.

Allocating Program Costs

Once an organization has set up a chart of accounts to help it properly code and classify its transactions, it must set up some type of system to allocate its costs. This is not a problem in the small, one program organization, because the organization knows that all the expenses it incurs are related to that one program. It becomes much more of a problem to allocate costs when there are a number of different programs in an organization. Methods of figuring costs were discussed in Chapter Seven. Methods of allocating program costs as well as fundraising costs were discussed in Chapter Four, Budgeting. The important thing to remember about setting up a system to allocate costs is that it must be rational and applied consistently based on documentation gathered by the organization.

Controlling Cash and Other Assets

Control was defined earlier as a system for setting standards, monitoring the fiscal activities of the organization, providing feedback regarding these activities, and taking corrective action if necessary. Control of the physical assets of the organization should be an integral part of any such system. Our concern here is in the development of "a system of procedures and cross checking which in the absence of collusion minimizes the likelihood of misappropriation of assets or misstatement of the accounts and maximizes the likelihood of detection if it occurs" (Gross et al., 1995, p. 404).

Two of the most important tools of internal controls are the cash flow budget and the monthly budget. These forms were discussed in Chapter Three; they give a quick overall review of cash received and disbursed, and any deviations from the norm for the month. In order for a control system to be effective, however, there must be control over receipt of cash, disbursement of cash, bank deposits of cash, and recording of cash, as well as other physical assets of the organization. Besides budgeting, the other important elements of internal control of assets are: personnel controls, transaction controls, and physical controls (Gross et al., 1995; Leduc & Callaghan, 1980).

Personnel Controls

Personnel controls really should form the heart of a control system for assets. They involve three main aspects: separation of duties, independent checks, and bonding of personnel. Some personnel controls are difficult to achieve in small nonprofits because there is often a limited number of personnel available to provide the appropriate separation of duties and operations are sometimes carried out by volunteers rather than employees (National Health Council, 1998). Nevertheless, the nonprofit organization should strive to achieve some level of these personnel controls:

Separation of Duties: Ideally, the receiving of cash should be separated from the recording of cash transactions. This may be difficult in small agencies where the receptionist may also be the one who receives money and records the receipt of it. But the principal of separation of duties applies here most of all if the organization is going to have a meaningful control system. Some other person besides the bookkeeper should have the designated responsibility of receiving cash and preparing receipts. If cash is received through the mail, two persons should open the mail, one of whom may be the person who records receipt of cash.

Separation of Duties: Two signatures should be required on all checks in order to have better control over payments. The signers should be the director of the organization and a board member, but not the bookkeeper as the bookkeeper has to record the transaction in the books. Someone other than the bookkeeper should do the receipt and reconciliation of the bank statements so as to provide a check on the bookkeeper's activities.

Bonding of Employees: This is another type of personnel control. Bonding is a process by which a fidelity company issues an insurance policy that protects the organization in case of loss or embezzlement. If assets are lost due to dishonest employees, the bonding company ensures that the organization can recover its loss. Bonding is seen as a deterrent to dishonesty, because in some cases bonding companies may screen employees for a company before they will cover them in a bond.

Transaction Controls

Transaction controls are concerned with insuring that transactions are executed and recorded properly. Some methods of transaction control involve using prenumbered documents, controlling the access to documents, making permanent indications on documents, and requiring cash received or disbursed to be made by check only.

Prenumbered documents help the organization keep track of every transaction in some chronological sequence. For example, with prenumbered receipts, it is simple to notice if a receipt is missing. Even voided receipts should be kept and filed so as to account for every prenumbered document.

Controlling access to documents means that not just anyone in the organization should be able to take petty cash slips to fill out, or even sign authorization documents for receipt or disbursement of funds. In small agencies this is sometimes again a problem, especially if there is a shortage of staff on occasion and some cash transactions need to take place. But the organization should have a standard set of policies and procedures to handle these contingencies and a clear line of responsibility when it comes to receipt and disbursement of cash.

Making permanent indications on documents in the form of stamping, hole punching, or some other means, insures that documents cannot be used again. In addition, they provide additional evidence as to date received, sent, disbursed, and so forth. Whatever mechanism used by the organization, having a distinctive logo reduces the risk that the markings will not be duplicated.

All disbursements should be made by check in order to have a permanent record of how much was paid to whom. This provides documentation to an auditor who will be able to trace the financial transaction. It also reduces the risk of loss from fraud or deception by staff in the organization.

Physical Controls

Along with personnel and transaction controls, there are physical control measures that can be taken by the organization. The objective of physical control measures is the safeguarding of assets and records. Equipment and other physical assets of the organization should be kept secured, with records of model numbers, identification numbers, and other such information on file. Supply rooms should be supervised, and periodic inventories made and recorded to determine patterns of usage as well as possible pilferage. Important documents relating to property and assets of the organization should be kept in a fireproof safe. Duplicates could be filed in a safe deposit as well as with the organization insurance company.

The internal control policies and procedures adopted by the human service organization help assure that its accounting data are accurate and reliable, that its assets are safeguarded, and that it is moving forward in promoting organizational efficiency to better serve its client population.

INFORMATION AND COMMUNICATION

Information and communication involves the flow of information down, up, and across all levels of an organization. It is not just enough to have written policies and procedures in place. The policies and procedures have to be communicated to all staff in the organization. Having manuals for staff is helpful, but not if they are not read. New policies, and even old ones, should be communicated to staff at staff meetings, staff trainings, and staff orientations.

Table 8-2
HUMAN SERVICES ORGANIZATION, INC.
QUARTERLY VARIANCE BUDGET

	Budgeted	Actual	Variance	Comments
Revenue/Public Support	$120,000	$150,000	$30,000	Unanticipated Bequest
Expenses	$120,000	$110,000	($10,000)	Budgeted item donated
Total Variance			$40,000	

MONITORING

Monitoring involves processes and mechanisms that assess the quality of an organization's performance and congruence with planned, measurable benchmarks of achievable outcomes as well as compliance with generally accepted accounting principles (GAAP). Some monitoring devices used are variance budgets, budget summaries, and internal audits.

Variance Budgets

Variance budgets show the differences between amounts budgeted and actual amounts. The variance budget is an important control tool because it may act as an important feedback or sensing mechanism, helping alert administrators and board members to deviations from anticipated expenditures and revenues. Analyzing the sources of the variances may also be helpful in subsequent budgeting, and information gleaned can result in more accurate forecasts of revenues and expenses (see Table 8-2).

While the variance in the budget shows how anticipated revenues and expenses vary from actual performance, the variance shown does not necessarily mean that this is an indication of poor or ineffective management. Any interpretation of variances must proceed with caution, for positive or negative variances may be misleading without a look at unforeseen factors, e.g., service volume over or under estimate, a cut in allocation or other public support, etc.

Two types of variance budgets of interest are revenue/public support budgets, and expense budgets, although they may also be combined into one budget for ease of analysis.

Revenue/Public Support Variances: Revenue and public support are resource inputs into the human service organization. Revenue is derived from fees earned due to service delivery efforts, while public sup-

Table 8-3
EFFECTS OF VARIANCES ON THE BUDGET

Type of Variance	Revenue Budget	Expense Budget
Over estimate	Favorable	Unfavorable
Under estimate	Unfavorable	Favorable

port includes allocations, grants, and donations. In examining the differences between actual and budgeted revenue and public support, a favorable variance is one in which actual amounts exceed budgeted ones (see Table 8-3 below).

In examining the reasons for a revenue/public support variance there are two components to be examined: **volume** and **rate** (Milani, 1982; Anthony & Govindarajan, 1995).

Volume refers to the number of units of service offered and/or delivered. Volume could be a factor in variance when the number of clients projected, or the number of service units projected to be delivered fall short of the estimated amount, or exceed it.

Rate refers to the amounts charged for services and /or products offered by the organization; in the case of public support, however, it may refer to amount of individual contributions to the organization. Rate could be a factor when client fees or estimated public support fall short of the projected amounts, or exceed it. In looking at these two components of variance, the socio-political and economic factors taken into account in the budgeting process need to be re-examined for possible clues for the variances.

Expense Variances: Expenses are costs incurred by a human service organization in delivering its services. In examining the differences between actual and budgeted expenses, a favorable variance is one in which actual amounts are less than budgeted ones. In examining the reasons for an expense variance, there are two components that need to be examined: **volume** and **cost.**

Volume could be a factor when the number of items budgeted, for example, office supplies, was used excessively during a period, or not totally used during the period.

Cost could be a factor when an item was projected in the budget to cost a certain price, and the actual price is either above or below this figure. Thus, patterns of usage and economic trends need to be examined in analyzing expense variances.

Consistently wide variances, whether positive or negative should be examined by the organization and adjustments made, either in levels or spending, in levels of funds sought, or in subsequent forecasts. Variance budgets should be prepared quarterly and then analyzed for trends at the end of the year when the new budget is being prepared. They should be prepared quarterly in order to show seasonal variations, which in and of themselves may explain some of the variances.

Budget Summaries

Budget summaries are a compilation and summarization of all the individual budgets of an organization. This summary enables the organization to see service volume, costs, revenue, utilization of capital, investments, and so forth, in their relation to one another. In this way, organization administrators can see how the organization as a whole is meeting its objectives.

In order to best use the budget summary as a control tool, the administrator and budget committee should be fairly comfortable in assuming that total budgets are an accurate reflection of organization plans and goals. The budgets that make up the summary should be scrutinized to ensure that a comparison of budgeted and actual costs really reveal the true nature of any deviations. Minor deviations from budget are not a matter of concern because the purpose of a control system is to draw attention to significant variations from the norm. If the budget summary reveals that the organization is not moving toward its objectives, then the summary provides a way of quickly discovering where the problems are occurring (see Table 8-4).

While the budget is an excellent control tool, it must be kept in mind that budgets do not replace a sound financial management system. Also, budgets are tools to be used by all program managers or others

Table 8-4
BUDGET SUMMARY
Human Services Organization, Inc.
All Programs
Quarterly Budget Summary

	1st Quarter	2nd Quarter	3rd Quarter	4th Quarter	Total
Public Support	$90,000	$93,000	$97,000	$136,000	$417,100
Revenue	24,500	16,700	25,350	25,200	101,750
Total Public Support & Revenue	$114,500	$109,700	$122,750	$171,900	$518,850
Expenses	$124,500	$124,600	$123,500	$126,350	$498,950

who have responsibility for organization programs and operations. And if budgetary control is to be workable in an organization, the budget committee should receive timely information on actual and estimated performance under budgets by those responsible for the budgets of their departments. Variance from budget must be communicated promptly to program managers to give them feedback as to how they are doing in order for them to take steps to avoid budget deviations.

Internal Audits

Internal auditing may be defined as "a staff activity intended to ensure that information is reported accurately in accordance with prescribed rules, that fraud and misappropriation of assets are kept to a minimum, and in some cases, to suggest ways of improving the organization's efficiency and effectiveness" (Anthony & Govindarajan, 1995, p. 17). Internal audits are usually performed by an employee of the organization, usually an accountant, who examines the accounting records, compliance, and internal controls of the nonprofit throughout the fiscal year. Some small nonprofits that cannot afford an internal auditor may set up an audit committee to oversee this function. Internal audits are a good way of making sure the organization's books are in order before the yearly audit that is performed by an outside Certified Public Accountant.

DESIGNING THE INTERNAL CONTROL SYSTEM

There are a number of important factors to consider in the structuring of such a system. An effective control system should:

- **Fit the organizational climate**

That is, the control system must be designed to be congruent with the particular demands and constraints of a given organization setting. Human service agencies are so unique and diverse that a control system set up to monitor one organization would be inappropriate in another.

- **Be tailored to plans and positions**

Any control system that is set up by the organization must reflect the long-range goals and plans of the organization, for, in effect, these are what the control system is set up to monitor. In addition, the system should be developed in such a way that it can quickly and accurately convey information to those in different positions in the organization.

The control system should be able to meet the varying needs of different persons in different positions in the organization. For example, information needed by the clinical director may not be the same as that needed by the director of budgeting and planning, or the administrator of the organization.

• Point up exceptions at critical points

An effective and efficient financial management system runs according to the rules of management by exception. That is, smoothly running activities are not routinely reported, rather those activities and events that deviate from the norm are reported so that analysis and corrective action may be taken.

• Be objective

While elements of subjectivity creep into any human system, an effective control system should be constructed in such a way that measurable standards of performance can be used in periodic review to judge the progress of organization and individual activities.

• Be flexible

No system should be so rigid that revisions cannot easily be made. Some provision should be made for periodic review, and revising, or modifying existing guidelines, policies and procedures.

• Be economical

A control system must efficiently do the job at a price that the organization can afford. This is a crucial factor in human service agencies, which usually have to operate with "bare-bones" budgets. How much a system will cost in terms of time, personnel, and materials must be evaluated in deciding on any control system.

• Have a reporting provision

This applies in several ways. First of all, standards and criteria must be communicated to all employees. Second of all, instances of deviations from the norm should be communicated through appropriate channels. In some cases, this communication may just be in the form of discussion between a worker and a supervisor. In more serious cases, written documentation may be needed. Thirdly, forms that concisely and graphically display pertinent report information should be developed and used.

• Be meaningful

There must be some logic and rationale for the system developed, and this must be communicated to employees. Any system developed will be counter-productive if employees feel as though they are engaged in "busywork" by having to fill out forms for which they see no use.

- **Be enforceable**

Some method must be built into the system to insure that policies, procedures, and rules will be enforced. That is, there must be sanctions for those who do not follow organization procedures, and there must be positive reinforcement or motivators for those that do (Koontz et al., 1982; Lohman, 1980).

Reading 8-1: Excerpts from NASW Code of Ethics (1999)

1. SOCIAL WORKERS' ETHICAL RESPONSIBILITY TO CLIENTS

1.03 Informed Consent

(a) . . . . Social workers should use clear and understandable language to inform clients of the purpose of the services, risks related to the services, limits to services because of the requirements of a third-party payer, relevant costs, reasonable alternatives, clients right to refuse or withdraw consent, and the time frame covered by the consent.

1.06 Conflicts of Interest

(b) Social workers should not take unfair advantage of any professional relationship or exploit others to further their personal, religious, political, or business interests.

1.07 Privacy and Confidentiality

(h) Social workers should not disclose confidential information to third-party payers unless clients have authorized such disclosure.

1.13 Payment for Services

(a) When setting fees, social workers should ensure that the fees are fair, reasonable, and commensurate with the services performed. Consideration should be given to clients' ability to pay.
(b) Social workers should avoid accepting goods or services from clients as payment for professional services. Bartering arrangements, particularly involving services, create the potential for con-

flicts of interest, exploitation, and inappropriate boundaries in social workers' relationships with clients.

(c) Social workers should not solicit a private fee or other remuneration for providing services to clients who are entitled to such available services through the social workers' employer or agency.

Section 1.16 Termination of Services

(c) Social workers in fee-for-service settings may terminate services to clients who are not paying an overdue balance if the financial contractual arrangements have been made clear to the client, if the client does not pose an imminent danger to self or others, and if the clinical and other consequences of the current nonpayment have been addressed and discussed with the client.

(d) Social workers should not terminate services to pursue a social, financial, or sexual relationship with a client.

2. SOCIAL WORKERS' ETHICAL RESPONSIBILITIES TO COLLEAGUES

2.06 Referral for Services

(c) Social workers are prohibited from giving or receiving payment for a referral when no professional service is provided by the referring social worker.

2.11 Unethical conduct of Colleagues

(a) Social workers should take adequate measures to discourage, prevent, expose, and correct the unethical conduct of colleagues.

3. SOCIAL WORKERS' ETHICAL RESPONSIBILITIES IN PRACTICE SETTINGS

3.05 Billing

Social workers should establish and maintain billing practices that accurately reflect the nature and extent of services provided and that identify who provided the service in the practice setting.

3.07 Administration

(a) Social work administrators should advocate within and outside their agencies for adequate resources to meet clients' needs.

(b) Social workers should advocate for resource allocation procedures that are open and fair. When not all clients' needs can be met, an allocation procedure should be developed that is nondiscriminatory and based on appropriate and consistently applied principles.

(c) Social workers who are administrators should take reasonable steps to ensure that adequate agency or organizational resources are available to provide appropriate staff supervision.

3.09 Commitments to Employers

(g) Social workers should be diligent stewards of the resources of their employing organizations, wisely conserving funds where appropriate and never misappropriating funds or using them for unintended purposes.

4. SOCIAL WORKERS' ETHICAL RESPONSIBILITIES AS PROFESSIONALS

4.04 Dishonesty, Fraud, and Deception

Social workers should not participate in, condone, or be associated with dishonesty, fraud, or deception.

4.07 Solicitations

(a) Social workers should not engage in uninvited solicitation of potential clients who, because of their circumstances, are vulnerable to undue influence, manipulation, or coercion.

5. SOCIAL WORKERS' ETHICAL RESPONSIBILITIES TO THE SOCIAL WORK PROFESSION

5.01 Integrity of the Profession

(c) Social workers should contribute time and professional expertise to activities that promote respect for the value, integrity, and competence of the social work professional. These activities may include teaching, research, consultation, service, legislative testimony, presentations in the community, and participation in their professional organizations.

6. SOCIAL WORKERS' ETHICAL RESPONSIBILITITES TO THE BROADER SOCIETY

6.01 Social Welfare

Social workers should promote the general welfare of society, from local to global levels, and the development of people, their communities, and their environments. Social workers should advocate for living conditions conducive to the fulfillment of basic human needs and promote social, economic, political, and cultural values and institutions that are compatible with the realization of social justice.

REFERENCES

American Institute of Certified Public Accountants. (1996). Statement on Auditing Standards (SAS) No. 78, *Consideration of Internal Control in a Financial Statement Audit.* New York: author.

Anthony, R.N & Govindarajan, V. (1995). *Management Control Systems* (8th Edition). Chicago: Richard D. Irwin, Inc.

Committee of Sponsoring Organizations (COSO) (1992). *Internal Control–Integrated Framework.*

Gross, M. J. Jr., Larkin, R.F., Bruttomesso, R.S. & McNally, J.J. (1995). Financial and *Accounting Guide for Not-for-profit Organizations* (5th ed.). New York: John Wiley.

Koontz, H., O'Donnell, C., Weirich, H. (1982). *Essentials of Management* (3rd Edition*).* New York: McGraw-Hill Book Co.

Leduc, R. & Callaghan, C.T. (1980). Accounting procedures for the nonprofit organization. pp. 6–63 to 6–81 in Tracy D. Connors (Ed.). *The Nonprofit Organization Handbook.* New York: McGraw-Hill.

Lohman, R.A. (1980). B*reaking Even.* Philadelphia: Temple University Press.

Milani, K. (1982). Overview of the budgeting process. In T. D. Connors & C. T. Callaghan (Eds.), *Financial Management for Nonprofit Organizations* (pp.10–13). New York: AMACOM.

National Association of Social Workers. (1999). *Code of Ethics.* Approved by the 1996 NASW Delegate Assembly and revised by the 1999 NASW Delegate Assembly. Washington, D.C.: author.

National Health Council, Inc. & the National Assembly of National Voluntary Health and Social Welfare Organizations, Inc. (1998). *Standards of Accounting and Financial Reporting for Voluntary Health and Welfare Organizations* (The Black Book)(4th Edition). Dubuque, Iowa: Kendall/Hunt Publishing Co.

Office of Management and Budget (OMB). (1997). Circular A-133, A*udits of States, Local Governments, and Non-Profit Organizations.*

Steinberg, Richard M. (1993). Internal control–integrated framework: A landmark study. T*he CPA Journal Online.* http://www.luca.com/cpajournal/old/14465853.htm

United Way of America. (1974). *Accounting and Financial Reporting: A Guide for United Ways and Not-for Profit Human Service Organizations.* Alexandria, VA: author.

INTERNET RESOURCES

Home Page of COSO–The Committee of Sponsoring Organizations of the Treadway Commission. http://www.coso.org

Internal Control Checklist at the homepage of the American Institute of Certified Public Accountants. http://www.aicpa.org/pubs/jofa/Sep97/check.htm

National Association of Social Workers. http://www.naswdc.org

Chapter Nine

INVESTMENTS

After reading this chapter you should be able to:

1. Describe the major types of investments;
2. Discuss the advantages and disadvantages of different investment strategies for nonprofit organizations;
3. Understand the varying degrees of risk involved in investments;
4. Develop an organizational investment plan;
5. Know how to choose an investment advisor.

INTRODUCTION

Investing may be defined as the current commitment of funds in order to receive a future financial gain. All nonprofit organizations have a need for secure, continuing sources of funds. In systems terms, the nonprofit receives inputs in the form of endowment monies or surplus funds. Through a planning process the nonprofit develops an investment strategy suitable for the organization within the constraints mandated by governing bylaws, legal statutes, and funder restrictions. The output of this investment process is an investment mix tailored to the special needs of the nonprofit human service organization (see Figure 9-1).

While some nonprofits barely have enough revenue and public support to go from one fiscal year to the next, others are fortunate enough to have surplus funds that can be used for investment. At times a nonprofit organization may receive restricted funds in the form of an endowment. An endowment is a monetary gift that is to be invested and the earned interest used for designated purposes or just general operating expenses. Other sources of funds for investment may include temporary excess resources from the cash accounts. Restrictions mandated by the donor are a factor in investment decisionmaking, as are any legal restrictions that may apply. While the nonprofit may not be bound by legal restrictions as to types of securities it may purchase, it may be bound by restrictions in its own charter or bylaws.

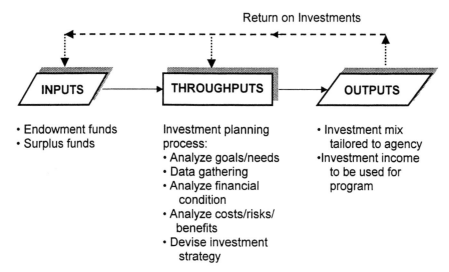

Figure 9-1: The Investment Subsystem

There are two types of investment return that can be gained by an investment. The first type of return is from interest and dividends, called *investment income.* The second type of return is from *capital gains (or losses).* Capital gains (or losses) occur when securities are sold at a price that is higher (or lower) from the original cost. If it is sold at a higher price, there is a capital gain; if at a lower price, a capital loss (Hirt & Block, 1993). When it comes to purchasing investment vehicles, the nonprofit is in a very different situation than the average investor. This is mainly due to Section 501(c)(3) of the Internal Revenue Code, which classifies most nonprofits as tax-exempt, as was discussed in Chapter One. One implication of this tax-exempt status is that the human service organization may not be motivated by some of the same considerations as other investors, such as the search for tax shelters, or the worry over capital gains taxes (Powell, 1978).

The purpose of this chapter is to familiarize human service professionals with some of the basics of investing. There are many different types of investments; the main types to be discussed in this chapter are the more conventional. There are other, somewhat more sophisticated, types of investments such as convertible securities and options that will not be discussed here. Also, other forms of investments such as art works, stamps, and coins will not be discussed; they take specialized knowledge that is beyond the realm of the typical human service nonprofit organization. As with much of the subject matter of this book, investing is an art–not a science. Many people have developed their own approaches to analyzing and choosing investments. The important thing to understand is the element of risk, for after all, the money to be invested has been given in trust that the nonprofit human service organization will use it wisely to further its humanitarian goals.

In this chapter investing by the nonprofit human service organization will be viewed within the context of risk and long-range planning. Different types of investment vehicles will be described, as well as the advantages and disadvantages of each investment type. Since the aim of this chapter is to make nonprofit human service organization staff informed investment clients, a discussion of factors to be considered in choosing an investment advisor will be presented. Reading 9-1 will hopefully facilitate an understanding of how investment information is presented to investors and to the general public in the financial pages of newspapers.

INVESTMENT PLANNING FOR HUMAN SERVICE ORGANIZATIONS

An effective investment plan for the nonprofit organization must reflect critical thought on the part of staff and board members. Such a plan should be the result of a process that includes the following steps: (1) an analysis of long-term organizational goals and needs; (2) gathering data from critical agency financial reports as well as information seeking about suitable investments; (3) an analysis of agency's financial condition; (4) an analysis of costs/risks/benefits of specific investments; (5) development of an investment strategy which involves an understanding and clarification of investment goals; (6) periodic review and evaluation of investments and investment plans.

Analysis of Long-term Organizational Goals and Needs

Key elements in investment planning are the goals of the investment within the context of the nonprofit organization's needs and the restrictions of any endowment gifts. The organization's board needs to have a clear idea of its goals before it embarks on an investment program, since its investments should be an integral part of its long-term plan. If the organization is not clear and explicit about its goals, what it does with its assets may result in disappointment. Without understanding what it is doing, a board and executive director may allow an investment advisor to assemble an inappropriate portfolio of investments that will not be in the organization's best interest.

If the nonprofit organization's long-range plans include the initiation or expansion of programs, the renovation or building of facilities, then it may want to target investment income to these ends. The key question for the nonprofit organization with funds for investment is—where is the greatest need for the extra income that could be generated with the prudent investment of this money? Of course, sometimes endowment monies come with restrictions. These may specify exactly how the interest from the investment is to be spent, for example, on a specific program or program activity. In this case, the agency must view the restriction in light of its organizational goals. If there is a fit, the agency should proceed with investing the donation. If not, it should return the money to the donor unless the donor can be persuaded to accommodate the nonprofit's specific interests.

In this planning phase, the nonprofit organization should also be clear as to what ethical values and principles it wants its investments to reflect. These principles should be codified and made a part of the nonprofit organization bylaws as a guide to an executive director or finance committee's deliberations.

Data Gathering

The persons responsible for investment decisions should assemble the agency's budgets, financial statements, external audits, cash flow charts, program reports, needs assessments, and any other pertinent data that could be helpful in analyzing the financial condition of the organization. Other information that needs to be gathered includes requirements of funding sources, information about various types of investments, and competent financial advisors in the area, their fees, and services.

One good place to find a wealth of information about all types of investments is the Internet. As with any information, the source of the information has to be considered, as well as its legitimacy and credibility. It is even possible for investors themselves to trade stocks and bonds on the Internet, although this is perhaps not advisable for a nonprofit to do.

Analysis of Financial Condition

Before the nonprofit organization embarks on an investment program, it must be sure that it has a financially secure enough base in case of emergency, for example, the loss of a major grant or a large cut in an allocation. Financial areas to check internally may include sufficient insurance on building and property, professional liability insurance for staff, low debt ratio, a satisfactory credit rating, sufficient cash flow, and an adequate, consistent source of public support from allocations and fundraising. Any shortcomings in these areas must be attended to before an investment program has begun, for there are some risks associated with any investment.

Analysis of Costs/Risks/Benefits

As in any financial endeavor, there are risks involved. The human service organization has to be more cognizant of risk factors in light of its stewardship function, for it is not investing its own money. Risk may be defined as "uncertainty concerning the outcome of an investment" (Hirt & Block, 1993, p. 775). The degree of risk in investments is related to the types and grades of securities involved. There are five major categories of risk: 1) business or financial risk; 2) price-level risk; 3) interest rate risk; 4) market risk; and 5) psychological risk (Huang, 1981).

Business or Financial Risk

Business risk is "concerned with the degree of uncertainty associated with an investment's earnings and ability to pay investors interest, dividends, and any other returns owed them" (Gitman and Joehnk, 1990, p. 120). Most businesses finance their operations by borrowing money. The larger the proportion of debt undertaken by a company, the greater the risk for itself as well as investors. Large debt financing means that a company has to not only repay the debt, but the interest as well before it can distribute any earnings to investors. If the company cannot meet its debt repayments, it may go out of business, resulting in financial loss for investors and creditors alike.

There is no guarantee as to how long any organization will remain in business; thousands of enterprises go out of business each year. In economic hard times, or periods of rapidly changing technology, businesses need to keep highly competitive to survive and make a profit. When a business does not make a profit over a period of time, it may eventually go bankrupt. In this case, the investors or shareholders of the business will lose their investments. The creditors of the business may receive something, but usually only a fraction of what they are owed. Thus business or financial risk is one type of risk that investors need to be concerned about.

Price-level Risk

Nonprofit investors must keep an eye to inflation. Price-level risk " . . . refers to the risk of losing purchasing power from returns of fixed income securities because of inflation" (Huang, 1981, p. 5). For example, the Consumer Price Index, which measures changes in the cost of living, rose from a base of 100 in 1983 to 166.2 in 1999, an increase of 67% (Bureau of Labor Statistics, 1999). Thus, an investor who purchased a bond at par value of $1000 in 1983 would find in cashing it in ten years later that it had lost about 54% of its original value due to inflation. Because of the constant loss in the value of the dollar and the constant rise in the price of living, this investor suffered from price-level risk. While recently economic forces in The United States have kept inflation largely contained, this remains an issue to watch.

Interest Rate Risk

Interest rate risk is usually borne by those who invest in fixed-income securities, as was mentioned previously. Because interest rates change over time, due to a large extent to federal monetary policies, the price of securities fluctuate. When interest rates are high, the prices of fixed-income securities tend to go down; when interest rates go down, the price of fixed-income securities tend to rise. Common stocks are also affected by changing money rates, but to a lesser degree. The reason for the fluctuation in price is an attempt to create attractiveness and competitiveness of yield. For example, when interest rates are 10% why would an investor want to buy a bond only paying 5%? In order to make the fixed-income bond more attractive to buyers, its par value of $1000 will decrease in price and be sold at a discount in the marketplace. Those who buy other fixed-income investments, such as CD's, may also be affected by interest rate risk.

Market Risk

External factors such as political, social, and economic occurrences, changes in consumer preference or taste, can influence the market for investments and their rate of return. These external factors thus cause market risk, that is, the fluctuation in the price of securities due to events perceived to be related to the earning power of the issuing corporation. For example, when one computer company recently announced reduced earnings, the prices of all microcomputer company stocks went down because of investor perceptions of weakness in the home computer market as a whole.

Psychological Risk

Psychological risk refers to the investor's emotional instability (Huang, 1981). When the market is up, investors become very enthusiastic; when it goes down, some investors panic and fear loss. They begin to sell their securities without regard for their real and potential earnings. This type of irrational behavior is due to the fact that the vagaries of investment markets are too stressful for some people to handle. This type of person should not be in charge of the investment function in your nonprofit organization.

These then, are the major types of risks associated with investing. There are other, more specific, risks that are related to the type of investment itself. Some of these risks have been described along with each particular type of investment mentioned previously.

Development of Investment Strategy

The best investment approach for any given human service nonprofit organization depends on many factors, including:

Degree of Risk

The nonprofit organization must decide how much risk it is willing to assume on loss of principal, fluctuation in price of security, and rate of return on investment. While considering degree of risk the organization is willing to incur, one must also consider risk management and those who are charged with it.

Expertise of Nonprofit Organization Staff

The nonprofit organization's board must decide whether someone in administration has sufficient knowledge, training, and expertise to be able to take the responsibility for the investment function. Or a board member with such expertise may be willing to assume this responsibility while at the same time taking care to avoid conflict of interest issues.

If there is no one on either staff or board who is able to meet the necessary criteria, the organization must depend on a professional investment advisor to make the investment decisions.

Assessment of the Investment Environment

The nonprofit organization's administrative staff and board need to discuss with a competent professional his or her assessment of the investment climate at the present time and in the near future. There are, of course, a number of factors of a socioeconomic and political nature that impinge on the investment environment at any given time. Try to evaluate the advisor's estimation of the importance of these factors for your nonprofit organization. Obviously, in economic downturns the organization will want to be particularly prudent with its money.

Nonprofit Organization Bylaws or Funder Restrictions

Occasionally, although not as often as is warranted, a nonprofit has corporate bylaws that restrict it to only certain types of investments. If its bylaws are specific as to investment vehicles, then the organization is bound by these restrictions. This, of course, makes the matter of investing much easier. For example, if bylaws state investments are limited to CD's or Treasury bonds, then decisions involve choosing the highest paying CD's or bonds for the period of time of the investment.

Nonprofit Organization Investment Goals

Obviously, the nonprofit organization wants maximum return on its investment coupled with minimum risk. At times, an organization may be willing to take small risks in order to get a higher return on investment. Some key investment considerations toward this end are: 1) safety of principal; 2) protection of purchasing power; 3) current income; 4) capital appreciation; 5) liquidity; and 6) ease of management (Huang, 1981; Stevenson & Jennings, 1984; Hirt & Block, 1993).

Safety of Principal: Principal is the amount of money originally invested. Because of the stewardship function of the human service organization, or the recognition that nonprofits serve as agents or managers of the property of others, in most cases the first objective of any investment strategy should be safety of principal. This means that the nonprofit organization should not engage in speculation, that is, high-risk ventures. Rather, the organization should try to avoid unsound and unnecessary risks. In attempting to meet the priority of safety of principal, the nonprofit organization should turn first to low-risk, highly rated

Table 9-1
INVESTMENT GOALS AND TYPES OF INVESTMENTS*

Type of Investment come	Investment Goal			
	Safety of Principal	Stability of Principal	Liquidity	Stability of In
Fixed Rate CD	High	High	Low	High
Variable Rate CD	High	High	High	Low
Money Market Mutual Fund	Med.-high	High	High	Low
Stock Mutual Fund	Variable	Medium	High	Low
Bond Mutual Fund	Variable	Medium	Medium	Med.-high
Treasury Bill	High	Medium	Medium	High
Stocks	Variable	Variable	High	Variable

*Adapted from: Consumer Reports, January 1984; Dunnan, 1994.

corporate and government bonds, money market funds, and certificates of deposit.

Diversification of portfolio is a strategy that can help the nonprofit organization attain safety of principal, as well as stability of investment income. However, safety of principal should be viewed within the context of the constant spiral of upward prices. Thus the constantly diminishing value of the invested dollars due to inflation needs to be taken into account in investment strategy by attempting to protect purchasing power. Table 9-1 shows the association between some investment goals, types of investments, and risk.

Protection of Purchasing Power: Constantly rising price levels have diminished the value of the dollar over time. Thus another goal of investment should be to try to create a hedge against inflation by investing in equities and tangible properties that increase in value at a higher rate than inflation. The uncertainties of politics, the market place, and future price trends again would dictate that the nonprofit organization diversify holdings as much as possible. In making decisions about the proportion of holdings between different investment types, the nonprofit organization and its investment advisor should carefully study economic trends and try to project: 1) the degree of price-level inflation expected; and 2) the possibilities of gain or loss on the investments available to the nonprofit organization, all within the limitations imposed by legal, moral, donor, funder, and board-imposed restrictions.

Current Income: Current income refers to the goal of insuring that an investment pays a regular amount of interest or dividend so that the nonprofit organization can have a steady cash flow. For the nonprofit organization, the goal of income should be subordinate to the main goal of safety of principal. Income, and the assurance of the regularity of income, is related to safety. Income and safety are related because those investment vehicles with a guarantee of income, or those companies with a stable, long-standing record of dividend and/or interest payment, tend to be the safest. Nonprofit organizations, for which stability of investment income is crucial, must view carefully the history, ratings, and prospects of any issuer of securities they consider purchasing. Those companies with long records in the payment of interest or dividends are the safest, and most likely to fulfill the goal of current, stable income (Huang, 1981).

Investments with a guaranteed stable rate of return include bonds, treasury notes, certificates of deposit, and preferred stocks. However, in looking for a fixed rate of return, the nonprofit organization must also take into account the factor of inflation. For example, an investor must think in terms of "real, or constant-dollar, returns rather than of conventional ones expressed in current dollars only" (Christy and Clendenin, 1978, p. 91). In inflationary periods, returns measured in terms of purchasing power are always lower than those expressed in terms of money. For example, if an investment was paying 10% and the inflation rate was 7%, the real rate of return would only be 3%. In order for the investor to make the 10% return during this period of 7% inflation, the return would have to be 17%.

Capital Appreciation: Capital appreciation refers to the increase in the price paid for an investment. If an investment appreciates in value, then some profit will be made when the investment is sold. Some investors are more interested in capital appreciation than anything else. Their motto is, "buy low, sell high". The difficulty for them is to know when the lows and the highs of the cycles have been reached. Many investors combine goals such as capital appreciation with others such as high yield and stability of income. But for the conservative investor, such as the human service organization, capital appreciation should be considered a secondary benefit if it should occur.

Liquidity: Liquidity is the ability to convert an investment into cash quickly at a value similar to the original amount of the principal invested. This may or may not be an important investment goal for a nonprofit organization. It depends on the purpose of the investment, that is, whether the investment is to generate operating monies, monies for the capital fund, or some other purpose. If the organization is to generate extra operating monies, then the nonprofit may want its investment, or part of it, to be liquid in case of emergency. On the other hand, investment for a capital building fund may not have to be as liquid.

In any case, a nonprofit organization should never let its funds sit in accounts that are not making any money, even funds that must be readily at hand. For example, organizations should make sure that they have their operating funds in interest-bearing checking accounts and short-term CD's so that no money is sitting idly. If there is enough cash in a bank account, an organization can set up a sweep account. In a sweep account, monies are taken out of an account every night, invested, and returned to the account the next morning with interest. There may be a minimum dollar threshold for this type of account, so a nonprofit should check with banks in its community.

Ease of Management: Most nonprofit human service organization staff have neither the time nor the expertise to manage investments. However, there are some simple types of investments, such as fixed-income investments, that a designated staff person of a nonprofit organization could be responsible for with minimum trouble. If ease of management is an important goal, then wisely choosing an investment advisor is the best route for the nonprofit organization. Factors involved in choosing such a person or institution will be discussed later in this chapter. If the nonprofit organization has a small amount of money to invest and wants more internal control over the investments, a mutual fund might be the best choice.

Given these factors, here are some important points to remember in developing a plan. The investment(s) chosen should be: safe, diversified, and reflect the values and ethics of the nonprofit organization and its mission.

Periodic Review and Evaluation

Nothing remains constant except change, and this is nowhere more true than in the world of investments. Therefore, it is imperative that the nonprofit organization's administrators and board periodically review the nonprofit organization's investment plan—at least annually, if not more. Not only can the investment climate change due to economic and political events, but the financial situation of the nonprofit organization can change as well. A periodic review involves a look at the current status of the investments and an evaluation as to their current suitability given the immediate and foreseeable goals of the nonprofit organization.

There are two main types of investments: *fixed-income* and *variable income*. Fixed-income investments, as the name implies, guarantee a given rate of return no matter how the economy fares over the life of the security. Variable-income investments, on the other hand, vary in their rate of return according to how well the company and the economy are doing. These investments vary in their degree of safety, an important consideration for nonprofit organizations.

FIXED-INCOME INVESTMENTS

Bonds

A bond is a debt instrument, that is, a loan by the person or organization that buys the bond to the issuer of the bond. These debt securities, or bonds, are issued for the purpose of raising money for the issuer. The major types of entities that issue bonds are corporations and governments (federal, state, and local).

Bonds are considered fixed income securities because the bondholder's return is limited to the fixed interest payments that the issuing organization agrees to pay. If bonds pay only a fixed amount, why would anyone invest in them? First of all, bonds do represent a stable source of current income for investors with that goal. It is a stable source of income precisely because the rate of interest is fixed. The second reason that investors buy bonds is for the possibility, for the more aggressive investor, of earning capital gains. This occurs with bonds because interest rates and prices of bonds tend to move in opposite directions, that is, when interest rates drop bond prices rise and when interest rates go up, bond prices fall (Dunnan, 1994). So the possibility of capital gains is the second reason that investors buy bonds.

Corporate Bonds

Bonds are debt instruments and investors who buy corporate bonds become creditors of the issuing institution. Corporations issue bonds to finance their projects such as expansion or other activities. Issuing bonds can help the issuer reduce the cost of financing its projects and use the money it receives as leverage to improve its rate of return on equity capital (Khoury, 1983). Debt for the company occupies an advantageous position in relation to equity because of the tax deductibility of interest expenses for the issuing company. All types of corporations issue bonds. There are many different types of corporate bonds, but they will not be discussed here. For further discussion of these and other types of investments, the reader is referred to the bibliography at the end of this book. For investors interested in bonds, there are rating companies, such as Moody's Investor Services and Standard and Poor's, that rate bonds. Highly rated bonds are those rated A+ or better, while some bonds may have no rating (junk bonds). A bond is rated based on an assessment of the financial stability and position of the entity issuing it. The higher the rating of the bond, the better it is.

Advantages and Disadvantages of Corporate Bonds

Advantages: Corporate bonds provide stability of income for investors with this goal as they pay a fixed rate of interest for the life of the bond, and the yield on corporate bonds is often higher than that for governmental securities. There is a high degree of safety of principal if a bond is highly rated, another important goal for some investors. The degree of safety on high quality bonds is comparable to government bonds. An investor may have capital gains if a bond is sold for more than was paid for it.

Disadvantages: As previously mentioned, bond prices and interest rates tend to move in opposite directions. Thus the investor who buys a bond when interest rates are rising may lose money due to loss of opportunity to invest in a higher yielding product. Also, because a bond has a guaranteed rate of interest that does not change, the investor may lose money due to inflation.

Government Bonds

All types of federal, state and local authorities issue government bonds. The United States Treasury issues three types of securities: bills, notes, and bonds. When an investor buys Treasury securities, s/he is in effect lending money to the government. A *bill* is a short-term type of debt instrument. *T-bills,* as they are called, usually have a maturity of one year or less. They are issued in denominations of $10,000 with $5,000 increments. They are sold at discount from face value (par) and do not pay interest before maturity. The interest earned on the bill is the difference between the purchase or discount price and the value of the bill at maturity. For example, if the discount or interest rate is 5%, the investor receives a discount of $500 (5% × $10,000), therefore pays $9,500 for the T-bill and at maturity receives $10,000. T-bills are purchased because they are considered to be a safe, secure investment. They are a good investment for nonprofits that do not want to tie up money for long periods of time and those required by funding sources to keep money in interest bearing accounts. As Dunnan (1994) said, "Think of them as interest bearing cash" (p. 124).

Notes are government coupon obligations with a fixed interest that is payable semiannually. These notes are medium-term debt instruments with a maturity of one to ten years. They are usually sold in denominations of $1,000 and $5,000. There are two kinds of notes, fixed-principal and inflation-indexed. The inflation-indexed bonds are adjusted to reflect inflation as measured by the Consumer Price Index.

Treasury *bonds* are long-term debt instruments with a maturity of more than ten years (U.S. Dept. of the Treasury). They are sold in denominations that start at $1,000 and go up to $1 million dollars. The Treasury Department suspended issuing the 30-year bond in October 2001, but they can still be bought on the open market.

State and local governments also sell bonds. Many government entities, such as cities, counties, water, and school districts issue bonds to raise money. For example, a county might issue a bond to finance construction of a community center. One feature that makes municipal bonds so attractive to some investors, even though they pay lower rates of interest, is that interest income from these bonds is exempt from federal income taxes. Even though capital gains are taxable, bonds are exempt from federal income taxes and most states also do not tax income from their own bonds or those of their local governments. Probably because of these features, most municipal bonds have yields that are much less than prevailing interest rates. One drawback to municipals is that some of them may have limited marketability, and thus this may mean lower liquidity for the nonprofit organization (D'Ambrosio, 1976).

Advantages and Disadvantages of Governmental Bonds

Advantages: There is minimal risk in acquiring U.S. Treasury bills, notes, or bonds. This low market-and-business risk is due to the high safety of principal and stability of income attached to the U.S. backed-securities. Governmental securities have high marketability; they can be acquired and disposed of easily and quickly. Long-term government bonds are not "callable", this means that an investor can lock in a high rate of return and keep it, even if interest rates go down.

Disadvantages: One disadvantage of buying bonds is related to the fixed yield, that is, return will not fluctuate with the market rates or inflation. Thus, they provide no buffer for the investor. There is no capital gain with governmental securities unless a bond is selling below par when purchased (Amling, 1984). Some municipal bonds are not as safe as U.S. Treasury bonds, or even highly rated corporate bonds. They pay a lower rate of interest because of their tax-exempt feature and therefore are not a good investment for nonprofits (who are already virtually tax-exempt).

Certificates of Deposit

Certificates of deposit (CD's) are time deposits issued by almost every bank. The certificate means that the investor has deposited a specified sum of money for a specific period of time at a guaranteed rate of return. CD's are issued in specific amounts usually ranging from $500 up to over $100,000. They are called time deposits because they can be issued with virtually any maturity date, but most frequent maturities start at 90 days and increase in units of 30 days. When a CD is purchased, it cannot be redeemed until maturity. If it is withdrawn before maturity, there is usually an early withdrawal penalty or loss of interest. However, since they are negotiable, the investor can sell the CD as any other market instrument could be sold.

Advantages of CD's: Certificates of Deposit offered by banks are very low risk; they are insured up to $100,000. They guarantee a specific rate of interest no matter what happens to interest rates in the economy.

Disadvantages of CD's: Certificates of Deposit may not be withdrawn or cashed in before the specified due date without penalty. So a nonprofit has to be sure that it can afford to have its money tied up for the specified period before it buys a CD. The major disadvantage of CD's however, has to do with interest rates. While CD's usually pay more than an ordinary savings account, the interest received may be lower than other types of investments. If a CD with a longer maturity period (3–5 years) is bought and interest rates rise during this period, the investor will be locked in for a long period with a lower rate.

Preferred Stocks

Preferred stocks possess characteristics of both common stocks and corporate bonds; thus they are considered a sort of hybrid security. Some of the characteristics they share with common stocks are that they represent equity ownership in a corporation and are issued without stated maturity dates as bonds are. They also pay dividends as common stocks do. Preferreds are like bonds in that the owners or investors have a claim on the income and assets of the company that supersedes that of the common stockholder. As with bonds, they provide a fixed level of current income for the life of the issue, and they are competitive with bonds because they are viewed as fixed income obligations (Gitman and Joehnk, 1990).

Advantages of Preferreds: The main advantage of preferred stock is as a source of income. There is also the possibility of capital gains in the price of the stock. Preferreds also usually pay higher dividends than common stock.

Disadvantages of Preferreds: As with all fixed-income investments, there is interest level risk. If interest rates rise, the investment loses money, as it gives no protection from inflation. And if a company's earnings rise, the investor does not share in the increased earnings.

VARIABLE-INCOME INVESTMENTS

Common Stocks

Common stocks represent shares of ownership in a corporation. If a corporation has 10,000 shares of common stock outstanding and a nonprofit organization buys ten shares of that stock, the nonprofit owns 10/10,000 of equity in the company. As owners, stockholders have the right to vote on decisions affecting the company. Stockholders are also entitled to earnings and dividends of the company.

Many investors are attracted to common stocks for the possibility of sharing in the growth of earnings of companies over time. This growth in earnings is usually translated into dividends for shareholders. Dividends are the amount of earnings distributed to shareholders (Domini & Kinder, 1985). A company's board of directors votes on what amount of dividends will be paid to shareholders from the profits of the company. These dividends are usually paid quarterly or semiannually. While many common stocks pay little or no dividends, some companies have a continuous record of paying dividends that goes back a hundred years and more. So, for investors interested in income, there are some common stocks that will fit the need for current income through quarterly dividends.

Advantages and Disadvantages of Common Stocks

Advantages: Common stocks have the most potential of many investments for profit through price appreciation when the stock is sold as well as through earning dividends. Quality stocks are almost as safe as corporate bonds. Stocks are highly liquid, that is, they can be bought or sold at any time.

Disadvantages: While common stocks represent the highest potential for gain, they also represent the most risk. The price of common stocks fluctuates, at times without logic or reason, and there is no guarantee of return in the form of principal or even dividends. Thus common stocks lack stability or safety of principal, as well as stability of income in the form of dividends. Investors who invest in common stocks should be willing to assume the market and business risks associated with such an investment; therefore most but not all, common stocks may be inappropriate for the majority of nonprofit organizations. Even the less risky stocks, such as utilities or the so-called "blue chips" (major corporations with a long history of growth and steady earnings), should only be considered as a small part of a nonprofit organization's investment portfolio.

MUTUAL FUNDS

Mutual funds are investment companies that sell their own shares or securities to the public and use the proceeds to invest in other securities. The managers of the investment company decide on the goals of the fund, the level of risk they will assume, and the types of securities to be bought. Buyers of the fund must evaluate whether their goals, needs, and risk factors mesh with those of the particular fund as reflected in its prospectus.

Mutual funds were not included in either the fixed or the variable income categories because there are a wide variety of mutual funds that fit in both categories as well as many other categories. There are funds available to meet any possible type of investor goal or combination of goals. Many mutual funds offer a number of different types of funds by one company, such as a money market fund, bond fund, growth fund, and so forth, and usually the investor is given the option, depending on market conditions, of being able to switch back and forth between funds. Investors are also given the option to reinvest their dividends rather than having them distributed. This helps accumulate more capital for investment.

Advantages and Disadvantages of Mutual Funds

Advantages: Financial professionals whose knowledge and expertise may give them an advantage over the lay investor manage mutual funds. Professional management also reduces commission costs on the buying and selling of securities as well as the costs incurred in information gathering. It is assumed that the professional manager will be able to outperform the investment amateur, but some have said that this is an unwarranted assumption based on the record of most mutual funds (Khoury, 1983). The pooling of funds with other investors is the most cost-efficient way for the small investor to diversify and minimize risk. One of the problems of the small investor is that excessive transaction costs are incurred in trying to buy a sufficient number of different securities for diversification. This is taken care of with mutual funds because the fund managers are able to buy large quantities at one time and therefore minimize costs.

Mutual funds may be redeemed or sold at any time by the shareholder, thus they have high liquidity. There is a small transaction fee, but orders are processed quickly and this is an advantage for organizations that do not want to have their money tied up in investments that take longer to liquidate. For example, real estate is not as liquid an investment because the seller has no idea as to if, when, and how long it will take to sell a property (Khoury, 1983).

Disadvantages: It is often difficult for an investor to determine the quality of a mutual fund and its management. It is often necessary to consult financial publications that periodically assess and rank mutual funds based on their current and past performance compared to the stock market. Over time, a number of mutual funds have not performed as well as the stock market. Thus, in some cases, an investor would have been better off to have looked to other vehicles for investment.

The cost of buying and selling mutual funds may in some cases be higher than purchasing stock. This is mainly due to the "load" or commission charged by some mutual funds (Amling, 1984). The human service nonprofit organization must remember that mutual funds are as safe or as risky as the securities they invest in. Investing in a mutual fund, as with any investment, should only be done after an analysis of the track record of the fund over time and its fit with nonprofit organization investment goals.

SOCIALLY RESPONSIBLE INVESTING

One approach to investing is known as socially conscious or socially responsible investing. This term describes an approach that integrates personal values and societal concerns with the investment decision-making process. For example, if one has certain values or principles about the environment, then one might want to invest in companies that are environmentally friendly. By investing in a socially responsible way, investors seek to make a statement about their own values as well as the kinds of companies they invest in.

The Social Investment Forum conducted a survey in 1984 to ascertain the extent of socially responsible investing. At that time, it found that social investment assets totaled $40 billion dollars. In 1997, they found that assets involved in socially responsible investment had grown to $1.185 trillion dollars (Social Investment Forum, 1997). Nearly ten percent of investment dollars are part of a responsibly invested portfolio.

There are three main approaches to socially responsible investing: screening, shareholder advocacy, and community investment (Social Investment Forum, 1999).

Screening: is the exclusion or inclusion of a particular investment based on certain criteria. The most common screens are for tobacco (84%), gambling (72%), weapons (69%), birth control/abortion (50%), environment (37%), labor issues (25%), human rights (23%), and animal welfare (7%) (Co-op America, 1999; Social Investment Forum, 1997).

Shareholder Advocacy: is the effort by investors to influence a company's policies by submitting and voting on corporate proxy resolutions. This is a strategy that was successful in influencing some corporations to withdraw or cease operations in South Africa. It has also been a help in improving corporate policies toward women and minorities, as well as the environment.

Community Investment: is the support of initiatives in low-income communities to provide affordable housing, create jobs, and help new business startups.

Socially responsible investment has begun to yield more than value choices. "One reason that the movement has gained respect is that the

Table 9-2
ANNUALIZED TOTAL RETURN OF SELECTED SOCIALLY
RESPONSIBLE MUTUAL FUNDS COMPARED TO
STANDARD & POOR'S 500 STOCK INDEX*

Fund	Annualized Total Return		
	1 year	3 years	5 years
Calvert Social Investment A	14.1%	16.8%	14.2%
Domini Social Equity	21.9%	28.2%	25.7%
Dreyfus Third Century	19.1%	24.6%	23.6%
Parnassus Fund	20.1%	14.3%	12.5%
Pax World Fund	20.7%	20.4%	19.3%
S&P 500 Stock Index	19.9%	26.6%	25.6%

*Source: Kiplinger's Personal Finance Magazine, August 1999.

returns of some ethical funds have far surpassed that of the Standard & Poor's 500, an index of the 500 stocks with the largest capitalization at a given time" (Judd, 1990, p. 2). In 1998, Morningstar, an investment research and analysis firm, found that socially responsible mutual funds were twice as likely as all mutual funds to earn its top five-star rating (Morningstar, 1999). While the number of socially screened mutual funds has increased over time, they, as with all mutual funds, vary in their performance. Some of the top ones have surpassed the S&P 500, others have not (see Table 9-2).

Guerard (1997) found that "there has been no significant difference between the average returns of a socially-screened and unscreened universe during the 1987–1994 period." This seems to indicate that an investor interested in socially responsible investing is not likely to have to worry about sacrificing performance for conscience as long as the same care is used as with choosing any investment.

SELECTING AN INVESTMENT ADVISOR

Analyzing investments and managing portfolios are specialized fields requiring the kinds of skill, training, and experience that most human service administrators do not have. While do-it-yourself investing has become popular and less expensive with the advent of discount Internet investment brokers, the nonprofit is in a very different situation than is the individual or even the large institutional investor. This chapter has tried to present a brief overview of investments to help the nonprofit board, administrator, and staff become more informed, but the safest and most prudent course of action is to seek professional advice. Granting this, how does one go about finding a competent financial advisor?

As an initial consideration, the financial planner or advisor hired by the nonprofit organization should be familiar with nonprofits. He or she should be able to look at the financial statements, cash flow, and budgets, and be able to mesh this information with the needs and goals of the nonprofit organization. In selecting such a person, it may be helpful to use criteria such as the following (O'Toole, 1984; Journal of Accountancy, 1997):

Credentials

What is the educational background of this person? What securities registrations, sales licenses, and professional designations does the advisor have? If an accountant, is the person a Certified Public Accountant (CPA)? If a planner, is the person a Certified Financial Planner or Chartered Financial Consultant? Does this person belong to the Institute of Certified Financial Planners or the International Association for Financial Planning? While the Certified Financial Planner or Chartered Financial Consultant designations are earned through a correspondence course, the participants must pass tests, and usually have experience in the financial field as insurance agents, stockbrokers, or other related occupations. If a stockbroker, the person must be registered and have passed the SEC (Securities and Exchange Commission) licensing exams.

Experience

What kinds of experience does this person bring to financial planning and investing? And how many years of experience has the advisor had in working with nonprofits? Can this person furnish verifiable references from other clients, as well as other professionals, such as bankers and lawyers, with whom this person may have worked? Is this person willing to show sample financial plans that have been done for others (without breaking confidentiality)? What historical rate of return has the advisor earned for clients over the years? It is also important that the person have experience and/or extensive knowledge of the nonprofit area, since nonprofits have unique characteristics that make their goal setting, planning, and needs different from other types of organizations.

Many large stock brokerage houses have nonprofit departments with staff who are able to provide services designed for the specialized needs of such organizations. These services include not only investments, but also designing annuity plans for nonprofit staff, advising on tax considerations, insurance, and similar matters.

Compensation

Financial planners or investment advisors make money in a variety of ways:

1) They may charge a fee for their advice. The fee is usually reasonable, and you are not obligated to purchase anything other than the advice;

2) They may give free advice, but receive a commission on whatever products they sell you. If you buy a mutual fund, stock, or bond through them they will earn a commission. This sort of advisor can give you unbiased opinions if he or she is not working for just one company (and thus is limited to offering the products of that company), but rather can sell anything on the market.

3) They may charge a combination of fees and commissions. In most cases, you will be encouraged to invest funds or purchase securities through such an advisor. In this way, the investment planner/advisor's services may cost from zero to $5,000 or more.

When working with advisors in the latter two categories, the nonprofit organization should ask how much the advisor would make on any product he or she sells. Avoid arrangements in which the advisor is employed by a parent investment company and therefore has a vested interest in the products s/he is recommending. This is not to say that all commission consultants should be avoided, rather that one be wary if an advisor is pushing a specific product rather than one that fits the nonprofit organization's needs.

Investment Philosophy

What is the advisor's investment philosophy as it pertains to nonprofits? How will s/he select investments and diversify the organization's portfolio to meet the goals it has articulated? How much risk will be involved for the nonprofit organization and how will the advisor work to reduce risk for the organization?

Content

What should the nonprofit organization expect for the money it pays an investment counselor? The result of the nonprofit organization's discussions with the advisor should be a written financial plan, with explanations of all assumptions made in the writing of it—such as estimated rate of inflation used, assumed rate of return on the investments, the nonprofit organization's financial goals and tolerance for risk. Using the financial statements, budgets, and other cost data made available to him or her, the advisor should be able to pinpoint trouble spots or special areas of concern. The last part of the plan should present alternative strategies, along with advantages and disadvantages of each approach, for the attainment of the nonprofit organization's financial goals. The planner may recommend types or categories of investments rather than specific investments. A well thought out financial plan should have the following components (Consumer Reports, 1986; Journal of Accountancy, 1997):

- A statement of the nonprofit organization's goals, objectives, and tolerance for risk
- An examination of the nonprofit organization's current investment portfolio, with suggestions for revising, if appropriate
- An examination of the current debt ratio of the nonprofit organization
- A cash flow analysis, before and after investment
- Recommendations that are clear and unambiguous
- Language that the users of the plan can understand

Along with the plan, once the organization has agreed to it, there needs to be a clear understanding of the kinds of reports that the nonprofit organization will receive regarding its investments. For example, will the advisor's performance reporting comply with Association of Investment Management Research standards? Be sure to ask if the reports will compare actual performance with established benchmarks such as the Standard and Poor's (S & P) 500 as well as with the investment goals of the organization.

Commitment

The nonprofit organization needs to clarify how much time the planner will spend with key personnel of the nonprofit organization and who will write the final report. In some firms, the planner spends time in consultation, but a junior staff person writes the final plan. This may not matter to your nonprofit organization, but you may want to know this in advance. When the plan is ready, it should be presented to administrative staff and/or board members in person so that any questions can be answered at that time. Final decisions on alternative courses of action should be deferred until board and staff have had time to study and analyze the plan and discuss it in private.

The nonprofit organization should also clarify what support from other professionals will be used in the drawing up of the financial plan. Since it is almost impossible to be an expert in all areas of insurance, tax laws, banking, and investments, the planner may consult with others on these matters. The nonprofit organization may want the planner to meet with its accountant and lawyer as well. Some large planning firms have accountants and lawyers on staff whom they will consult with.

If a nonprofit organization does have money it wishes to invest, a competent financial planner, tax accountant, and lawyer should be consulted. A board member may be able to recommend someone competent who understands nonprofit organizations. Remember that a financial plan is not an end, it is a beginning. It is the beginning of some hard-decision making on the part of the nonprofit organization as to the best avenue to use in investing money given for the public good.

IMPLICATIONS OF INVESTING FOR NONPROFITS

In 1995, the Financial Accounting Standards Board issued *Statement of Financial Accounting Standards (SFAS) No. 124: Accounting for Certain Investments Held by Not-for-profit Organizations.* This statement was formulated to provide guidance to nonprofits in the accounting and reporting of their investments as well as to bring uniformity to nonprofit reporting. SFAS-124 applies to nonprofit investments in equity securities (common and preferred stocks) and to all investments in debt securities (corporate and governmental bonds). It holds that all of these types of investment securities have to be accounted for at fair value. How is fair value determined? For an equity security, the sales price or the bid-and-asked quotation on a securities exchange registered with the SEC or in the over-the-counter market can be considered a stock's fair value. For an investment in a mutual fund, the published value per share that is the basis of the current transaction is the fair value. For debt securities, the best measure of fair value is the quoted market prices (Clark & Jordan, 1997; Williams, 1999; FASB, 1995). SFAS-124 also considers endowments and how they should be treated in accounting and reporting. This topic will be more fully discussed in the chapter on nonprofit accounting.

There are many small nonprofits whose boards think that because they have no excess revenues for investment the topic of investment is irrelevant to them. However, even small nonprofits have opportunities for investment. For example, all cash accounts of a nonprofit should be interest-bearing accounts. Payments made quarterly by allocation agencies can be invested in safe, short-term vehicles. All nonprofit organizations should have policies and procedures in place that address the issues of cash accounts, grant and contract accounts, and endowments. No monies of a nonprofit should be sitting idly in accounts that do not pay interest, rather, agency funds should be considered in terms of the opportunities they represent for investment in the future of the nonprofit organization and its mission.

REFERENCES

Amling, F. (1984). *Investments, An Introduction to Analysis and Management* (5th Edition). Englewood Cliffs, NJ: Prentice-Hall.

Christy, G. A. and Clendenin, J. C. (1978). *An Introduction to Investments*. New York, McGraw-Hill.

Clark, S. J & Jordan, C. E. (1997). SFAS 124: Accounting for investments by not-for-entities. *National Public Accountant,* 42(1): 49–52.

Co-op America. (1999). *Socially responsible mutual fund screens.* http://www.coopameria.org/mfsc.htm

D'Ambrosio, C. A. (1976). *Principles of Modern Investments.* Chicago, Science Research Associates, Inc.

Domini, A.L. & Kinder, P.D. (1986). *Ethical Investing.* Reading, MA: Addison-Wesley Publishing Co., Inc.

Dunnan, N. (1994). *Dun & Bradstreet Guide to Your Investments: 1994,* New York: Harper Perennial.

Financial Accounting Standards Board. (1995). Statement of Financial Accounting Standards (SFAS) No. 124: *Accounting for Certain Investments Held by Not-for-profit Organizations.* Stamford, CT.

Gitman, L. J. and Joehnk, M. D. (1990). *Fundamentals of Investing.* New York: HarperCollins.

Guerard, J. B. (1997). Is there a cost to being socially responsible in investing? *Journal of Investing,* 6(2):11-14.

Hirt, G.A. & Block, S.B. (1993). *Fundamentals of Investment Management* (4th Ed.). Homewood, IL: Richard D. Irwin, Inc.

Huang, S. S.C. (1981). *Investment Analysis and Management.* Cambridge, Winthrop Publishers, Inc.

Journal of Accountancy. (1997), Selecting an investment advisor, Monthly Checklist Series, Online Issues, 183(7). www.aicpa.org . . . /cklist.htm

Judd, E. (1990). *Investing with a Social Conscience,* New York: Pharos Books.

Khoury, S. J. (1983). *Investment Management: Theory and Application.* New York: McGraw-Hill Book Co.

Kiplinger's Personal Finance Magazine, August 1999.

O'Toole, P. (1984). Picking the right financial planner. *Money,* 13(3): 131-138.

Powell, R. M. (1978). *Accounting Procedures for Institutions.* Notre Dame, University of Notre Dame Press.

Social Investment Forum. (1999). *Introduction to Socially Responsible Investing.* http://www.socialinvest.org/Areas/SRIGuide/Default.htm

Social Investment Forum. (1999). *Social Screening.* http://www.socialinvest.org/Areas/SRIGuide/Screening.htm

Social Investment Forum. (1999). *Shareholder Advocacy.* http://www.socialinvest.org/Areas/SRIGuide/Shareholder.htm

Social Investment Forum. (1999). *Community Investment.* http://www.socialinvest.org/Areas/SRIGuide/Community.htm

Stevenson, R.A. and Jennings, E.H. (1984). Fundamentals of Investments (3rd Edition). St. Paul:West Publishing Co.

United States Department of the Treasury. http://treasury.gov

Williams, J.R. (1999). *The 1999 Miller GAAP Guide: Restatement and Analysis of Current FASB Standards.* New York: Harcourt Brace & Co.

INTERNET RESOURCES

The Basics of Treasury Securities at the Treasury Department online. http://publicdebt.treas.gov/of/ofbasics.htm

Ameritrade Information Center. http://www.ameritrade.com/education/html

The Motley Fool. http://www.fool.com

IV. RESOURCE RECORDING
AND REPORTING

Chapter Ten

THE BASICS OF ACCOUNTING

After reading this chapter you should be able to:

1. Explain basic accounting principles and concepts;
2. Understand accounting differences between for-profit and nonprofit organizations;
3. Demonstrate effects of organization transactions on the accounting equation;
4. Follow simple transactions through the accounting cycle.

INTRODUCTION

Accounting is the art of analyzing, recording, summarizing, and reporting the financial activities of an organization using generally accepted accounting principles (GAAP). In systems terms, the organization is taking in resources and converting them into usable goods and services. Therefore, the accounting subsystem in the human service organization is concerned with analyzing and recording these activities in a consistent, generally accepted manner so that the accumulated information can be used by management as well as interested outsiders (see Figure 10-1). As an art, accounting is a dynamic process that is evolving to meet the changing needs of economic organizations, regulatory agencies, and the general public. This is especially true in the area of nonprofit accounting because it is only quite recently that the accounting profession has taken note of the peculiar characteristics of nonprofit human service organizations, and therefore, their special accounting needs.

The art of recording business transactions is as old as civilization itself (Henderson & Peirson, 1977). Ancient Babylon, Greece, and Rome all had some sort of bookkeeping systems. Though different than the kind of system we are familiar with today, they were still forms of business recording. The present cost-based system of double-entry bookkeeping was developed in Italy in the twelfth and thirteenth centuries. This bookkeeping method spread across Europe, and the first book describing this system, written by a monk named Pacioli, was printed in

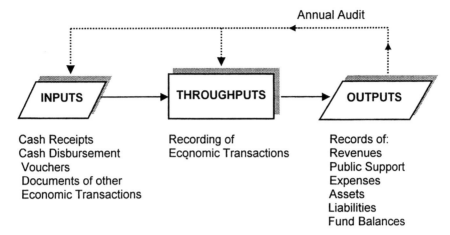

Figure 10-1: A Systems View of Accounting

1494. There were virtually few changes in the basic system for three hundred years thereafter. In the nineteenth century, some writers began to try to formulate general theories of accounting. These formulations laid the cornerstone for some of the commonly accepted accounting principles of today. In the 1950's, efforts moved toward more research on improving accounting practice. After the 1970's, attempts to provide a general theory of accounting were to some extent abandoned and energy directed toward applying the scientific method to problems of the discipline (Racek, 1982).

While all this had gone on, however, very little attention had been directed toward the nonprofit side of accounting. Until recently, the general public or even contributors did not consider financial reporting by nonprofit organizations very important. The prevailing attitude was that, as charities, human service organizations provided the kind of help difficult to quantify or measure. Thus often some nonprofit organizations issued confusing, misleading, and inconsistent financial reports. There were very few laws regulating nonprofits. There was also a lack of clear direction from the accounting profession, which tended to overlook the specific differences between for-profit and nonprofit organizations. At times, nonprofits were treated as special cases in which certain accounting principles did not apply (Racek, 1982).

During the 1950's, awareness of the need for guidelines and regulations for nonprofits began to develop. A well-publicized case of fraud by a charitable organization in the 1950's was the impetus for some states to pass legislation requiring nonprofit organizations to file certain types of financial information with their state governments on an annual basis. The nonprofit sector itself also took steps toward self-regulation. In 1964, the *Standards of Accounting and Financial Reporting for Voluntary Health and Welfare Organizations* (called The Black Book) was published by a joint committee of the National Health Council and the National Social Welfare Assembly. This was the first time that an attempt had been made to establish uniformity in accounting principles and financial reports for nonprofit organizations. The organizations that were members of the National Health Council agreed to voluntarily follow the guidelines set forth in the *Standards*.

The American Institute of Certified Public Accountants (AICPA) is the body which, along with the Financial Standards Accounting Board (FASB), sets standards for the accounting profession. Generally accepted accounting principles are adopted through usage, but they are not strictly binding unless given sanction by the professional regulatory bodies, in much the way standards are set in the human service professions. In the mid-1960's, the AICPA began to provide some direction for human service accounting by issuing "audit guides". The first one, entitled *Audits of Voluntary Health and Welfare Organizations;* was published in 1967. Although this guide was useful in providing information regarding auditing procedures, it did not go far enough in helping to develop uniformity in accounting practices in the nonprofit field.

Thus, at the beginning of the 1970's, the nonprofit sector was being provided with very little guidance from the accounting profession. Nonprofits tended to be excluded from most accounting principles, and their financial reports were viewed as "special-purpose reports" (Racek, 1982). But pressure had been mounting during the 1960's for some more definitive guidelines, due to the need for greater accountability on the part of human service organizations as well as the increased federal involvement in the health and welfare field.

Early in the 1970's a number of significant measures were taken. The AICPA's 1967 audit guide was revised and reissued in 1974. Also in 1974, the United Way published *Accounting and Financial Reporting–A Guide for United Ways and Not-for-profit Human Service Organizations.* The same year a revision of the 1964 work by the National Health Council and the National Social Welfare Assembly was co-published with the United Way of America. In 1980, the FASB published *Objectives of Financial Reporting by Nonbusiness Organizations,* an attempt delineate fundamentals and objectives that could be used as a basis to develop financial accounting and reporting standards. Later in the 1980's the Financial Accounting Standards Board began working on a project to determine and resolve some of the issues related to accounting for nonprofit organizations. The results of their work were a number of standards developed specifically for nonprofits. These standards were all released in 1993 and were to be implemented over a period of two years, depending on the size of the nonprofit. These include Financial Accounting Standard *(SFAS) 116: Accounting for Contributions Received and Contributions Made; SFAS 117: Financial Statements of Not-for-profit Organizations;* and *SFAS 124: Accounting for Certain Investments Held by Not-for-profit Organizations,* as discussed in the previous chapter. SFAS 116 was discussed in Chapter 5, on fundraising. SFAS 117 will be discussed in Chapter 12, Financial Statements.

The AICPA also updated its standards for nonprofits, especially as they relate to fundraising costs and audits. The AICPA standards of relevance here are SOP (Statement of Position) *98-2: Accounting for Joint Activities of Not-for-profit Organizations and State and Local Entities* and SOP *98-3: Audits of State, Local Governments, and Not-for-profit Organizations Receiving Federal Awards.* SOP 98-2 was discussed in Chapter 5, Marketing and Fundraising, and also in Chapter 9, Internal Control. SOP 98-3 will be discussed in Chapter 12, Financial Reporting and Analysis. In the late 1990's, a new edition of the black book was published to reflect the changes that had occurred in the field.

As can be seen, there are now a number of standards and guides for nonprofits. Most of them have tried to coordinate with one another so as to diminish, rather than increase, confusion, anxiety, and inconsistent reporting by nonprofits. Unfortunately, they have not always succeeded, for sometimes new guidelines are just as confusing or controversial as the ones they replace. In any case, it is imperative that human service staff develop fiscal capability if their organizations are to survive in an increasingly competitive world. In developing this capability, some understanding of the basics of accounting is essential. In this chapter, basic accounting principles and practices as they apply to the human service organization will be reviewed. These practices and their relationship to the accounting cycle and the financial reporting of the organization will also be explained.

BASIC ACCOUNTING PRINCIPLES AND CONCEPTS

While no definitive list of basic accounting principles and concepts has yet been published, there are generally accepted principles in use in the accounting profession. Not all of them are pertinent to human service organizations; the principles discussed here are the ones that appear to be the most applicable. In keeping with a systems framework, we will use the categorization developed by Wolk et al. (1992) to describe these accounting principles and concepts. The concepts consist of two parts, postulates and principles:

"*Postulates* are basic assumptions concerning the [organizational] environment.

Principles are general approaches utilized in the recognition and measurement of accounting events. Principles are, in turn, divided into two main types:

Input-oriented principles are broad rules that guide the accounting function.

Output-oriented principles involve certain qualities or characteristics that financial statements should possess if the input-oriented principles are appropriately executed" (Wolk et al., 1992, pp. 119–120).

Postulates

Accounting Entity

Accounting is concerned with data gathered from a discrete economic unit. An accounting or business entity is any economic unit that takes in resources and engages in some form of economic activity. For our purposes, the accounting entity in the human service organization is the organization itself or possibly each of its separate programs or funds. But it does not include any of the economic activities of any of its employees that are unrelated to, or take place outside of, the main objectives and tasks of the organization. This book will review the accounting activities of two types of human service organizations. The first type is the simplest in structure and has only one source of revenue: fees from clients. The accounting activities of this type of organization will be reviewed in this chapter. The second type is a nonprofit with multiple funding sources. The accounting activities of this more complex type of organization will be reviewed in the next chapter.

Going Concern or Continuity

Most of the time it is impossible to predict the longevity of an organization, but most human services agencies are not formed with the intention of closing shop in a year or two. Thus the going concern postulate means that an assumption is made that the accounting entity will continue operating indefinitely into the foreseeable future. This assumption affects the way financial transactions are recorded in organization books and reported in financial statements. Thus assets are recorded at the cost that was paid for them, not their liquidation value.

Monetary Unit

In accounting the monetary principle states that all financial transactions and statements are reflected in terms of money. There are some shortcomings in this from the point of view of some accountants, however. First of all, because of the cost principle (discussed below), assets that may have been acquired many years ago and recorded at cost will not reflect the current value of the asset. Secondly, the monetary principle assumes a stability in the value of the dollar that does not exist. So an asset acquired for $20,000 fifteen years ago, such as land, will at the present time be worth much more than that because of appreciation. Also, $20,000 today does not have the same value that $20,000 did fifteen years ago. Some large corporations are now trying to take these factors into account in their financial statements, but most human service organizations have not developed the financial sophistication to be able to do so.

Time Period

Users of financial reports need some periodic feedback about the financial position of an organization and the results of its financial activities for decision-making purposes. Thus while we assume an indefinite life for accounting entities, this indefinite life is broken into short time intervals for accounting and reporting purposes. For example, an organization usually has monthly cash flow reports and trial balances, monthly or quarterly budget variance reports, and yearly financial statements. The usual time period for both nonprofits as well as for-profits is a calendar year or a fiscal year. The fiscal year of a nonprofit may be the same as the calendar year, but it may be different. Some nonprofits adopt the same fiscal year as their major funding sources; for example, October to September is the fiscal year for the federal government, while July to June is the fiscal year for some state governments, and so forth.

Principles
Input-Oriented Principles

The Matching Principle

In order to measure income accurately, revenue from one accounting period is matched or compared with expenses incurred during the same accounting period. The matching principle is important in the accrual method of accounting, which we will discuss later in this chapter.

The Realization Principle

In accrual accounting, revenue should be recognized when it is earned. However, it is sometimes difficult to judge at times exactly when revenue is earned. Therefore, accountants commonly do not recognize revenue until it is realized. Two conditions have to be met for revenue to be realized. First, there must be objective evidence that this is so. Objective evidence is usually in the form of documentation, so for the nonprofit this would be an appointment kept by the client with a payment given or a bill processed for which the client received a receipt. Secondly, the earning process must be essentially complete. In the case of the human services, this usually means that earnings would be realized at the time of the rendering of the services.

The Cost Principle

The cost principle refers to the traditional, widely used method of recording the acquisition of assets. Thus, assets are initially recorded in the accounting books of the organization at their actual cost, and no adjustment for inflation or appreciation is made in the books at a later time. The only adjustments made are to allocate a portion of the cost to expenses as the assets expire or depreciate. While there is some debate over the usefulness of this principle because of inflation, it is supported by many accountants as an objective way to value an asset. It is objective because it can be verified by supporting documents such as receipts, bills of sale, and cancelled checks, whereas later estimates of asset value are only that–estimates.

Disclosure Principle

Material and relevant facts upon which outsiders can evaluate the economic activities of the organization should be disclosed either in its financial statements or in the notes accompanying them. These kinds of disclosures make the statements less misleading and therefore more useful to readers. While the information does not have to be in great detail, it should include all relevant information that an interested outsider might need to know.

Materiality

The concept of materiality may be applied to procedures in recording transactions as well as in preparing financial statements. Materiality is the relative importance of any amount, event, or procedure. It is relative because what is material in one organization may not be in another, depending of the size of the organization's budget and the size and nature of the item in question. If an item is not considered important enough to influence the users of the organization's statements, then it is probably immaterial. Materiality is not guided by theoretical principles, but more by the professional judgment of the accountant who makes such a decision.

Conservatism

The principle of conservatism is aptly illustrated in the old saying, "anticipate no profits and provide for all losses" (Meigs & Meigs, 1990). This means that accountants often choose among alternative methods or procedures that result in lower amounts of net revenue or asset value being reflected in the financial statements. Today some accountants have moved away from this principle and believe that other principles such as materiality, consistency, disclosure, and objectivity should take precedence (Fess & Warren, 1993).

Objectivity

In order to accept the accounting records of an organization as an accurate reflection of its economic activities, the principle of objectivity is used. Objective evidence is necessarily the basis upon which cost and revenue are recorded. Objective evidence is in the form of documents such as receipts, invoices, checks, vouchers, and so forth. They form the bases of the journal entries that are made. Despite the goal of objectivity, however, there will always be judgments made that are open to differing interpretations.

Output-Oriented Principles

Consistency

It is important that management and interested outsiders have a basis upon which to compare the economic performance of the organization from one year to the next. It would be very confusing if an organization changed its system every other year. So the principle of consistency means that once an accounting system is adopted by an organization it will not be changed from period to period. Obviously, changes in a system can take place when appropriate and they must be pointed out in the notes accompanying the financial statements of the organization.

Comparability

Comparability as an output principle applies to the degree of reliability users can find in financial statements when comparing the financial condition or cash flows of similar organizations. Comparability is dependent on the amount of uniformity in recording transactions and preparing financial statements. This principle has reached more attainability with the publication of SFAS 117.

The key word here is similar organizations. So if funding sources or other interested users want to compare nonprofits in terms of administrative overhead or indirect costs, then like organizations should be compared, for example, child care organizations with child care organizations, other counseling organizations with each other, and so forth.

Uniformity

Uniformity is concerned with similar accounting treatment of economic transactions and therefore influences comparability. There are three approaches to uniformity in accounting: finite, rigid, and flexible (Wolk et al., 1992). *Finite uniformity* occurs when similar accounting procedures take into account different economic circumstances. For example, when accounting standards make exceptions for nonprofits or when nonprofits apply GAAP to fund accounting this would be finite uniformity. *Rigid uniformity* is when similar accounting treatment is required in similar economic circumstances, but possible different circumstances are ignored. For example, cash flow statements that are required of both for-profits and nonprofits provide an example of rigid uniformity. *Flexible uniformity* obtains when more than one possible accounting treatment is possible and any one may be chosen by an organization.

TYPES OF ACCOUNTING SYSTEMS

There may be one of three types of accounting systems used in a nonprofit human service organization: a cash basis accounting system, an accrual accounting system, or a modified accrual accounting system.

Cash Basis Accounting: records only those transactions in which cash is received or disbursed. Thus, in this system revenue and expenses are only recognized or realized when money is paid to the organization or paid out by the organization. While a very simple method of accounting, the cash basis method has many disadvantages. First of all, it does not provide an accurate picture of the organization's financial condition at any point in time. Secondly, in any but the simplest fee-for-service organization, it compounds the possibility of error and manipulation of records. Some organizations may use a cash basis of accounting, but then convert their records to the accrual basis to prepare financial reports (Listro, 1983). It is the author's experience that the majority of human service nonprofits do not use cash basis accounting. With managed care and many other third-party payer systems in use today, many nonprofits do not even actually take in revenues in the form of cash.

Accrual Basis Accounting: records not only transactions involving the receipt and disbursement of cash, but also transactions in which the organization incurs obligations or others incur obligations to the organization. An example of accrual basis accounting is when an agency bills a client for service and records the client's bill in its records. Most for-profit business organizations as well as nonprofits keep their records on an accrual basis.

A Modified Accrual Accounting System: has characteristics of both the accrual and cash bases. That is, an organization may record certain transactions on a cash basis, usually revenue, and record other transactions on an accrual basis, usually unpaid bills (Gross et al., 1995). However, there may be many variations as to what is kept on a cash vs. accrual basis. This method is not generally considered an appropriate system.

According to the Audit Guide, "The accrual basis of accounting is required by generally accepted accounting principles for a fair representation of financial position and results of operations" (AICPA, 1974, p. 33). If an organization uses a cash or modified accrual basis, its reports may be acceptable only if they do not differ materially from reports prepared on an accrual basis. An organization's reports will also be acceptable only if they are prepared using generally accepted accounting principles.

The application of these principles and concepts will be illustrated within the context of the human service organization. Before this is done, however, it must be pointed out that just as there are organizational and environmental differences between for-profit and nonprofit organizations, there are also some differences in accounting procedures and functions characteristic of these two types of organizations. There are six main areas of distinction that will be discussed in the next section.

UNIQUE ACCOUNTING CHARACTERISTICS OF NONPROFIT HUMAN SERVICE ORGANIZATIONS

Nature and Purpose of Financial Statements

The purpose of nonprofit human service organizations is service, while the purpose of for-profit organizations is profit. This basic distinction is also the basis of the difference in the financial statements of the two types of organizations. The financial statements of for-profit organizations are concerned with the bottom line—how much net profit was earned? The financial statements of nonprofits are concerned with reflecting stewardship and fiduciary responsibility of public monies, as there is no profit (Gross et al., 1995; United Way, 1974; National Health Council et al., 1988; AICPA, 1974).

Fund Accounting

In fund accounting, separate accounting entities, or funds, are set up to segregate and report on those resources available to be used at the discretion of the board (unrestricted funds); as well as those available to be used for specific purposes only (restricted funds). In business organizations there is no such thing as fund accounting, whereas it is widely used in nonprofits because it reflects accountability to various funding entities. Fund accounting is the most unique aspect of nonprofit accounting and will be discussed more fully in the next chapter.

Transfers and Appropriations

Transfers are monetary transactions between funds. For example, earnings from investments may be transferred from an endowment fund to the current fund for operating expenses. Excess cash from a current fund may also be transferred to an endowment fund. Appropriations are monies that may be set aside for specific future uses. These transactions are unique to nonprofit organizations because for-profit organizations do not use fund accounting.

Allocations, Contributions, Grants, Pledges, and Noncash Contributions

For-profit organizations do not receive allocations from community organizations, contributions or pledges from the public, or noncash (in-kind) contributions. They may, at times, receive grant monies, but this is not a major source of income for profit-oriented organizations. Yet these sources of funds constitute a large proportion of the available resources of nonprofit organizations. These sources of funds may constitute unique accounting problems for the nonprofit organization. If a for-profit is owed money, for example, it is recorded as an account receivable. If a nonprofit receives a pledge, the obligation created may not be legally binding, though some may consider it morally so. But most organizations do record these pledges on their books as receivables.

Functional Basis Accounting

The AICPA Audit Guide requires functional basis accounting. It is an accounting device for separating an organization's expenses into two main categories: program services and support services. Distributing all expenses between these two functions does this. Since organization staff and other resources may be reflected in more than one category, this functional separation of expenses can sometimes be difficult, as was discussed in Chapter Six.

Treatment of Fixed Assets

While business enterprises usually record fixed assets as assets and depreciate them over their period of expected life, nonprofits have varied tremendously in their recording of fixed assets. According to the Audit Guide, generally accepted accounting principles "require fixed assets to be carried at cost and donated assets to be recorded at their fair value at the date of the gift" (AICPA, 1974, p. 10). The Audit Guide also states that depreciation should be included as an element of expense in the appropriate financial statements of the organization. Even with these guidelines, there are some nonprofit organizations that neither record fixed assets nor depreciate.

These then, are some of the major distinctions between nonprofit and for-profit accounting. The particular accounting characteristics of non-profits will be seen more clearly in the next chapter, which uses a case to illustrate simple fund accounting procedures in a nonprofit human service organization. In order to understand these procedures and their relationship to the accounting cycle, the financial statements, and the organization as a whole, the fundamental accounting equation will be discussed. The accounting equation is the basis of the double-entry bookkeeping system.

THE ACCOUNTING EQUATION

Assets are things of monetary value that are owned by an individual or business entity. *Equities* are claims on assets. The relationship between assets and equities can by illustrated by the equation:

Assets = Equities

There are two components of equities. *Liabilities* are the claims that creditors may have on assets. In other words, liabilities are the debts owed by the firm. These are called *Accounts Payable* when merchandise or other goods are bought on credit, while *Notes Payable* are debts that are incurred by signing a promissory note to repay the monies owed at a definite future time.

The other component of equities is called *Capital or Owner's Equity.* Capital or owner's equity is the rights of the owners of the assets. Capital represents the residual of the resources of the firm after all the liabilities are satisfied or paid. It is important to emphasize that capital does not equal cash, capital only exists as a concept on a piece of paper. It cannot be put in the bank, as it is just the result of a mathematical equation (Solomon et al., 1986). As a result of this residual concept, the basic accounting equation can be expanded as follows:

Assets = Liabilities + Capital

Traditionally and in law, the rights of creditors have precedence over the rights of owners in regard to the assets. This is mainly because assets are frequently used as collateral in securing loans from creditors to acquire more assets for expansion or operations. Thus a corollary to the basic equation is one that illustrates these rights:

Assets - Liabilities = Capital

Effects of Transactions on the Accounting Equation

In order to illustrate the effects of some simple transactions on the basic accounting equation, a hypothetical human service organization will be set up to see its initial transactions and their effects on the equation. In the following example, the accrual basis of accounting will be used.

Suppose John Jones, M.S.W., decides to open up a private practice to be called "John Jones Counseling Services". The first thing that Jones does is open a bank account in the name of his new agency with $10,000. The effect of this transaction is to increase the asset, cash, by

$10,000 and at the same time to increase capital by a similar amount. Changes in capital are the result of factors such as:

1. **Investments by the owner:** As can be seen here Jones has taken his personal assets and invested them in this new counseling service. This money is not considered a loan, its effect is to increase assets and therefore it increases capital.

2. **Withdrawals by the owner:** If Jones were to withdraw assets from the practice for his personal use, this would decrease capital.

3. **Net Income/net loss:** Net income is the excess of revenue over expenses during an accounting period. This is illustrated by the following equation:

Net income = Revenue - Expenses

Net loss is calculated the same way, except that in the case of a loss, expenses exceed revenues. ***Revenues*** are amounts earned by an organization for providing a service. ***Expenses*** are costs borne by the organization in providing the service. To help us remember these factors as they relate to capital, they will be listed individually next to it. Revenues and Expenses are combined in financial statements later.

This first transaction of John Jones Counseling Services, the depositing of $10,000, would effect the accounting equation as follows:

	ASSETS		=	CAPITAL	
a)	Cash	$10,000	=	John Jones, Capital	$10,000

Remember that according to the accounting entity concept, we are only concerned with the entity John Jones Counseling Services, not any other assets that Jones might have such as a house, car, or any other personal property.

Jones next secures an office to rent, for which he pays one month's rent of $400. The effect of this transaction is to decrease the asset cash by $400 and to decrease capital by the same amount. The equation would then look like this:

	ASSETS		=	CAPITAL	
b)	Cash	$10,000		John Jones, Capital	$10,000
	Rent	- 400			- 400
	Cash	$ 9,600		John Jones, Capital	$ 9,600

Jones now needs to secure office equipment such as a desk, chairs, and a filing cabinet. He finds office equipment that costs $850, and he pays for this on credit. This creates a debt called ***Accounts Payable*** as well as a new asset, Office Equipment. The accounting equation now looks like this:

	ASSETS			=	LIABILITIES	+	CAPITAL
			Office		Accounts		John Jones,
c)	Cash	+	Equipment	=	Payable	+	Capital
	$ 9,600	+	$850	=	$850	+	$ 9,600

In actual practice, each piece of equipment would be recorded separately in the organization's books, but equipment has been grouped together here just to illustrate the effects of the transaction. What has occurred is that assets have increased by $850 and liabilities have increased by $850.

By the first two weeks of the month Jones has started getting referrals for clients. He saw eight clients who paid $480 in fees. These fees are called **Revenues**; they are the amounts earned by the organization for providing a service. In this case, these fees increased his asset cash and increased his capital as well.

	ASSETS			=	LIABILITIES	+	CAPITAL
			Office		Accounts		John Jones,
d)	Cash	+	Equipment	=	Payable	+	Capital
	$ 9,600						$ 9,600
	+480						+480
	$10,080	+	$850	=	$850	+	$10,080

During the month Jones pays $250 to his creditors for the office furniture that he purchased. This has the effect of reducing the asset cash and reducing the liability accounts payable:

	ASSETS			=	LIABILITIES	+	CAPITAL
			Office		Accounts		John Jones,
e)	Cash	+	Equipment	=	Payable	+	Capital
	$10,080				$850		
	-250				-250		
	$ 9,830	+	$850	=	$600	+	$10,080

If you will add the assets cash and office equipment you will see that the total of the two is $10,680 and that the equity side of liabilities and capital also is $10,680. Therefore, the amount of assets equals the amount of equity.

During the month Jones also had some clients who did not pay him at the time the services were rendered. Instead, they agreed to pay him at sometime in the near future. This created a new account called **Ac-**

counts Receivable. By creating this new account, Jones is using the accrual method of accounting. Jones had $725 in accounts receivable, which had the following effect on the accounting equation:

	ASSETS			=	LIABILITIES	+	CAPITAL
		Office	Accounts		Accounts		John Jones,
f)	Cash +	equipment +	receivable	=	Payable	+	Capital
							$10,080
		+	$725			+	+725
	$ 9,830 +	$850 +	$725	=	$600	+	$10,805

The money due Jones by his clients increased the asset called accounts receivable as well as increased his capital. When the clients pay there will be no change on the right side of the equation, only the left side will be effected as accounts receivable will decrease and cash will increase.

At the end of the month Jones paid $300 in expenses. Expenses are assets used or consumed by the organization during the course of business. These include such things as supplies, wages, telephone, rent, and so forth. The excess of revenue after deducting all expenses is called ***Net Profit.*** Since a nonprofit human service organization does not make a profit, this excess is called a ***Surplus.*** The effect of paying the expenses was to decrease cash as well as capital:

	ASSETS			=	LIABILITIES	+	CAPITAL
		Office	Accounts		Accounts		John Jones,
g)	Cash +	equipment +	receivable	=	Payable	+	Capital
	$ 9,830						$10,805
	−300						−300
	$ 9,530 +	$850 +	$725	=	$600	+	$10,505

The last transaction Jones completed during the month was to draw $1000 for himself. The purpose of this drawing was to pay himself a salary. The effect was to decrease cash and capital:

	ASSETS			=	LIABILITIES	+	CAPITAL
		Office	Accounts		Accounts		John Jones,
h)	Cash +	equipment +	receivable	=	Payable	+	Capital
	$ 9,530						$10,505
	−1,000						−1,000
	$ 8,530 +	$850 +	$725	=	$600	+	$ 9,505

These then would reflect the transactions of John Jones Counseling Services during the month. If you will add all the assets you will find that they equal $10,105 and if you add the liabilities and capital you will note that they also equal $10,105.

There are two points to be drawn from the illustration provided here:

1. In the accounting equation the left side should always equal the right side, that is, assets should always equal liabilities plus capital.

2. The effect of every monetary transaction that takes place in the organization can be stated as an increase or decrease in one or more components of the accounting equation, that is assets, liabilities, or capital.

In the next section will be a brief description of the relationship between the basic accounting equation and one of the required financial statements, the Statement of Position or Balance Sheet.

FINANCIAL STATEMENTS

Financial statements are one of the end products or outputs of the accounting cycle, but they are mentioned here in brief to facilitate an understanding of the accounting process. The purpose of financial statements is to provide a picture, for management and interested outsiders, of the financial position of an organization at one point in time as well as to show changes in net assets that have occurred. Since the financial statements are issued at the end of the cycle, understanding them and how they reflect changes in transactions will help one appreciate the preceding steps.

While there are four types of financial statements required for nonprofit human service organizations, the only one we will be concerned with here is the ***Statement of Position*** (also called the Balance Sheet) because the Statement of Position is essentially a reflection of the accounting equation: assets = liabilities + capital. To illustrate what the Statement of Position represents, take the previous example of John Jones Counseling Services and let us see the effect of its transactions on the Statement of Position. Briefly, the transactions were:

a) Jan. 1. Began business by depositing $10,000 in a bank account. On Jan.1 John's Statement of Position would look like this:

John Jones Counseling Service
Statement of Position
January 1, 200X

| ASSETS | LIABILITIES AND CAPITAL |
| Cash $10,000 | John Jones, Capital $10,000 |

The Statement of Position for January 1 shows that the organization has cash of $10,000. Since there are no liabilities, Jones also has capital of $10,00 in his practice. Remember that although in this case capital is equal to the amount in the bank, this is rarely the case because capital is just the result of a mathematical equation.

b) Jan. 3. Paid rent of $400 for the month.
c) Jan. 4. Purchased office equipment for $850 on credit.
d) Jan. 15. Received fees of $480.

On Jan. 15 the Statement of Position of the Counseling Service would look like this:

John Jones Counseling Service
Statement of Position
January 15, 200X

ASSETS		LIABILITIES AND CAPITAL	
Cash	$10,080	Accounts payable	$850
Office equipment	850	John Jones, Capital	10,080
	$10,930		$10,930

Jones has cash of $10,080 because while he paid rent of $400, he also received fees of $480. He also increased his assets by acquiring office equipment.

e) Jan. 17. Paid $250 on office equipment.
f) Jan. 20. Billed clients $725 for services.
g) Jan. 25. Paid expenses of $300.
h) Jan. 30. Drew $1000 salary.

On January 30, the Statement of Position of John Jones Counseling Service would look like this:

John Jones Counseling Service
Statement of Position
January 30, 200X

ASSETS		LIABILITIES AND CAPITAL	
Cash	$ 8,530	Accounts payable	$600
Office equipment	850		
Accounts receivable	725	John Jones, Capital	9,505
Total	$10,105	Total	$10,105

These then are the transactions of John Jones Counseling Services. All of them effect one or more components of the accounting equation, all of them make up components of the Statement of Position. As you will notice, one side of the Statement of Position, the assets, equals the other side, the liabilities and capital. The Statement of Position shows how these components are distributed, and how much is left over for capital.

In the next chapter an overview of fund accounting and the accounting cycle will be presented, using a multi-funded human service organization as an example.

REFERENCES

American Institute of Certified Public Accountants. (1974). *Audits of Voluntary Health and Welfare Organizations*. New York: author.

Fess, P.E. & Warren, C.S., (1993). *Accounting Principles* (17th Ed.). Cincinnati, OH: South-Western Publishing Co.

Financial Accounting Standards Board (FASB). (1980). *Objectives of Financial Reporting by Nonbusiness Organizations*. Stamford, Conn: author.

Gross, M.J. Jr., Larkin, R.F., Bruttomesso, R.S., & McNally, J.J. (1995). *Financial and Accounting Guide for Not-for-profit Organizations* (5th Ed.). New York: John Wiley & Sons, Inc.

Henderson, S. & Peirson, G. (1977). *An Introduction to Financial Accounting Theory*. Melbourne: Longman Cheshire Pty.

Listro, J.P. (1983). *Accounting for Nonprofit Organizations*. Dubuque, IA: Kendall-Hunt.

Meigs, R.F. & Meigs, W.B. (1990). *Accounting: The Basis for Business Decisions* (8th Ed.). New York: McGraw-Hill.

Racek, T.J. (1982). Nonprofit accounting and financial reporting, pp. 6–3 to 6–46 in Tracy D. Connors (Ed.). *The Nonprofit Organization Handbook*. New York: AMACOM.

Solomon, L., Vargo, R.J. & Walther, L.M. (1986). *Accounting Principles* (2nd Ed.). New York: Harper & Row.

National Health Council, the National Assembly of Health and Human Service Organizations & the United Way of America. (1988). *Standards of Accounting and Financial Reporting for Voluntary Health and Welfare Organizations (Revised 3rd Edition)*. New York: National Health Council, Inc.

United Way of America. (1974). *Accounting and Financial Reporting: A Guide for United Ways and Not-for Profit Human Service Organizations*. Alexandria, VA: author.

Wolk, H.I., Francis, J.R., & Tearney, M.G. (1992). *Accounting Theory: A Conceptual and Institutional Approach* (3rd Ed.). Cincinnati, OH: South-Western Publishing Co.

INTERNET RESOURCES

American Institute of Certified Public Accountants (AICPA). http://www.aicpa.org
Financial Accounting Standards Board (FASB). http://www.fasb.org

Chapter Eleven

NONPROFIT ACCOUNTING

After reading this chapter you should be able to:

1. Understand fund accounting;
2. Discuss appropriate funds for the nonprofit organization;
3. Follow simple transactions through the accounting cycle;
4. Understand the relationship of accounts to the financial statements.

INTRODUCTION

The example of John Jones Counseling Service was a very simple agency with only one source of revenue—fees from clients. However, as you know, a nonprofit may have a multiplicity of funding sources, all with differing goals, purposes, restrictions, requirements, guidelines, and fiscal periods. For example, one human service organization may have one or more of the following sources of support all at the same time:

- Federal government
- State government
- County and/or municipal government
- Allocation agency, e.g., United Way, Jewish Federation, Catholic Charities, Black United Fund, Women's Way, and so forth
- Private foundation grant
- Fees from clients
- Contributions and pledges from donors
- Membership dues
- In-kind donations
- Revenue from sales of goods
- Revenue from fundraising activities
- Investment income

These various sources do not always give money for the organization to dispose of at its sole discretion. Many times agencies receive gifts that are restricted by the donor in some way; that is, the organization is not free to use the money for its operating expenses or for just anything it chooses. Rather, it must hold and use the monies as stipulated by the donor if it accepts them. If an organization is not willing to abide by the restrictions as set forth by the donor, it must decline the money. Because of the possible multiplicity of funding sources and the problems that ensue in trying to meet organization as well as donor needs and requirements, nonprofits, as public stewards, often up separate accounts called "funds" in order to be better able to account for the monies received from various sources.

FUND ACCOUNTING

The "fund" concept is the basis for accounting and reporting in many multi-funded human service agencies. "A fund is a separate accounting entity with a self-balancing set of accounts for recording assets, liabilities, fund balance, and changes in fund balance" (National Health Council et al., 1988, p. 8). Funds are used for two main reasons in nonprofit human service agencies: 1) to account for resources that are earmarked for specific programs or projects; and 2) to ensure and be able to demonstrate that the organization has complied with legal and/or administrative requirements (Lynn & Freeman, 1983; Freeman & Shoulders, 1999). There is a difference, however, between fund accounting and "funder" accounting. The mechanism for fund accounting is done by actual separation of sets of books or separation in the chart of accounts for each fund (Whalen, 1982).

Funder accounting is a type of accounting by sources and uses of revenue by funding source. For example, if an organization received funds from three different organizations and kept separate books for each funder, it would be doing funder accounting. Funder accounting has no set format or method; there are a variety of ways of designing a system to be able to report disposition of funds to funding sources. The organization should be guided by its accountant and funder requirements. In this chapter we will not discuss funder accounting in detail, rather we will concentrate on fund accounting.

While no longer required for financial reporting, most nonprofit human service organizations still use fund accounting internally (National Health Council & National Assembly, 1998). The appropriate funds for nonprofit human service agencies include the following (AICPA, 1998):

Current Unrestricted Fund

Current unrestricted funds are those resources that have no donor-imposed restrictions on them and may be used to carry out the day-to-day operations of the organization. Current unrestricted funds usually come from program service fees, contributions, membership dues and investments. Decreases in unrestricted funds may be the result of expenses incurred in the carrying out of organization programs. Therefore, current unrestricted funds are usually used for general operating expenses. Even though in acquiring these funds they were unrestricted, the agency board may "appropriate" or restrict part of the funds for specific purposes or projects.

Current Restricted Fund

Current restricted funds are often established to account for those resources that are expendable only for operating purposes specified by a donor or other funding source. In other words, the organization may receive gifts, donations, grants, or even income from an endowment fund in which the resource has specified the purpose for which the monies are to be used. For example, a donor may give an organization some money with the stipulation that it only be used to provide services to unwed mothers, or teen-age drug abusers, or whatever special interest the donor might have. Therefore, the organization sets this money aside in a restricted account so that it will not be used for general operating expenses and the organization will be able to account for it properly.

Fixed Asset Fund

This fund is sometimes called the land, building and equipment fund or the plant fund. It " . . . is often used to accumulate the net investment in fixed assets and to account for the unexpended resources contributed specifically for the purpose of acquiring or replacing land, buildings, or equipment for use in the operations of the organization" (National Health Council et al., 1988, p. 12). This means that after an organization has decided to purchase land or a building or major equipment, it would store up its surplus or set aside money in this fund in order to accumulate enough to complete the purchase. It uses this fund in order to be able to account for the money so set aside. Mortgages and other liabilities arising from the acquiring of land, buildings, or equipment are included in this fund, as are depreciation expenses and gains or losses from the sale of these fixed assets.

Endowment Fund

An endowment fund is made up of the " . . . principal amount of gifts and bequests accepted with the donor-stipulation that the principal be maintained intact in perpetuity, until the occurrence of a specified event, or for a specified period, and that only the income from investment thereof be expended either for general purposes or for purposes specified by the donor" (National Health Council et al., 1988, p. 13). In other words, an endowment fund is made up of money that is to be invested. The organization may use the income earned from the investment, while the original amount (the principal) stays intact either to be used indefinitely or to be returned to the donor at some time in the future as agreed. The money earned may be used for general operating expenses unless the donor restricts the money for a specific purpose. If the investment income is available for any general purpose, then it must be transferred to the current unrestricted fund.

Other Funds

A Custodian Fund is a fund set up "to account for assets received by an organization to be held or disbursed only on instructions of the person or organization from whom they were received" (National Health Council et al., 1988, p. 14). Since the monies in this fund are being held temporarily for someone else, they are not assets of the organization and should not be considered as part of the revenue or support of the organization. A Custodian Fund may be set up, for example, for "pass through" funds. These are funds that are given to the organization to be passed on to someone else as when an organization receives funds to distribute to unemployed youth for summer stipends.

A fifth fund, called the Loan and Annuity Fund, may be used if needed. This fund may be used for making loans or paying annuities, but it is not usually an important or common fund in the nonprofit human service organization.

THE ACCOUNTING EQUATION

For the nonprofit human service organization with one or more of these funds, the accounting equation would be basically the same as that discussed in Chapter Ten except that capital is now replaced by the term *"Net Assets"*. Capital represents the ownership equity in a business, and is replaced by the term net assets because, by its very nature, the nonprofit human service organization has no owners or stockholders. Therefore, the use of the term capital would be inappropriate. The accounting equation for the human service organization states that assets equal liabilities plus net assets. Thus, the accounting equation for the human service organization would look like this:

Assets = Liabilities + Net Assets

Conversely, net assets represent the residual resources of the organization after all liabilities are satisfied or paid. This is illustrated by the following equation:

Assets - Liabilities = Net Assets

Fund accounting is unique to nonprofit accounting and more than anything else, is what distinguishes nonprofit from for-profit accounting. In being able to account for the disposition of resources by purpose or fund, fund accounting is reflecting the public responsibility and stewardship function of the human service organization. In addition, this type of accounting is reflecting the obligation of human service agencies to separate restricted from unrestricted funds. Let us now view fund accounting within the framework of the accounting cycle.

THE ACCOUNTING CYCLE

According to the time period principle, the economic activities of the human service organization are divided up into periods of equal length for purposes of recording and reporting. The longest fiscal period is usually one year. The beginning and end of an organization's fiscal year may depend on its major funder. For example, if an organization's major source of funds is a United Way or other federated funder, it may have a fiscal year to coincide with that allocation organization. Other fiscal periods may be divided into shorter periods of time, such as quarters of a year. In any case, in each time period there is a similar cycle of events that take place in all financial subsystems. Some of these are quite routine in nature and make up the accounting cycle. Steps in the accounting cycle include the following (Meigs and Meigs, 1990):

Occurrence of an Economic Transaction

An economic transaction is any event that occurs in which a representative of the organization and monies are involved. For example, a client pays for casework or counseling services rendered, the case-

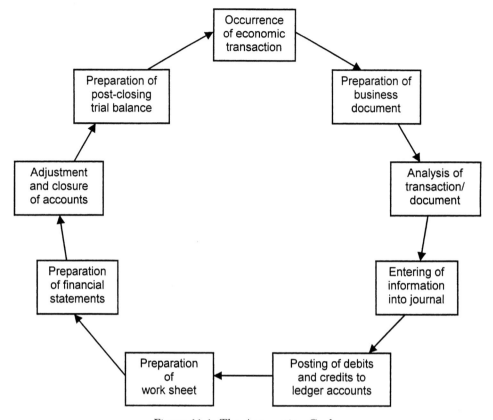

Figure 11-1: The Accounting Cycle

worker makes a home visit and submits a travel voucher for reimbursement for mileage, the office manager buys office supplies, and so forth (see Figure 11-1).

Preparation of a Business Document

After an economic transaction has taken place, as in the case of the client paying for services rendered, a business document is prepared. In most cases the business document is a receipt or a voucher. This document represents the objective evidence needed to ascertain the value or cost of the exchange in the economic transaction.

Analysis of Transaction/Document

After receiving the document that reflects that a transaction has taken place, the person in charge of the recording function must decide what effect it has on the fund balances of the organization. That is, does the transaction increase them or decrease them? The person in charge, usually a bookkeeper, must also decide what accounts are effected by the transaction. The accounts that make up the accounting system of the organization are asset, liabilities, fund balance, expense, and revenue accounts. The bookkeeper is helped in this task if a chart of accounts has been established by the organization. You may recall from Chapter Nine that a chart of accounts is a listing of the main accounts used by the organization in which every account is assigned a code number. If the organization is a United Way organization, it may use the chart of accounts codes of the United Way (see Chapter Eight for an example). If expenses are involved in the economic transaction, the bookkeeper must also decide how to allocate the costs by program or support service functions. This task is also made easier if the organization has set up a control system that allows for automatic recording by department or function.

Entering of Information in Journal

Every monetary transaction that occurs is first recorded in a journal. The journal is called the book of original entry and it is a day-to-day, chronological listing of each transaction and the debit and credit changes caused by each (see Table 11-1). At periodic intervals in the accounting cycle, the debit and credit entries recorded in the journal are *posted,* or transferred from the journal to the appropriate accounts in the ledger. The updated ledger accounts then serve as the bases of the financial statements prepared by the organization.

There may be many different types of journals used by an organization, generally, the larger the organization the more specialized journals it may use. Some common journals are the cash receipts

Table 11-1 GENERAL JOURNAL				
Human Services Organization, Inc.				
General Journal				
				p. 7
Date	Description	Chart of Accts No.	Debit	Credit
July 15	Cash	1-1001	35,000.00	
	Public Support	1-4001		35,000.00
July 17	Cash	1-1001	4,725.00	
	Revenue	1-6005		4,725.00
July 28	Cash	1-1001	16,000.00	
	Pledges Receivable	1-4002		16,000.00

Table 11-2
RULES FOR CHANGES IN ACCOUNTS

Account	Debit		Credit	
	Normal Balance	Affect of Entry	Normal Balance	Affect of Entry
Asset	X	Increase		Decrease
Liability		Decrease	X	Increase
Fund Balance		Decrease	X	Increase
Revenue		Decrease	X	Increase
Expense	X	Increase		Decrease

and revenue journal, the cash disbursements journal, the voucher register and purchase journal, and the general journal (Meigs and Meigs,1990).

The general journal has the format shown in Table 11-1. You will note that the journal has the date, a place for an explanation, a posting number, and columns for debits and credits. The terms *debit* and *credit* mean only one thing in accounting. Debit means the left side column and credit means the right side column and that is all. Whether an entry is placed on the right (or credit) side or the left (or debit) side depends on the nature of the transaction and the nature of the account. This is because the normal balance of some accounts, assets and expenses, is a debit, while the normal balance of other accounts, liabilities, fund balances, and revenues, is a credit. Whether a transaction increases or decreases the balance in an account determines whether it will be debited or credited.

Table 11-2 above summarizes the rules for debits and credits. You will note, for example, that the effect of debiting an asset account is to increase the balance in the account, while crediting an asset account decreases the amount in it. One important point to remember in journalizing is that, because of the accounting equation, debits must always equal credits. So every entry in the journal must be balanced by another entry in the journal.

Posting of Debits and Credits to Ledger Accounts

A ledger is made up of the total group of accounts used by the organization. A ledger account is used to record the increases and decreases in every balance sheet item. In a manual accounting system all these separate accounts are kept in a loose-leaf binder and collectively called the ledger. In a computerized accounting system, ledger accounts

Table 11-3
GENERAL LEDGER

Human Services Organization, Inc.				
General Ledger				
Date	Cash Account No. 1-1001	Debit	Credit	Balance
July 1	Beginning Balance			23,250.00
July 15	Gen. Journal, pg. 7	35,000.00		58,250.00
July 17	Gen. Journal, pg. 7	4,725.00		62,975.00
July 28	Gen. Journal, pg. 7	16,000.00		78,975.00

are stored on computer disks, tapes, zip drives, CDs or special backup systems. Computerized accounting systems will be discussed in Chapter Thirteen.

The general ledger is the heart of an organization's accounting system. While the journal is the book of original entry, the ledger is the book of final entry in which all the financial transactions of the organization are summarized by account title and number. (see Table 11-3 for an example of a ledger entry).

A general ledger may have subsidiary ledgers for handling specific types of transactions, for example, an organization may use an accounts receivable ledger, a pledges receivable ledger, an accounts payable ledger and a land, building and equipment ledger (Meigs and Meigs, 1990).

In posting, the bookkeeper transfers the debits and credits from the journal and records them in the general ledger in their proper account. This facilitates the identification and isolation of specific information regarding any particular account. For example, if an organization director wanted to know the balance in the Revenue from Fees Account, rather than having to go day-by-day through the general journal, the bookkeeper can go straight to the appropriate account in the ledger.

Preparation of Work Sheet

The work sheet is a multi-column form that helps in making adjustments, in preparing the trial balance, and in the construction of the financial statements. The worksheet has columns for the unadjusted trial balance, any necessary adjustments, the adjusted trial balance, the Statement of Activities and the Balance Sheet.

There are a number of steps in using a worksheet, usually the book-keeper or account will (NIMH, 1983):

a. Enter all end of period unadjusted account balances;
b. Check to make sure that total debit balances equal total credit balances (preliminary trial balance);
c. Make all necessary adjusting entries in the adjustments columns;
d. Obtain new adjusted trial balance;
e. Transfer account balances to Balance Sheet or Statement of Activities. The excess of revenue over expenses or vice versa is found by noting the difference on the Statement of Activities between total credits and total debits. The amount needed to balance is entered in the appropriate column of the Statement of Activities.
f. Next the balance sheet debit and credit totals are determined. Then the amount needed to balance the totals is entered. This amount should equal the amount needed to balance the Statement of Activities totals, but should be of the opposite type, i.e., a credit if there is an excess and a debit if there is a deficit.
g. If all sets of columns are now balanced, and excess or deficit is found, then the financial statements can be prepared.

Preparation of Financial Statements

All of the required financial statements of the human service organization can be prepared from the information in the worksheet. The required statements are:

- The Statement of Activity and Changes in Net Assets;
- The Balance Sheet or Statement of Position;
- The Cash Flow Statement;
- The Statement of Functional Expenses.

There will be a complete discussion of financial statements in the next chapter, but Figure 11-2 illustrates the relationship of the organization accounts to the required financial statements.

But before the statements can be prepared, the funds need to be re-arranged into net asset groupings. Since each fund account, except custodian funds, recognizes revenues and expenses as well as fund balances, this makes it relatively simple for agencies to prepare the financial statements (Wilson et al., 2001). As mentioned previously, *net assets* are similar to fund balances, that is, the excess of assets over liabilities. There are three classes of net assets that are used in the finan-

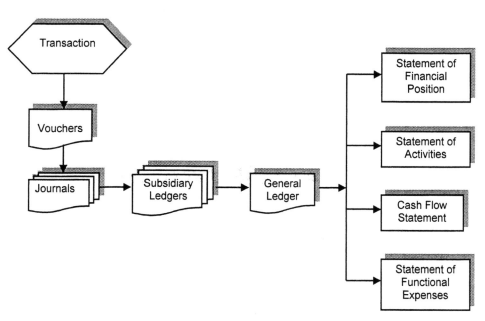

Figure 11-2: The Relationship of Accounts to the Financial Statements

cial statements: unrestricted, temporarily restricted, and permanently restricted.

Unrestricted net assets have no donor imposed restrictions upon them, while temporarily and permanently restricted assets do have donor-imposed restrictions. The difference is that temporary restrictions will usually be fulfilled by some action of the organization, for example, a specific project is implemented. Permanent restrictions, on the other hand, never expire, for example, an endowment given for the principal to be invested. Unrestricted net assets include all unrestricted monies, including board-imposed appropriations or restrictions. Permanently restricted net assets are basically endowment monies given in perpetuity. Table 11-4 shows the relationship of the funds to the net asset classes.

Adjustment and Closure of Accounts

After preparation of the financial statements, two types of entries should be made: adjusting entries and closing entries.

a. Adjusting entries are part of the accrual accounting system. Because of the matching concept used in accrual accounting, the organization wants to match revenue with expenses incurred during any particular fiscal period. However, because of the fact that revenue and

Table 11-4
RELATIONSHIP OF FUNDS TO NET ASSET CLASSES

| | Net Asset Classes | | |
Fund	Unrestricted	Temporarily Restricted	Permanently Restricted
Unrestricted	X		
Restricted		X	
Land, Building, Equipment		X	
Endowment			X
Custodian		X	

expenses may not always fall exactly within a fiscal period, it is necessary to make adjusting entries. Also, certain activities that may take place during a period will not be recorded in the books and have to be taken care of by means of adjusting entries. Some items that may be included in adjusting entries are depreciation of buildings and equipment, uncollectible accounts and pledges (National Health Council et al., 1988).

Adjusting entries may be done on the same work sheet that is used for the trial balance and the preparation of interim financial statements.

b. Closing entries are usually only done at the end of the fiscal year. Closing entries "close" or reduce the balance of all revenue and expense accounts and transfer them to an Income Summary (or Revenue Summary) Account. The purpose of this is to be able to start the new fiscal period with zero balances so that the organization can accurately "match" expenses and revenues during the new period. Remember that these entries will not be done at the end of a quarter or a month, they are usually done at the end of the fiscal year.

Preparation of Post-closing Trial Balance

The purpose of the post-closing trial balance is to see if the ledger account debits equal account credits. As in any trial balance, just the fact that debits and credits balance does not mean that there are no errors in the records, but if they do not balance it is an obvious indication of error.

One important aspect of the accounting cycle to remember is that while the processing of transactions does have a logical flow, many of the activities discussed occur continuously and simultaneously. For example, even though journalizing must take place before posting to the ledger, they both may occur on the same day. Other activities, such as the preparation of financial statements, will occur much less frequently—once a month, once a quarter, or once a year. The concern is that you, as a human service professional, have an overall picture of the accounting process as it may take place in the human service organization.

The previous discussion was a basic conceptual overview of the accounting cycle based on a manual system. Most nonprofits today use computers to do much of this work, although humans are needed to analyze and make decisions about the proper coding of economic transactions. While most of the preceding discussion is relevant to both manual and computerized accounting systems, one difference is that in computerized systems data is entered into a data base rather than a journal first. In the computerized system, "data posted to the ledger accounts comes directly from the data base, rather than from the journal" (Meigs & Meigs, 1990, p. 61). There will be a fuller discussion of computerized financial information systems in Chapter 13, but now let us turn to financial statements in the next chapter.

REFERENCES

American Institute of Certified Public Accountants (AICPA). (1999). *Audit and Accounting Guide: Not-for-profit Organizations.* New York: author.

Freeman, R. J. & Shoulders, C.D. (1999). *Governmental and Nonprofit Accounting: Theory and Practice* (6th Edition). Upper Saddle River, NJ: Prentice Hall.

Lynn, E.S. & Freeman, R.J. (1983). *Fund Accounting: Theory and Practice* (2nd Edition). Englewood Cliffs: Prentice-Hall.

Meigs, R.F. & Meigs, W.B. (1990). *Accounting: The Basis for Business Decisions* (8th Ed.). New York: McGraw-Hill.

National Health Council, the National Assembly of Health and Human Service Organizations & the United Way of America. (1988). *Standards of Accounting and Financial Reporting for Voluntary Health and Welfare Organizations* (Revised 3rd Ed.). New York: National Health Council, Inc.

National Health Council, Inc. & the National Assembly of Health and Human Service Organizations. (1998). *Standards of Accounting and Financial Reporting for Voluntary Health and Welfare Organizations* (4th Ed.). Dubuque, Iowa: Kendall/Hunt Publishing Co.

National Institute of Mental Health (NIMH), Series FN No. 6, *Accounting and Budgeting Systems for Mental Health Organizations,* by Sorensen, J.E., Hanbery, G.B., & Kucic, A.R. DHHS Pub. No. (ADM) 83–1046. Washington, D.C., Supt. Of Docs: U.S. Govt. Printing Office.

Whalen, W.J. (1982). The basis of accounting, pp. 269–277 in Tracy D. Connors and

Christopher Callaghan (Eds.). *Financial Management for Nonprofit Organizations.* New York: AMACOM.

Wilson, E.R., Kattelus, S.C., & Hay, L.E. (2001). *Accounting for Governmental and Nonprofit Entities* (12th Edition). New York: McGraw-Hill/Irwin.

INTERNET RESOURCES

Management Assistance Program for Nonprofits. http://www.mapfornonprofits.org

Chapter Twelve

FINANCIAL REPORTING

After reading this chapter you should be able to:

1. Understand the purposes and uses of financial statements;
2. Know the required financial statements;
3. Read financial statements;
4. Be familiar with IRS reporting requirements.

INTRODUCTION

Until recently, financial reporting by human service organizations was of very little interest to most people, including the accounting profession. An attitude of "laissez-faire" permeated public thinking about these agencies and was even perpetuated by the nonprofits themselves. The idea was that these organizations did "good works" that were unquantifiable and needed no justification. This, along with the tendency of human service administrators to be poorly prepared in the financial aspects of nonprofit management, led to a situation in which financial statements of nonprofits were often incomplete and misleading. So prevalent was this attitude that even the accounting profession took very little leadership in the setting of standards and guidelines for nonprofit agencies (Racek, 1980, Williams, 1999). In the 1960's, this attitude began to change for a variety of reasons: increased pressure from the public, funding agencies, and the federal government for greater accountability of public spending; competition from the private sector; and the need for greater efficiency due to cutbacks in funding for social services. There are now explicit guidelines and requirements for human service agencies to follow in the preparation of financial statements.

In 1964, *Standards of Accounting and Financial Reporting for Voluntary Health and Welfare Organizations* ("the Black Book") was published by the National Health Council and the National Assembly. Three years later, in 1967, *Audits of Voluntary Health and Welfare Organizations* was published by the American Institute of Certified Public Accountants

(AICPA) to guide auditors in the audit review of the financial statements of nonprofit health and welfare organizations. In 1974, the audit guide and the Black Book were revised, and the United Way published a guide as well. In 1988 the Black Book was revised again and its latest version was published in 1998 to reflect changes that have occurred since that time.

In the late 1980's, the Financial Accounting Standards Board (FASB) began working to review and revise the required financial statements of nonprofits, to bring some uniformity in the variety of requirements for various types of nonprofits, and to make them more understandable to interested users. In 1989, the AICPA issued a Report, *Display in the Financial Statements of Not-for-profit Organizations* in which it presented its recommendations for improvements in presentation and format (Kay & Seafoss, 1995).

Based on the Task Force Report of the AICPA, and comments received from the public, the FASB issued the final standard in June 1993, known as *Standards of Financial Accounting Statement (SFAS) No. 117: Financial Statements of Not-for-profit Organizations.* "The purpose of this standard is to establish standards for general purpose external financial statements provided by a not-for-profit organization" (Kay & Seafoss, 1995, p. 32–10). SFAS-117 was effective December 15, 1995 for all nonprofits. SFAS-117 was issued simultaneously with SFAS-116 as discussed previously.

As you will recall, in the accounting cycle financial reports are an output of the financial management subsystem of the organization. These financial reports are prepared from information gathered from the accounting records. As such they are, or should be, a mirror to the outside world, a reflection of the organization's activities expressed in monetary terms. What are the purposes served by such reports? Who are the target audiences or interested receivers of this information? What are the guidelines one should be familiar with when the organization's accountant prepares the financial reports? What type of information can one glean from them? This chapter will address these questions.

In addition, the Internal Revenue Service (I.R.S) has also increased interest in nonprofit organizations. Accordingly, in 1999, the IRS released regulations as part of the Taxpayer Bill of Rights Act of 1996, in which it required almost all tax-exempt organizations to provide public access to their three most recent federal tax returns as well as their Application for Recognition of Exemption. These tax returns are compiled using a document called Form 990 and are based on a nonprofit's financial statements. These IRS requirements will also be discussed in this chapter.

PURPOSES OF FINANCIAL STATEMENTS

Financial statements are reports that describe financial activities at different points in the financial management process. Some of the purposes of financial statements are the following:

To Describe Inputs

Financial statements describe the importation of resources such as revenues into the organization (see Figure 12-1 below). As historical documents, financial statements show the types of public support and revenue received by the organization during a specified accounting period. They explain to the reader where resources were obtained and in what amount. By looking at these reports, major funding sources can be spotted easily.

To Describe Throughputs

There are two types of processes that take place within the organization that can be reflected in financial statements: accounting processes and management processes. In addition to reflecting management processes, financial statements, as end products of the accounting cycle, are also used by management to facilitate its activities.

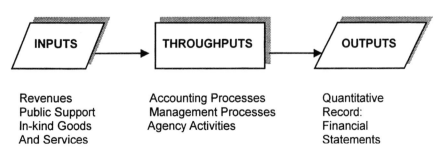

Figure 12-1: A Systems View of Financial Statements

Accounting Processes

Accounting processes are those activities that take place in the human service organization that involve monetary transactions. Some of the activities that can be seen in perusing the agency's financial statements are:

- The allocation and deployment of resources by the organization among its various components, for example, the allocation of revenues to various programs and objects of expenditure. Because of the need for accountability by human service organizations, it is important for users of financial statements to be able to quickly discern how resources have been used by the organization for its various programs.
- The consumption of assets by the organization, for example, expenses for office supplies and materials. The expense statement format used for nonprofits shows not only expenses, but further breaks them down by program area so that the reader can see how much was spent by each program.
- The acquisition of new assets by the organization during the period being reported in the statement, for example, new office equipment.
- The assumption of new liabilities by the organization, often related to acquisition of assets. As an example, the organization may acquire new office equipment on credit.
- The division of operating expenses among the various programs. By allocating or attributing costs such as staff or administrative time to each of the agency's programs, the comparison of program expenses is facilitated.

Management Processes

In addition to accounting processes, there are many other activities going on in the human service agency. Besides the major function of providing services, there are a myriad of management tasks that must take place to ensure the continual operation of an organization and to provide support to service delivery staff. One important management process reflected in the human service financial statements is:

- The operationalization of the agency's goals and objectives during a specific period of time. Many small human service organizations do not have written goals and objectives, strange as it might seem. It is assumed by the people who work in the organization that there is an implicit consensus among staff, board members, and even clients as to what the goals of the organization might be. But often the perceptions of management, staff, and the board are very different. Whether the organization's goals are written or not, its financial statements are a reflection of these goals and should reflect its service efforts.

In addition, financial statements are important tools in human service management decision making and planning. Some of the uses of these statements that help facilitate the management process are:

- To provide information to be used by the organization and its officers for planning purposes. The financial statements of the organization are crucial for budgeting and other planning that takes place in the organization. The information can also be used for marketing purposes, for example, parts of the nonprofit's financial statements may be printed in a brochure that is distributed to the public and other funding sources.
- To provide a basis of comparison from one fiscal period to the next. By looking at past performance over time and taking into account any environmental factors such as changes in level or source of funding, state of the economy, changes in function or goals of the agency, changes in the demography of the client population, and so forth, one can discern trends in the organization's acquisition, allocation, and use of resources.
- To have data available that can be used in evaluating the effectiveness and efficiency of the organization's programs. Measuring efficiency (maximum use of resources) and effectiveness (reaching stated goals) are important functions that can be measured in an agency and are often scrutinized by outside funders. By looking at measures such as ratios and percentages one can evaluate efficiency, economic stability, and stewardship. Measuring effectiveness, on the other hand is a much more difficult evaluative process. Something that can nevertheless be gleaned from the financial reports is whether the agency's stated priorities are in fact reflected in the allocation of resources and expenses.

To Describe Outputs

Financial statements provide a quantitative record of an organization's activities during a specific period of time, usually one year. One can get a more accurate picture of organizational activities by taking these "snapshots" of financial position at any one moment in time.

Sometimes the statements are broken up into smaller units of time, as in quarterly or monthly reports. This documentation can be presented to funding sources as a basis for current and future funding decisions. Funding sources need some information upon which to base decisions about an organization's performance, whether or not it is meeting its stated goals, and providing the services for which it was initially funded. In addition, "doing good works" is no longer enough; in an era of accountability funders are also concerned about efficient use of resources and look to management to provide some evaluative indicators of effectiveness as well.

USERS OF FINANCIAL REPORTS

Among the potential audiences of an organization's financial statements and reports, such as federal and state tax returns, are interested groups with overlapping memberships such as the following (FASB, 1980, AICPA, 1998):

Constituents

Constituents are those who are served by the organization, such as members, clients, and potential clients. In addition to members of the board of directors or board of trustees, there may be other members who pay dues to belong to a given voluntary organization, taxpayers whose taxes may help support the organization, and clients who may pay on a sliding fee-scale for services. Thus, in the last analysis, the organization's constituency is made up of the community itself.

Resource Providers

Resource providers are individuals, groups, and organizations that provide inputs into the organization in the form of human and material capital (see Chapter One). They may contribute directly in the form of grants, loans, credit, contributions, or volunteer time. They include both those who are directly compensated for providing resources, such as creditors, suppliers, and employees, as well as those who are not directly compensated, such as members, contributors, and taxpayers.

Some resource providers, such as contributors, are interested in organization financial statements because this information can help them make decisions regarding continued financial or material support on the basis of how efficiently the agency has met or tried to meet its goals. Other resource providers, such as creditors, are interested in whether or not the agency has the ability to meet its financial obligations to them as well as the ability to generate sufficient cash flow for present and future operating expenses.

There is, or may be, an overlap between resource providers and constituents. However, a constituent's concerns may be different from those of providers. The resource provider wants to know whether the organization is using its resources to meet organizational goals and financial obligations. The constituent may be interested in another set of issues, that of whether resources are being allocated in such a manner as to meet the social and material needs of the community. This has been a particular sore spot for some groups, such as ethnic minorities who have pressured agencies for change because of a perceived lack of sensitivity to the needs of the constituent community.

Governing and Oversight Bodies

Governing and oversight bodies include accrediting agencies, regulatory agencies, taxing agencies, other units of government, federated fund raising and allocation agencies, legislatures, and boards of trustees. These bodies are responsible for setting policies, administrative rules, and laws that regulate nonprofit human service organizations. They are also responsible for overseeing, reviewing, and sometimes evaluating top management performance as well as agency conformance and compliance with the various laws and regulations that govern the agency. These groups therefore use financial statements to help them carry out their oversight/evaluative mission, and perhaps to suggest changes in goals, policies, or programs when necessary. These suggestions can provide important feedback to an organization.

Managers

Managers of human service organizations have the responsibility of implementing policy formulated by the board of directors and other governing bodies, as well as overseeing day-to-day operations. Managers include organization heads, program directors, supervisors, and directors of fund-raising activities. They, along with the governing board, may be considered internal users of financial reports.

Managers can use the information garnered from financial statements along with other accounting information for purposes of planning and control, as was discussed earlier. The information may be needed for decision making related to asset acquisition, or for capital projects. The information may also be needed in order for the manager to carry out his or her stewardship function regarding proper use of resources, whether restricted or not. The manager also needs information from the statements to oversee and demonstrate compliance with established guidelines of funding sources.

In summary, the human service agency has a responsibility to provide useful information to users of its financial statements to help them:

- In making resource allocation decisions;
- In assessing services and ability to provide services;
- In assessing management's stewardship and performance;
- In being aware of economic resources, obligations, net resources, and any changes that have occurred in them;
- In evaluating organizational performance during the period;
- In understanding service efforts and accomplishments of the organization (FASB, 1980).

QUALITATIVE ASPECTS OF FINANCIAL STATEMENTS

The information reflected in financial reports is affected by many factors because human service organizations do not operate in a vacuum, but in a highly charged socio-political and economic environment. Changing social values, social policies, and economic conditions affect the financial condition of the nonprofit. Along with environmental factors that affect the organization's financial statements are constraints due to the nature of the reports themselves. That is, information contained in the financial statements is quantitative and expressed in monetary terms. Thus, money is the common denominator that depicts economic activities and events in the statements. The problem with this is that accounting is an art, not a science, and even though it is surrounded by an aura of preciseness due to its numerical format, it is subject to an enormous amount of judgment, estimates, classifications, and summarizations. Therefore, often what appears to be unequivocal are in fact "approximations which may be based on rules and conventions rather than exact amounts" (FASB, 1980, p. 13).

What are largely reflected in financial statements are historical data, events and transactions that have occurred in the past. These statements may be contrasted with budgets, which reflect future goals and plans. Even so, this historical information can be extremely useful to many groups, as has been pointed out. It is important to remember that the information from financial statements needs to be used in conjunction with, and in the context of, other social, political, and economic information about an organization. Such important aspects of a nonprofit's functioning as the following are not shown on financial statements:

Social Information: addresses questions such as, what is the demographic profile of the clients served by the agency? Are clients served representative of a cross-section of the community and/or target population? Do minorities use the agency in proportion to their numbers in the population? Is the agency responsive to the needs of the community?

Political Information: addresses questions such as, what is the background and makeup of members of the board and agency administrators? What political interests are represented on the board? Is the composition of the board representative of the client group? What community issues is the board concerned with? What political factors facilitate or hinder the delivery of services? Have political views regarding the client group or the services offered affected funding?

Economic Information: addresses such questions as, what is the economic level of the clients being served? Does the agency serve indigent clients as well as those able to pay or that have third-party payers? Are the outcomes of the program producing a positive result in relation to the material and human costs incurred? How are inflation and other economic indicators affecting requests for service as well as fundraising efforts?

Certain types of nonmonetary information can be found in the notes accompanying financial statements or from budget information on number of clients served, and so forth. Other nonmonetary information may be needed to understand and evaluate the significance of information contained in financial statements. Thus, financial reports are only one type of information about an agency that is needed by interested parties; there are other types of information that must be considered. In trying to assess financial reports the constraints of trying to quantify human service endeavors and their outcomes must be kept in mind. "Financial reporting by nonbusiness organizations . . . is limited in its ability to provide direct measures of the quality of goods and services provided in the absence of market-determined exchange prices or the degree to which they satisfy the need of service beneficiaries and consumers" (FASB, 1980, p. 13).

REQUIRED FINANCIAL STATEMENTS

Interested users of a nonprofit's financial statements obviously want to know the sources and disposition of its assets. As mentioned previously, SFAS-117 (1993) established standards for nonprofit financial statements. There are now four required financial statements for nonprofit human service agencies: 1) a Statement of Financial Position (also known as a Balance Sheet); 2) a Statement of Activities (also called a Statement of Support, Revenue, and Expenses, and Changes in Net Assets); 3) a Statement of Cash Flows; and 4) a Statement of Functional Expenses. In addition, for those organizations receiving federal funds, the Office of Management and Budget (OMB) Circular A-133, *Audits of States, Local Governments, and Non-Profit Organizations* (revised June 24, 1997), and the AICPA's Statement of Position (SOP) *98-3, Audits of States, Local Governments, and Not-for-profit Organizations Receiving Federal Awards,* require a schedule of expenditures of federal awards for the period covered by the financial statements.

SFAS-117 does not require financial reports by fund nor does it use the terms "fund balance" or "changes in fund balance". Rather, SFAS-117 requires that net assets (assets minus liabilities) be presented as a whole in three net asset classes: unrestricted net assets, temporarily restricted net assets, and permanently restricted net assets. Also, changes in net assets for each net asset class are to be disclosed. The purpose of this approach is to focus on the agency as a whole, rather than any of its specific funds. These asset classes are defined as follows:

Unrestricted Net Assets: These include all assets with no restriction on them, for example, a donation given to the agency to be used for operations, or fees for services. It can also include assets that were previously temporarily restricted, but had met donor stipulations and were released for use.

Temporarily Restricted Net Assets: These are assets whose use is limited due to donor-imposed restrictions, for example, a donation limited to one program or organization activity.

Permanently Restricted Net Assets: These are assets whose use is limited by donor-imposed restrictions that are permanent in nature, as for example, an endowment.

Nonprofits may be required to prepare other types of special reports for internal use or for funders, and the format of these other reports will vary depending on the needs of the users. But the format of the financial statements has become standardized since the publication of SFAS-117, although not all organizations will use all of the categories listed in the sample statements shown here. Organizations should check with their state's civil codes regulating nonprofit corporations to ascertain any state requirements for reporting. Most states use the FASB standards.

Statement of Financial Position (Balance Sheet)

As you will recall from Chapter Eleven, the Statement of Financial Position is a reflection of the accounting equation (Assets = Liabilities + Net Assets). Thus, the objective of the statement of financial position is to present information about assets, liabilities, and net assets in order to facilitate analysis of credit, liquidity, ability to meet obligations, and the need to obtain external financing. It is a reflection of the financial condition of an organization at one point in time, the date it is presented (see Table 12-1).

The sample statement shown here has two columns, one of the current year and, for comparative purposes, a column of the previous year's totals. Although not required by SFAS-117, displaying the previous year is useful to the reader as it gives a reference point and some idea of trends.

The Statement of Financial Position must provide information about the entity's liquidity, that is, its cash and near-to-cash assets. This can be accomplished (1) by sequencing assets in the order of diminishing liquidity or by current/noncurrent classification or (2) by sequencing liabilities according to their nearness to maturity (SFAS-117, par 12). The statement must also disclose the amount and nature of the restrictions on net assets either in the statements or the notes accompanying the statements. As can be seen in the sample Statement of Position, assets are presented as current or fixed as well as to their nearness to cash.

Current assets: are cash or other assets expected to be converted to cash within one year or less. On the sample statement shown here, these current assets would be cash and cash equivalents, marketable securities, accounts receivable, pledges receivable, and prepaid expenses.

Cash equivalents: are those cash items held in interest-bearing accounts such as money market or savings accounts with a maturity date of less than three months.

Marketable securities: are investments that can be easily converted to cash and whose maturities are less than one year. Some examples of these types of investments would be CDs and Treasury bonds.

Accounts receivable: are monies owed to the organization.

Table 12-1
STATEMENT OF FINANCIAL POSITION
Human Services Organization, Inc.
Statement of Financial Position
December 31, 2011 with Comparative Totals for 2010

			Total	
ASSETS	**Unrestricted**	**Restricted**	**2011**	**2010**
Current Assets:				
Cash and cash equivalents (Note 3)	$110,400	$ 11,000	$121,400	$127,000
Marketable securities (Note 5)	121,500	149,000	270,500	297,400
Accounts receivable	122,600		122,600	112,100
Pledges receivable (Notes 4 & 6)	58,900		58,900	46,000
Grants	152,800	10,000	162,800	126,400
Prepaid expenses	54,800		54,800	39,600
Total Current Assets	621,000	170,000	791,000	748,500
Fixed Assets, Net (Note 7)	173,800		173,800	167,500
Total Assets	794,800	170,000	964,800	916,000
LIABILITIES AND NET ASSETS				
Current Liabilities:				
Accounts payable and accrued expenses	39,300		39,300	36,500
Salaries and payroll taxes payable	41,600		41,600	39,700
Current portion of notes payable	3,200		3,200	3,600
Total Current Liabilities	84,100		84,100	79,800
Long-term Liabilities:				
Mortgage payable, net of current portion (Note 14)	28,200		28,200	31,400
Total Liabilities	112,300		112,300	111,200
Net Assets:				
Unrestricted	682,500		682,500	639,800
Temporarily restricted (Note 10)		50,000	50,000	55,000
Permanently restricted (Note 10)		120,000	120,000	110,000
Total Net Assets	682,500	170,000	852,500	804,800
Total Liabilities and Net Assets	$794,800	$170,000	$964,800	$916,000

Adapted from: *Standards of Accounting and Financial Reporting . . . , 1998*

Pledges receivable: pledges of donations that have not yet been paid.

Grants: monies given by an individual, foundation, corporation, or a governmental agency for services to be provided by the human service organization.

Prepaid expenses: are expenses that have been paid in advance, for example, insurance or property taxes. They are included if they can be expected to expire within one year or less.

As was discussed in Chapter Ten, *Liabilities* are the claims that creditors may have on assets. In other words, liabilities are the debts owed by the firm. These are called Accounts Payable when merchandise or other goods are bought on credit, while Notes Payable are debts that are incurred by signing a promissory note to repay the monies owed at a definite future time.

Current liabilities on the Statement of Position are those debts that must be satisfied in one year or less. The sample Statement shown here has sequenced liabilities according to current or long-term as well as to their nearness to maturity as suggested in SFAS-117. In this Statement, *Mortgage payable* would not be considered a current liability.

Statement of Activities

The Statement of Activities shows revenues, expenses, and changes in net assets in three classes: *unrestricted net assets, temporarily restricted net assets,* and *permanently restricted net assets.* The statement also includes a total change (increase or decrease) in net assets for the fiscal period (see Table 12-2). The statement may use the term *changes in net assets* or *changes in equities* to describe equity. As noted above, SFAS-117 does not use the terms *fund balance* or *changes in fund balance.* Rather, SFAS-117 sees net assets or equities as encompassing the whole of the net assets of the nonprofit organization, while fund balance has historically been used to refer only to certain groups of assets. The other operating statement, the Statement of Functional Expenses, gives a more detailed breakdown of the expenses listed in the Statement of Activities.

Shown here is one suggested type of suggested format for the Statement of Activities. In this format, all revenues and expenses, as well as net assets, are presented in columns by each class of net asset—unrestricted, temporarily restricted, and permanently restricted. This makes it easy for the reader to see not only the allocation of monies between asset classes, but also the reclassification between classes due to expirations on donor restrictions. For example, one can see in the Statement that $23,600 of temporarily restricted net assets were reclassified as unrestricted once the donor restrictions were met. The Statement also refers the reader to the notes that accompany the statements, which gives more explanation.

Being able to see whether assets of a nonprofit are restricted or not is useful in being able to gauge the organization's ability to respond to short-term needs or whether it has the flexibility to do so.

Table 12-2
STATEMENT OF ACTIVITIES

Human Services Organization, Inc.
Statement of Activities
For the year ended December 31, 2011 with Comparative Totals for 2010

		Restricted		Total	
	Unrestricted	Temporarily	Permanently	2011	2010
SUPPORT AND REVENUE:					
Public Support:					
Received directly:					
Contributions (Note 2)	$230,350	$ 3,000	$ 10,000	$243,350	$246,800
Donations–in-kind	28,400			28,400	25,500
Donated Services (Note 8)	17,600			17,600	16,000
Received Indirectly:					
Federated fundraising					
organizations	83,500			83,500	82,000
Total Public Support	359,850	3,000	10,000	372,850	370,300
Revenues and grants from					
governmental agencies	350,000			350,000	382,000
Other Revenues:					
Program service fees	10,850			10,850	9,000
Investment income	16,200	15,000		31,200	26,000
Other	2,800			2,800	3,600
Gain (loss) on investments		600		600	27,200
Total Other Revenue	29,850	15,600		45,450	65,800
Net Assets released from					
restrictions					
Satisfaction of program					
restrictions	23,600	(23,600)			
Total Revenue	763,300	(5,000)	10,000	768,300	818,100
EXPENSES:					
Program Services:					
Program A	141,400			141,400	136,500
Program B	54,400			54,400	48,500
Program C	61,800			61,800	51,600
Program D	257,800			257,800	273,600
Total Program Services	515,400			515,400	510,200
Supporting Services:					
Management and General	57,400			57,400	63,800
Fundraising	65,400			65,400	54,600
Total Supporting Services	122,800			122,800	118,400
Payments to national					
organization (Note 13)	82,400			82,400	85,400
Total Expenses	720,600			720,600	714,000
Excess (deficiency) of revenue					
over expenses	42,700	(5,000)	10,000	47,700	104,100
CHANGE IN NET ASSETS	42,700	(5,000)	10,000	47,700	104,100
NET ASSETS, BEGINNING					
OF YEAR	639,800	55,000	110,000	804,800	700,700
NET ASSETS, END OF YEAR	$682,500	$50,000	$120,000	$852,500	$804,800

Adapted from: *Standards of Accounting and Financial Reporting . . . , 1998.*

Statement of Cash Flows

Previously, nonprofits were excluded from the requirement to produce a cash flow statement. SFAS-117 extended the requirement to nonprofits. A Statement of Cash Flows is now required for nonprofit human service agencies. The Statement of Cash Flows reflects the amount of net cash given to, and used by, a nonprofit as the result of: 1) operating activities, 2) investing activities, and 3) financing activities during the fiscal period being reported (see Table 12-3). The governing standard here is Statement of Financial Accounting Standard *(SFAS) No. 95: Statement of Cash Flows* (FASB, 1987).

Operating activities include those cash transactions related to the day-to-day activities of the organization, including revenue from fees, unrestricted donations, and payment of operating expenses.

Investing activities include "cash transactions related to the acquisition and disposal of long-term assets such as land, buildings, and equipment and investment securities" (National Health Council & The National Assembly, 1998, p. 37).

Financing cash flows include transactions related to borrowing and repayment of loans as well as receipt of resources such as permanently or temporarily restricted endowment gifts.

The Statement of Cash Flows helps the reader determine whether a nonprofit has the ability to meet its cash obligations as well as its ability to manage its investing activities. Although prepared at the end of an organization's fiscal year along with all of the other required statements, it may be useful for planning purposes for an organization to divide the Statement into smaller periods, for example, quarters, especially if it has seasonal variations in revenue inflows.

The Statement is important because it is possible for an organization to have a large amount of net assets and yet still have difficulty in meeting its expenses (Fraser & Ormiston, 2001). It is even more useful when the Statement is presented in a comparative format, that is, with one or two previous years along with the current one.

SFAS-117 encourages nonprofits to use the direct method in reporting cash flows. A cash flow statement using the direct method is prepared in a similar way as the cash flow budget discussed in Chapter Four. That is, all inflows are added to the beginning balance for a period and all outflows are deducted. The resulting net balance becomes the beginning balance for the next period. One difference is that the statement is separated into three categories: cash flows from operating

Table 12-3
STATEMENT OF CASH FLOWS (DIRECT METHOD)
Human Services Organization, Inc.
Statement of Cash Flows
For the year ended December 31, 2011 with Comparative Totals for 2010

	Unrestricted	Restricted	Total 2011	2010
Cash flows from operating activities:				
Cash received from service recipients	$ 22,300		$ 22,300	$ 18,300
Cash received from contributors	667,300		667,300	720,000
Cash collected on pledges receivable	46,300		46,300	54,000
Interest and dividends received	16,200	15,000	31,200	27,000
Cash paid to employees and suppliers	(728,100)		(728,100)	(758,500)
Miscellaneous payments	(3,800)	(20,500)	(24,300)	(7,400)
Net cash provided (used) by operating activities	20,200	(5,500)	14,700	53,400
Cash flows from investing activities:				
Purchase of fixed assets	(11,500)		(11,500)	(7,000)
Proceeds from sale of investments	1,000		1,000	51,000
Purchase of investments	(19,600)	(10,000)	(29,600)	(86,000)
Net cash used by investing activities	(30,100)	(10,000)	(40,100)	(42,000)
Cash flows from financing activities				
Proceeds from contributions restricted for:				
Investment in endowment		10,000	10,000	41,000
Other financing activities:				
Payments on mortgage payable	(400)		(400)	(400)
Proceeds from capital lease obligation	10,200		10,200	–
Net cash provided by financing activities	9,800	10,000	19,800	40,600
Net increase (decrease) in cash and cash equivalents	(100)	(5,500)	(5,600)	52,000
Cash & cash equivalents, beginning of year	110,500	16,500	127,000	75,000
Cash & cash equivalents, end of year	$110,400	$11,000	$121,400	$127,000
Reconciliation of change in net assets to net cash provided (used) by operating activities				
Change in net assets	$ 42,700	$ 5,000	$ 47,700	$104,100
Adjustment to reconcile change in net assets to net cash provided (used) by operating activities:				
Depreciation & amortization	5,200		5,200	4,600
Net (gains)/losses on sales of securities	(1,000)	500	(500)	(27,500)
(Increase)/decrease in receivables	(12,900)	(1,000)	(13,900)	7,000
(increase)/decrease in inventory	(900)		(900)	1,500
(increase)/decrease in prepaid expenses	(4,200)		(4,200)	(2,000)
(increase)/decrease in accounts payable	(6,700)		(6,700)	5,000
Contributions restricted for long-term investment		(10,000)	(10,000)	(40,000)
Net cash provided (used) by operating activities	$ 20,200	$(5,500)	$ 14,700	$ 53,400

Adapted from: *Standards of Accounting and Financial Reporting . . . , 1998* activities, cash flows from investing activities, and cash flows from financing activities. Usually for each of these categories figures are aggregated for the three classes of net assets (unrestricted, temporarily restricted, and permanently restricted), otherwise the statement would be too cumbersome to read.

Statement of Functional Expenses

Not all nonprofits are required to report expenditures by functional classification, but SFAS-117 requires all voluntary health and welfare organizations (VHWO's) to do so. This statement has been required for some time by the *Standards* and other guidelines. The Statement of Functional Expenses is similar in format to the functional expense budget discussed in Chapter Four. The difference is that while the functional expense budget is an estimate of future costs, the statement of functional expenses is a record of actual expenditures of unrestricted net assets (Freeman & Shoulders, 1999). The information needed to prepare the Statement of Functional Expenses is obtained from the various expense ledgers. Table 12-4 shows a representative Statement with the main types of expenses included.

As you will recall, the functional classification separates program services and support services and shows the natural or object classification for each expense. Support services are to be apportioned between management and general, fundraising, and membership development (SFAS-117, par. 28). Classification of fundraising expenses was discussed in Chapter Five. M*embership development* is the cost of membership recruitment and maintenance for those organizations with such costs, such as YMCAs, YWCAs, Mental Health Associations, Boys and Girls Clubs, and so forth. *Management and general* is a category that encompasses all other support services necessary for the maintenance of the organization. The purpose of the Statement of Functional Expenses is to disclose how the organization spent its money in each of these categories.

Object expense categories represent specific classifications for objects such as salaries, telephone, travel, and so forth. Obviously, the number of program service categories and object expense classifications will depend on the size and nature of the reporting agency.

Besides the usual object expense categories such as salaries, employee benefits, payroll taxes, equipment, supplies, travel, and telephone, the following categories may be found in some statements:

Table 12-4
STATEMENT OF FUNCTIONAL EXPENSES
Human Services Organization, Inc.
Statement of Functional Expenses
For the year ended December 31, 2011 with Comparative Totals for 2010

	Program Services					Supporting Services			Total Expenses	
	Prog. A	Prog. B	Prog. C	Prog. D	Total	Mgt & Gen	Fund-raising	Total	2011	2010
Salaries	$ 75,817	$29,100	$35,200	$189,600	$329,717	$33,100	$36,800	$ 69,900	$399,617	$233,300
Employee benefits	4,100	1,400	2,000	12,800	20,300	2,200	1,500	3,700	24,000	12,500
Payroll taxes, etc.	6,069	2,600	3,500	16,400	28,569	3,000	3,100	6,100	34,669	21,500
Total salaries and related expenses	85,986	33,100	40,700	218,800	378,586	38,300	41,400	79,700	458,286	267,300
Professional fees	16,487	3,500	300	1,200	21,487	2,600	1,000	3,600	25,087	5,200
Supplies	4,297	2,300	1,300	1,900	9,797	1,800	2,400	4,200	13,997	5,200
Telephone	1,481	1,300	1,000	2,350	6,131	1,500	2,300	3,800	9,931	6,800
Postage & shipping	2,603	2,000	1,300	5,900	11,803	1,350	5,100	6,450	18,253	6,500
Occupancy	2,105	1,300	1,100	2,400	6,905	1,500	1,300	2,800	9,705	5,300
Equipment maintenance	2,284	1,300	1,100	2,300	6,984	1,500	1,300	2,800	9,784	6,200
Travel & transportation	5,639	2,200	2,000	2,350	12,189	2,100	2,100	4,200	16,389	10,200
Conferences	5,358	2,900	7,100	2,000	17,358	3,950	400	4,350	21,708	14,500
Printing & publications	12,760	3,100	4,700	4,500	25,060	1,500	7,000	8,500	33,560	17,400
Membership dues		500			500				500	500
Research Expense				10,000	10,000				10,000	9,000
Insurance	700	200	100	800	1,800	600	200	800	2,600	1,000
Other expenses	500	200	500	400	1,600	100	500	600	2,200	1,600
Depreciation	1,200	500	600	2,900	5,200	600	400	1,000	6,200	4,600
Total functional expenses	$141,400	$54,400	$61,800	$257,800	$515,400	$57,400	$65,400	$122,800	$638,200	$628,600
Payments to National Organization									82,400	85,400
Total expenses									720,600	714,000
Direct benefit cost									18,000	16,300
Total expenses and direct benefit cost									$738,600	$730,300

Adapted from: *Standards of Accounting and Financial Reporting . . . , 1998*

Professional Fees: are for those outside consultants such as doctors, lawyers, accountants, and auditors, who may have a contract for services with the agency.

Occupancy: includes rental, utilities, mortgage and any other costs associated in using a building and land for the agency's purposes. It does not include depreciation because this is covered elsewhere in the statement.

Awards and Grants: are monies paid by the agency to support research, scholarships, or other welfare programs. For example, some organizations provide seed money to community groups to start new projects, while other organizations provide money to encourage research in a specific problem area such as alcohol abuse, teenage pregnancy, child abuse, and so forth.

Depreciation or Amortization: allocates the cost of an asset over its useful life. Its useful life is the time that it benefits the agency. Some types of assets that may be depreciated are equipment, buildings, and automobiles.

The method of classifying expenses by object categories across programs requires that those expenses falling into more than one program area be coded at the time they are entered into the books. This will facilitate the preparation of the statement. But sometimes nonprofits find it difficult to ascertain what proportion of an expense falls under two or more programs. This uncertainty may be minimized by instituting some procedures to allocate costs such as those discussed in Chapter Nine, and certainly the organization should consult with its accountant regarding the procedures. The accountant must determine whether the methods used are reasonable and constitute a sufficiently accurate reflection of agency activities so as to be able to render an unqualified opinion in the notes accompanying the statements. While some methods for allocating costs have been previously discussed, it must be remembered that accounting is an art and therefore "it may be impossible, even with the most meticulous accounting, completely to isolate and precisely report ALL of an agency's expenses for any single function, whether fund-raising, management and general, or a particular program service" (United Way, 1974, p. 93).

There are two additional components that make up a complete financial statement package. They are: 1) the notes that accompany the statements, and 2) for organizations receiving federal funds, a listing, or schedule, of expenditure of awards.

Notes to Financial Statements

Usually accompanying the required financial statements are notes that explain or expand upon some items in the statements. For example, the notes may contain the following information (see Appendix for sample notes):

The nature of the organization: that is, a charitable 501(c)(3) organization;

A summary of significant accounting policies: including:

- Its basis of accounting, i.e., accrual or other;
- Its IRS status, 501 (c)(3) or some other status;
- Whether its contributions are recorded in accordance with SFAS-116;
- Any comments regarding its functional expenses;
- A listing of its fixed assets;
- Its definition of revenue recognition;
- Its definition of cash equivalents, for example, in the Appendix one can see that this organization considers all investments available for current use with a maturity of three months or less to be cash equivalents;
- Any other notes deemed material by the organization.

Schedule of Expenditure of Federal Awards

As was mentioned previously, all nonprofits receiving federal grants or contracts are required to list such a schedule. The guiding standard here is OMB Circular A-133, *Audits of States, Local governments, and Nonprofit Organizations* (1997). This is not a required part of the basic financial statements as enunciated by SFAS-117, but it is convenient and common for these schedules to be included with the financial statements (see Table 12-5).

The Schedule shown here shows that the grantor (or funding source) was the United States Department of Health and Human Services. The grant money that was awarded passed through the State Department of Human Services for the listed programs of the organization. The first program listed, Mentoring, had a budget period of July 1 to June 30. It was awarded $106,053 and spent the same amount. The information listed in these schedules is not only important to the federal or state funding source, but also to other potential funders and the general public.

Table 12-5
SCHEDULE OF EXPENDITURE OF FEDERAL AWARDS
Human Services Organization, Inc.
Schedule of Expenditure of Federal Awards
For the year ended June 30, 200x

Federal Grantor Pass Through Grantor ments/ Program Title	Federal CFDA Number	Budget Period	Pass-through Grantor's Number	Contract Amount	Disburs Expenditures
U.S. Department of Health and Human Services					
Passed through: State Department of Human Services *Division of Family Services*					
Mentoring	95.123	7/1/2010– 6/30/2011	01AABBCC	$106,053	$106,053
Foster Care	95.123	1/1/2010– 12/31/2010	01AABBCC	$1,768,455	$1,768,455
Family Preservation	95.123	7/1/2010– 6/30/2010	01AABBCC	$782,468	$782,468

Etc.

INTERNAL REVENUE REQUIREMENTS: FORM 990

Even though they are tax-exempt, nonprofit organizations are required to file annual tax returns, called Federal Form 990. This requirement applies to all 501(c)(3) organizations with annual receipts of more than $100,000 or total assets of more than $250,000. A shorter form, Form 990-EZ, may be filed by those nonprofits with annual receipts between $25,000 and $100,000 and total assets of less than $250,000. Small nonprofit organizations that fall below the $25,000 threshold do not have to file a return at all (see Reading 12-2 for a copy of 990-EZ).

In addition to Form 990, nonprofit organizations are required to file another form along with it, Schedule A. Schedule A asks for a listing of the highest paid employees and other information. Form 990 is due every year four and a half (4½) months after the close of the organization's fiscal year. For example, if an organization's fiscal year ends on December 31, the return would be due on May 15 and so forth (U.S. Department of the Treasury).

In looking at the 990-EZ in reading 12-1, one may note Part I, "Revenue, Expenses, and Changes in Net Assets or Fund Balances" is very similar to the Statement of Activities. Part II, Balance Sheets, is similar to the Statement of Position. Part III, "Statement of Program Service Accomplishments" is an important part of the return and one that is not found on any of the financial statements. It asks for information that cannot be gleaned from the financials by themselves. This section asks for a description of the services provided, the number of persons benefited, and other relevant information.

Part IV, "List of Officers, Directors, Trustees, and Key Employees", asks for the names and addresses as well as the average hours per week worked, compensation, pension, and expense account information. Part V, "Other Information ", asks a number of questions such as questions about unrelated business income, political expenditures, loans to officers or key employees, and so forth. There is also an attachment, called "Schedule A", in which the organization must list its sources of financial support, the names and addresses of all donors, the salaries of the highest paid employees, and other information.

What makes this return so important is that, for a large number of nonprofits, these Form 990's can be viewed by anyone on the Internet. As mentioned before, the I.R.S. began in 1999 to require nonprofits to make their three most recent Form 990's available to the public. They are not, however, required to release the section of Schedule A that contains the names and addresses of contributors. In order to implement the new I.R.S. regulations on public disclosure, the Urban Institute's National Center for Charitable Statistics (NCCS) and Philanthropic Research, Inc. (PRI) teamed together to make these forms available on the Web.

The Form 990's have been compiled in a database and are available through PRI's website (http://www.guidestar.org) as well as the NCCS website (http://nccsdataweb.urban.org). In addition, NCCS also offers a Unified Chart of Accounts (UCOA) free to nonprofits to help them translate their financial statements into the categories required by the Form 990, as well as the Office of Management and Budget and other standard reporting formats. What is unique is that many organizations have come together to make reporting less difficult for nonprofits while at the same time making these reports widely accessible to the public.

This chapter briefly discussed I.R.S. requirements of human service nonprofits. It also presented an overview of financial statements and the various components that make up the statements. The next chapter will discuss the audit function related to financial statements as well as approaches to analyzing each of the statements.

Reading 12-1: Form 990-EZ

		Short Form	OMB No. 1545-1150
Form **990-EZ**		**Return of Organization Exempt From Income Tax** Under section 501(c), 527, or 4947(a)(1) of the Internal Revenue Code (except black lung benefit trust or private foundation) ► For organizations with gross receipts less than $100,000 and total assets less than $250,000 at the end of the year.	**2002**
Department of the Treasury Internal Revenue Service		► *The organization may have to use a copy of this return to satisfy state reporting requirements.*	**Open to Public Inspection**

A For the 2002 calendar year, or tax year beginning _____ , 2002, and ending _____ , 20___

B Check if applicable:	Please use IRS label or print or type. See Specific Instruc- tions.	**C** Name of organization	**D** Employer identification number
☐ Address change ☐ Name change ☐ Initial return ☐ Final return ☐ Amended return ☐ Application pending		Number and street (or P.O. box, if mail is not delivered to street address)	Room/suite	**E** Telephone number ( )
		City or town, state or country, and ZIP + 4	**F** Enter 4-digit (GEN) ►

• *Section 501(c)(3) organizations and 4947(a)(1) nonexempt charitable trusts must attach a completed Schedule A (Form 990 or 990-EZ).*

G Accounting method: ☐ Cash ☐ Accrual
Other (specify) ►

I Web site: ► _____

H Check ► ☐ if the organization is **not** required to attach Schedule B (Form 990, 990-EZ, or 990-PF).

J Organization type (check only one)— ☐ 501(c) ( ) ◄ (insert no.) ☐ 4947(a)(1) or ☐ 527

K Check ► ☐ if the organization's gross receipts are normally not more than $25,000. The organization need not file a return with the IRS; but if the organization received a Form 990 Package in the mail, it should file a return without financial data. **Some states require a complete return.**

L Add lines 5b, 6b, and 7b, to line 9 to determine gross receipts; if $100,000 or more, file Form 990 instead of Form 990-EZ. . ► $ _____

Part I Revenue, Expenses, and Changes in Net Assets or Fund Balances (See page 36 of the instructions.)

Revenue	1	Contributions, gifts, grants, and similar amounts received	**1**	
	2	Program service revenue including government fees and contracts	**2**	
	3	Membership dues and assessments	**3**	
	4	Investment income	**4**	
	5a	Gross amount from sale of assets other than inventory	**5a**	
	b	Less: cost or other basis and sales expenses	**5b**	
	c	Gain or (loss) from sale of assets other than inventory (line 5a less line 5b) (attach schedule) .	**5c**	
	6	Special events and activities (attach schedule):		
	a	Gross revenue (not including $ _____ of contributions reported on line 1)	**6a**	
	b	Less: direct expenses other than fundraising expenses	**6b**	
	c	Net income or (loss) from special events and activities (line 6a less line 6b)	**6c**	
	7a	Gross sales of inventory, less returns and allowances	**7a**	
	b	Less: cost of goods sold	**7b**	
	c	Gross profit or (loss) from sales of inventory (line 7a less line 7b)	**7c**	
	8	Other revenue (describe ► _____)	**8**	
	9	**Total revenue** (add lines 1, 2, 3, 4, 5c, 6c, 7c, and 8) . . . . ►	**9**	
Expenses	10	Grants and similar amounts paid (attach schedule)	**10**	
	11	Benefits paid to or for members	**11**	
	12	Salaries, other compensation, and employee benefits	**12**	
	13	Professional fees and other payments to independent contractors	**13**	
	14	Occupancy, rent, utilities, and maintenance	**14**	
	15	Printing, publications, postage, and shipping	**15**	
	16	Other expenses (describe ► _____)	**16**	
	17	**Total expenses** (add lines 10 through 16) . . . . ►	**17**	
Net Assets	18	Excess or (deficit) for the year (line 9 less line 17)	**18**	
	19	Net assets or fund balances at beginning of year (from line 27, column (A)) (must agree with end-of-year figure reported on prior year's return)	**19**	
	20	Other changes in net assets or fund balances (attach explanation)	**20**	
	21	Net assets or fund balances at end of year (combine lines 18 through 20) . . . . . . ►	**21**	

Part II Balance Sheets—If Total assets on line 25, column (B) are $250,000 or more, file Form 990 instead of Form 990-EZ.

	(See page 39 of the instructions.)		**(A)** Beginning of year		**(B)** End of year
22	Cash, savings, and investments			**22**	
23	Land and buildings			**23**	
24	Other assets (describe ► _____)			**24**	
25	**Total assets**			**25**	
26	**Total liabilities** (describe ► _____)			**26**	
27	**Net assets or fund balances** (line 27 of column (B) **must** agree with line 21) . .			**27**	

For Paperwork Reduction Act Notice, see the separate instructions.   Cat. No. 10642I   Form **990-EZ** (2002)

Form 990-EZ (2002)   Page **2**

Part III	**Statement of Program Service Accomplishments** (See page 39 of the instructions.)	**Expenses**

What is the organization's primary exempt purpose? _____
Describe what was achieved in carrying out the organization's exempt purposes. In a clear and concise manner, describe the services provided, the number of persons benefited, or other relevant information for each program title.

(Expenses — Required for 501(c)(3) and (4) organizations and 4947(a)(1) trusts; optional for others.)

28 ....
....
_____ (Grants $ _____) | **28a** |

29 ....
....
_____ (Grants $ _____) | **29a** |

30 ....
....
_____ (Grants $ _____) | **30a** |

31 Other program services (attach schedule) . . . . (Grants $ _____) | **31a** |

32 Total program service expenses (add lines 28a through 31a) . . . . ▶ | **32** |

Part IV	**List of Officers, Directors, Trustees, and Key Employees** (List each one even if not compensated. See page 40 of the instructions.)

(A) Name and address	**(B)** Title and average hours per week devoted to position	**(C)** Compensation (If not paid, enter -0-.)	**(D)** Contributions to employee benefit plans & deferred compensation	**(E)** Expense account and other allowances
....				
....				
....				

Part V	**Other Information** (Note the attachment requirement in General Instruction V, page 14.)	**Yes**	**No**

33 Did the organization engage in any activity not previously reported to the IRS? If "Yes," attach a detailed description of each activity . .

34 Were any changes made to the organizing or governing documents but not reported to the IRS? If "Yes," attach a conformed copy of the changes.

35 If the organization had income from business activities, such as those reported on lines 2, 6, and 7 (among others), but **not** reported on Form 990-T, attach a statement explaining your reason for not reporting the income on Form 990-T.

  a Did the organization have unrelated business gross income of $1,000 or more or 6033(e) notice, reporting, and proxy tax requirements?

  b If "Yes," has it filed a tax return on **Form 990-T** for this year? . . . .

36 Was there a liquidation, dissolution, termination, or substantial contraction during the year? (If "Yes," attach a statement.)

37a Enter amount of political expenditures, direct or indirect, as described in the instructions. ▶ | **37a** |

  b Did the organization file **Form 1120-POL** for this year? . . . .

38a Did the organization borrow from, or make any loans to, any officer, director, trustee, or key employee **or** were any such loans made in a prior year and still unpaid at the start of the period covered by this return? . . . .

  b If "Yes," attach the schedule specified in the line 38 instructions and enter the amount involved. | **38b** |

39 *501(c)(7) organizations.* Enter: **a** Initiation fees and capital contributions included on line 9 | **39a** |

  b Gross receipts, included on line 9, for public use of club facilities . . . . | **39b** |

40a *501(c)(3) organizations.* Enter: Amount of tax imposed on the organization during the year under: section 4911 ▶ _____ ; section 4912 ▶ _____ ; section 4955 ▶ _____

  b *501(c)(3) and (4) organizations.* Did the organization engage in any section 4958 excess benefit transaction during the year or did it become aware of an excess benefit transaction from a prior year? If "Yes," attach an explanation. . . . .

  c Amount of tax imposed on organization managers or disqualified persons during the year under 4912, 4955, and 4958 ▶ _____

  d Enter: Amount of tax on line 40c, above, reimbursed by the organization . . . . ▶ _____

41 List the states with which a copy of this return is filed. ▶ _____

42 The books are in care of ▶ .... Telephone no. ▶ (___) _____
Located at ▶ .... ZIP + 4 ▶ _____

43 *Section 4947(a)(1) nonexempt charitable trusts filing Form 990-EZ in lieu of* **Form 1041**—Check here ▶ ☐
and enter the amount of tax-exempt interest received or accrued during the tax year . . . ▶ | **43** |

Please Sign Here

Under penalties of perjury, I declare that I have examined this return, including accompanying schedules and statements, and to the best of my knowledge and belief, it is true, correct, and complete. Declaration of preparer (other than officer) is based on all information of which preparer has any knowledge.

▶ _____   _____
Signature of officer   Date

_____
Type or print name and title.

Paid Preparer's Use Only	Preparer's signature ▶	Date	Check if self-employed ▶ ☐	Preparer's SSN or PTIN (See Gen. Inst. W)
	Firm's name (or yours if self-employed), address, and ZIP + 4 ▶		EIN ▶	
			Phone no. ▶ ( )	

✪   Form **990-EZ** (2002)

REFERENCES

American Institute of Certified Public Accountants. (1967). *Audits of Voluntary Health and Welfare Organizations*. New York: author

American Institute of Certified Public Accountants. (1974). *Audits of Voluntary Health and Welfare Organizations*. New York: author.

American Institute of Certified Public Accountants .(1998), Statement of Position 98-3, *Audits of States, Local Governments, and Not-for-profit Organizations Receiving Federal Awards*. New York: author.

Financial Accounting Standards Board. (1980). *Objectives of Financial Reporting by Nonbusiness Organizations*. Statement of Financial Reporting Concepts No. 4, Stamford, CT: Author.

Financial Accounting Standards Board. (1987). *Statement of Financial Accounting Standards No. 95: Statement of Cash Flows*. Norwalk, CT: author.

Financial Accounting Standards Board (1993). *Statement of Financial Accounting Standards No. 117: Financial Statements of Not-for-profit Organizations*. Norwalk, CT: author.

Fraser, L.M. & Ormiston, A. (2001). *Understanding Financial Statements (6th Edition)*. Upper Saddle River, NJ: Prentice-Hall, Inc.

Freeman, Robert J. & Shoulders, Craig D. (1999). *Governmental and Nonprofit Accounting* (6th ed.). Upper Saddle River, NJ: Prentice-Hall, Inc.

Kay, R. S. & Seafoss, D. G. (Eds.) (1995). *Handbook of Accounting and Auditing* (2nd Edition). Boston: Warren, Gorham & Lamont.

National Health Council, National Assembly of National Voluntary Health and Social Welfare Organizations, Inc., United Way of America. (1974). *Standards of Accounting and Financial Reporting for Voluntary Health and Welfare Organizations*. New York: author.

National Health Council, the National Assembly of Health and Human Service Organizations & the United Way of America. (1988). *Standards of Accounting and Financial Reporting for Voluntary Health and Welfare Organizations (Revised 3rd Edition)*. New York: National Health Council, Inc.

National Health Council, Inc. & the National Assembly of Health and Human Service Organizations. (1998). *Standards of Accounting and Financial Reporting for Voluntary Health and Welfare Organizations* (4th Ed.). Dubuque, Iowa: Kendall/Hunt Publishing Co.

Office of Management and Budget, *OMB Circular A-133, Audits of States, Local Governments, and Non-Profit Organizations* (revised June 24, 1997). Washington, D.C.

Racek, T. J. (1982). Nonprofit accounting and financial reporting. In T. D. Connors (Ed.), *The Nonprofit Organization Handbook* (pp.6–3 to 6–46). New York: AMACOM.

United Way of America. (1974). *Accounting and Financial Reporting: A Guide for United Ways and Not-for Profit Human Service Organizations*. Alexandria, VA: author.

U.S. Department of the Treasury. Internal Revenue Service.

Williams, J.R. (1999). *The 1999 Miller GAAP Guide: Restatement and Analysis of Current FASB Standards*. New York: Harcourt Brace & Co.

INTERNET RESOURCES

Alliance for Nonprofit Management. http://www.allianceonline.org

Guidestar website that is a repository of nonprofit 990's as well as other information: http://www.guidestar.org

IRS website: http://www.irs.ustreas.gov

Quality 990: a website trying to improve the quality of 990 reporting: http://www.qual990.org

The Urban Institute, National Center for Charitable Statistics (NCCS): http://www.nccsdataweb.urban.org/

Website for filing Form 990 electronically: http://efile.form990.org

Chapter Thirteen

FINANCIAL STATEMENT AUDITS AND ANALYSIS

After reading this chapter you should be able to:

1. Understand the audit function;
2. Have an understanding of the types of financial information that can be gleaned from financial statements;
3. Use ratios and other techniques to analyze financial statements.

AUDITS OF FINANCIAL STATEMENTS

After a nonprofit has prepared its financial statements, it is required by law in many states to have a periodic check or "audit" of its records by an accountant. In many cases, the accountant must be a Certified Public Accountant (CPA) who will examine agency records and render an opinion as whether the agency's financial statements fairly represent its financial position. "The auditor's purpose in performing an audit is to render a report expressing his or her opinion that the financial statements present fairly the financial position, results of operations, and, where appropriate, cash flows of the organization" (Wilson et al., 2001, p. 506).

In addition to this opinion, the auditor will attach notes to the financial statements that give fuller explanations, if needed, to any of the financial transactions presented in the statements. Nonprofit human service organizations are generally required to have an annual audit by a number of different oversight bodies, such as state attorneys general who enforce laws regulating nonprofit corporations, funding sources, and, for those agencies receiving federal funds, the federal government. As mentioned previously, the AICPA issued guidelines for audits of nonprofits for the first time in 1968. These guidelines have been updated a few times; the latest guidelines are called *Statement of Position (SOP) 98-3, Audits of Not-for-profit Organizations Receiving Federal Awards.* These guidelines were issued as a guide to auditors to help them make sure that the nonprofits they audited were in compliance with federal government requirements.

Many nonprofit human service organizations receive federal funds, indeed, for some, federal funding is the major source of support. In light of this, the Federal Office of Management and Budget (OMB, 1997) has also issued guidelines for audits of agencies receiving federal funds. Nonprofits expending more than $300,000 or more in a fiscal year are subject to what is called the Single Audit Act (P.L. 104–156) and OMB Circular A-133. For those organizations, there are two different types of audits they may have:

- *A single audit:* includes an audit of the organization's financial statements as well as a reporting on expenditures of federal awards and a compliance audit.
- *A program specific audit:* for organizations that have only one program expending federal award monies.

The auditor is required by Circular A-133 to produce four types of reports. These reports are: an audit opinion (or disclaimer of opinion); a report on internal control; a report on compliance; and a schedule of findings and questioned costs (see Reading 13-1).

In an audit, the auditor does not examine every recorded transaction in the books; rather he or she selectively tests transactions and internal controls to form an opinion as to the fairness of the representation of the financial statements. The auditor looks at a random representative sample of the transactions, but there are two tests the auditor cannot omit:

- *Confirmation of accounts receivable:* this involves contacting those owing money and asking them to confirm that they do. This is especially important if the agency shows a large amount of pledges receivable.
- *Observation of physical inventories:* this involves checking the existence of the inventory to make sure that assets are not overstated (Gross et al., 1995).

Even though to some an audit may appear to be a nuisance, there are some benefits to be gained from it. Some of these benefits are:

- The audit lends credibility to the financial statements of the agency.
- The auditor can provide assistance in the preparation of statements so that they meaningfully reflect the monetary transactions of the agency.

- The auditor can provide advice on developing internal controls.
- The auditor can help the agency meet its legal requirements for compliance as well as in tax reporting (Gross et al., 1995).

Types of Audit Opinions

After the auditor has examined the agency's books, he or she will write an audit opinion. Depending on the individual circumstances of the agency, there are four types of formal opinions that the auditor may write (Gross et al., 1995):

Unqualified Opinion

An unqualified opinion is given if the auditor thinks that the financial statements were prepared in accordance with generally accepted accounting principles and accurately reflect the financial position of the agency, its operations and changes in net assets (see Reading 13-2).

Qualified Opinion

A qualified opinion is given in those cases in which the auditor thinks that there are certain aspects of the financial statements that vary from generally accepted accounting principles, yet are not material enough to require an adverse opinion.

Disclaimer of Opinion

A disclaimer of opinion may be given when the auditor is not satisfied with the statements. This may occur for a number of reasons, for example, the auditor was not able to examine sufficient documentary evidence, or not able to contact donors to verify pledges receivable, and so forth.

Adverse Opinion

An adverse opinion is given when the auditor thinks that the agency's financial statements are not a fair reflection of its financial position and were not prepared in accordance with generally accepted accounting principles.

In the end, the responsibility for accurate records prepared in accordance with generally accepted accounting principles rests with the agency, its administrator and board of directors. As officers of the agency, the board may be legally liable for any mishandling of funds. Therefore, it is in the best interest of everyone concerned–board, administration, staff, and clients–that a CPA knowledgeable in non-profit accounting conduct an annual audit, whether or not it is required by the state.

In addition to knowing which financial statements are required by state, federal and other funding authorities, to achieve maximum usefulness from the statements one must have an idea of how to interpret them according to one's own needs. In the next section of this chapter, methods of analyzing financial statements will be discussed.

ANALYSIS OF FINANCIAL STATEMENTS

Financial statements provide neutral information, that is, in and of itself, the information is neither good nor bad. Thus, it is only within the context of the agency, and the analyses applied to the statements, that value inferences may be made. Users of financial statements have a need for financial information that can be classified into four main categories: questions regarding 1) fiscal compliance; 2) stewardship; 3) financial strength; and 4) operating efficiency (Ramanathan, 1982). In this section, discussion will center on how interested users can meet their information needs utilizing quantitative methods of analysis, especially regarding financial strength and operating efficiency.

Fiscal Compliance

Fiscal compliance refers to whether or not the agency is complying with the regulations, laws, guidelines, and rules of its funding sources as well as those of governmental bodies. Questions regarding compliance address issues that are rather straightforward, for example, has the agency filed required reports and statements in a timely manner, in a format prescribed by the regulatory agency, and with the required information? Has the organization expended monies in the manner spelled out in its grant or contract? These and other compliance issues are of particular interest to the auditors of the organization's financial statements as well as funding sources and will certainly be addressed by them, as was discussed previously.

Table 13-1
PERCENT OF COSTS ALLOCATED

Formula	Source of Data
$\dfrac{\text{Program Expense}}{\text{Total Program Expense}}$	Statement of Functional Expenses

Stewardship

An agency may adhere to legal requirements and its funding guidelines and yet not benefit a single client. Stewardship, an important consideration, refers to whether or not the agency is really spending its money for its stated goals, and whether it is doing this in a way that is really benefiting its constituency. It is not here a question of costs with respect to benefits, or even of compliance. Rather, it is a question of the degree to which stated goals and priorities are reflected in actual spending distribution patterns.

One method that the user of financial reports can employ to measure spending priorities versus stated goals is to examine the Statement of Functional Expenses (SFE). In looking at the SFE, one can get an idea of the percentage of costs allocated for each program by turning the money spent for each program into a percentage of the total program expenses (see Table 13-1). To do this, one divides total amount spent for a program by total program expenses. In this instance, we are not counting support service expenses, only those expenses spent on programs. Thus, the percentage spent for each program is a reflection of organizational goals, stated or unstated.

For example, using the Statement of Functional Expenses presented in Chapter 12, we can see that the organization had expenses of $141,400 for Program A, $54,400 for Program B, $61,800 for Program C, and $257,800 for Program D. Thus, total program expenses (for Programs A, B, C, and D) for this organization amount to $515,400 and total expenses are $638,200. We can thus compute the following:

$$\text{Program A:} \quad \frac{\$141{,}400}{\$515{,}400} = 27.4\%$$
Total Program Expenses:

$$\text{Program B:} \quad \frac{\$\ 54{,}400}{\$515{,}400} = 10.6\%$$
Total Program Expenses

$$\text{Program C:} \quad \frac{\$\ 61{,}800}{\$515{,}400} = 12\%$$
Total Program Expenses

$$\text{Program D:} \quad \frac{\$257{,}800}{\$515{,}400} = 50\%$$
Total Program Expenses

This shows that 27.4% of total program expenses went to Program A, while 10.6% of expenses were for Program B, 12% went to Program C, and 50% went to Program D. This allocation of expenses should be compared with the agency's mission statement or statement of goals in its annual report. Such comparisons sometimes reveal that the organization is pursuing goals other than those stated, perhaps goals even unrelated to its main mission and original purpose, or that the priorities of goals have shifted. In such a case, the organization's board and administrators need to rethink or clarify its goals, or re-write its mission statement and goals to reflect its new reality. Otherwise, this contradictory evidence may be misleading to funders, clients, and other interested readers of the financial statements. Thus, stewardship is a managerial as well as a fiduciary function.

Financial Strength

Financial strength refers to whether the agency has adequate resources to carry out its mandated objectives, and whether its resources help it to maintain viability and flexibility of operations. Whether the agency has financial strength depends to some extent on the composition of its resources, for example, the liquidity of its assets, the extent to which funds are restricted, the degree of dependency on one or two major funding sources, and so forth. Some measures used to determine financial strength are the following:

Working Capital

As users of financial statements, creditors are interested in whether the agency has the ability to pay its bills on time. The ability to pay bills promptly is increased if the organization's cash and near-to-cash assets are high in comparison to current liabilities. Remember that **current assets** are cash, or liquid assets that can be converted to cash in one year or one operating cycle such as stocks, bonds, mutual funds, certificates of deposit (CD's), and so forth (Fraser, 1988). Pledges receivable also fall into this category. **Current liabilities,** on the other hand, are those monies owed by the agency that are due within one year or less. In order to assess working capital one must examine the Statement of Position (Balance Sheet). Working capital is found by subtracting current unrestricted liabilities from current unrestricted assets (See Table 13-2).

Table 13-2
WORKING CAPITAL

Formula

Current Unrestricted Assets–Current Unrestricted Liabilities

Source of Data

Statement of Financial Position

For example, in looking at the Statement of Position in Chapter 12, we can see that the agency reported the following current assets:

Cash and cash equivalents	$110,400
Marketable securities	121,500
Accounts receivable	122,600
Pledges receivable	58,900
Grants	152,800
Prepaid expenses	54,800
Total current assets	$794,800

The organization had a total of $794,800 in current unrestricted assets. The other assets listed in its Statement of Financial Position, fixed assets, usually includes land, buildings, and equipment and long-term investments. These are not considered current assets.

The agency also had the following current liabilities:

Accounts payable and accrued expenses	$39,300
Salaries and payroll taxes payable	41,600
Current portion of notes payable	3,200
Total current liabilities	$84,100

This organization had a total of $84,100 in current liabilities. Its other liability, Mortgage payable, is not considered a current liability. Thus, if we subtract the current assets from the current liabilities, we see that the organization has working capital of $710,700.

A high working capital figure is indicative of financial solvency, that is, of the ability of the nonprofit to pay its bills in a timely manner. However, a very high amount of working capital may be an indication that there are idle current assets that could either be put into existing programs, fixed assets, or income-producing investments.

Current Ratio

The current ratio is used in business frequently by credit and financial analysts to ascertain the risk of insolvency or bankruptcy. This ratio shows the ability of the agency to pay its bills from current funds.

Table 13-3
CURRENT RATIO

Formula	Source Of Data
Current Unrestricted Assets	Statement of Financial Position
Current Unrestricted Liabilities	

To find the current ratio, we must again examine the Statement of Financial Position and divide current unrestricted assets by current unrestricted liabilities (See Table 13-3).

Using the same figures for the current assets and current liabilities, we find that the current ratio for this organization is 9.5 to 1:

$$\frac{\$794,800}{\$\ 84,100} \ = \ 9.5$$

Traditionally, a ratio of 2 to 1 is considered adequate. An appropriate ratio is one adequate to meet current expenses, but a large surplus would be questionable. It may be the result of some unexpected large contribution, or grant. But a very high ratio would not necessarily be good, as with the working capital ratio, it may be reflective of idle assets that could be used for investment or programs.

Before a final conclusion from the analyses can be made, these figures should be compared with agency trends over time. Data from other agencies providing similar types of services would be useful as a way of comparing whether the figures are too high or too low. Working capital and the current ratio should only be interpreted after taking into account any restrictions on the use of current assets.

Unrestricted Net Assets Balance

It is desirable, although not always possible, for human service agencies to have an excess of revenues over expenses at the end of the fiscal year. If an organization does have an excess, it could be used to cover unanticipated expenses, revenue shortfalls, or anticipated increases in variable costs such as travel, utilities, or telephone. Unfortunately, some funders have policies that do not allow carryover of funds from one fiscal period to the next. These types of policies encourage inefficient use of funds, such as the common practice of expending all unused funds in the last quarter in order to avoid a decrease in funding in the next year.

In recent years, however, many allocation agencies have begun to recognize the importance of nonprofits having a "cushion" available for investment, for emergency needs, and so forth. On the other hand, nonprofits with a large amount of net assets at the end of the year should be

Table 13-4
UNRESTRICTED NET ASSETS BALANCE
Formula

Unrestricted Net Assets at Beginning of Year–Unrestricted Net Assets at End of Year

Source of Data

Statement of Activities

examined closely. Organizations with large accumulations of reserves (up to 20% of their annual budget) may tend to engage in another type of inefficiency, that is, the initiation or expansion of unneeded or duplicative services (Hall, 1982). Or a large reserve may reflect that an organization may not be responsive to meeting needs in its community.

To determine unrestricted net asset balance, examine the Statement of Activities. Subtract the unrestricted net assets at end of year from the unrestricted net assets at beginning of year (See Table 13-4).

In looking at the Statement of Activities from Chapter 12, no calculations are necessary as the change in unrestricted net assets are given in the Statement. The organization had an increase of $42,700 from the previous year. This Statement should be compared with those from previous years to determine trends. Has the amount of unrestricted net assets increased or decreased? An important trend to watch for is whether the organization's unrestricted net assets show a decline over a period of time. If it has decreased, see if you can ascertain why. This may indicate that an organization will have a difficult time if it is subject to budget cutbacks by funding sources.

Percent of Revenue/Public Support from Various Sources

In a time of declining availability of funds for human service agencies and programs, agencies that are dependent on only one or two funding sources are in a precarious financial position. Funding instability may result from dependency on too few funding sources. In addition, agencies with large amounts of restricted funds are in the situation of being less able to respond to necessary programmatic changes or client needs.

Many agencies are seeking to diversify their funding bases in order to avoid or minimize fiscal dependence. The degree of diversification of an agency can be measured by calculating the percentage each funding source represents of the total funding base. For example, what percentage of total revenue/public support is from government sources? From membership fees and contributions? From client fees? To find

Table 13-5

PERCENT OF REVENUES FROM VARIOUS SOURCES

Formula	Source of Data
$\dfrac{\text{Revenues from all Government Sources}}{\text{Total Public Support/Revenue}}$	Statement of Activities
$\dfrac{\text{Membership Dues}}{\text{Total Public Support/Revenue}}$	Same
$\dfrac{\text{Contributions}}{\text{Total Public Support/Revenue}}$	Same
$\dfrac{\text{Revenues from Client Fees}}{\text{Total Public Support/Revenue}}$	Same

these figures, examine the Statement of Activities and divide each source of support and revenue by total support and revenue (See Table 13-5).

For example, in reviewing the Statement of Activities one can see that the organization had a total of $243,350 in contributions, $28,400 in donations-in-kind, $17,600 in donated services and $83,500 in allocations from federated fundraising organizations. It also received $350,000 in revenues and grants from governmental agencies, the revenues probably in the form of contracts. In addition, it received $10,850 in program service fees, and the balance was from investment income and gains on long-term investments. It had no revenues from membership dues. Its total revenues were $768,300. Its contributions made up 31.7% of the total revenues, while governmental revenues and contracts made up 45.6%. As can be seen, 77.3% of revenues for this organization are from two sources.

$$\frac{\text{Contributions}}{\text{Total Revenue}} \quad \frac{\$243,350}{\$768,300} \; = \; 31.7\%$$

$$\frac{\text{Donations in-kind}}{\text{Total Revenue}} \quad \frac{\$\ 28,400}{\$768,300} \; = \; 3.7\%$$

$$\frac{\text{Allocations}}{\text{Total Revenue}} \quad \frac{\$\ 83,500}{\$768,300} \; = \; 10.9\%$$

$$\frac{\text{Governmental agencies}}{\text{Total Revenue}} \quad \frac{\$350,000}{\$768,300} \; = \; 45.6\%$$

These percentages will tell the reader to what extent the agency is being funded from any one source, and how potentially unstable its funding base may be. For example, if 50 percent or more of revenue from client fees is from clients who are on Medicaid, this could be a warning signal as federal changes may affect a significant portion of the organization's revenues. If over 80 percent of revenue comes from government sources, this should also be a sign that the agency is in a potentially vulnerable position (Hall, 1982). The agency must then take steps and develop strategies to expand its funding base. In the example above, the organization receives a large amount of income from two sources and it may want to review its vulnerability in this area.

Operating Cash Flow (OCF) Ratio

Some have said that cash flow information is more reliable than either Statement of Financial Position (SFP) or Statement of Activities (SOA) information because the SFP just reflects one point in time and the SOA is subject to many subjective choices (Mills & Yamamura, 1998). Thus, the cash flow statement reflects the changes in the other statements and focuses on cash available for operations. One ratio that is presumed to be a more accurate depiction of an organization's ability to meet its current liabilities is the operating cash flow (OCF) ratio. The formula for this ratio is: net cash from operating activities divided by current liabilities (see Table 13-6). While one would obtain the net unrestricted cash figure from the Cash Flow Statement, the amount of current liabilities must be obtained from the Statement of Financial Position.

Table 13-6
OPERATING CASH FLOW (OCF) RATIO

Formula	Source of Data
Net Cash From Operating Activities	Cash Flow Statement
Current Liabilities	Statement of Financial Position

In looking at the Cash Flow Statement from Chapter 12, one can see that the organization had $20,200 of net cash used by operating activities. In looking at the Statement of Financial Position, the organization had current liabilities of $84,100. If we divide the net cash by the current liabilities, we find that the agency has an operating cash flow ratio of less than 1:

$$\frac{\text{Net cash}}{\text{Current liabilities}} \quad \frac{\$20,200}{\$84,100} \quad = \quad .24$$

An OCF ratio of 2.0 means that an organization has enough cash to cover its current liabilities twice over, while an OCF ratio of less than 1.0 means that an organization is not receiving enough cash to meet its current financial commitments. The resulting ratio should still be viewed within the context of other similar type nonprofit organizations.

Operating Efficiency

Operating efficiency refers to how much unrestricted money was obtained by the agency during the report period, how successful the agency has been in diversifying its funding base, the proportion of costs allocated to programs as opposed to administrative or other support costs, how reasonable the costs of operations are, personnel costs per client, and other sorts of similar measures. Some tests to measure operating efficiency are the following:

Support Test

As you know, the main purpose of human service organizations is to provide services. It is important to be able to measure the efficiency of these services. One way to do this is to compare the percentage of resources used for agency programs to the percentage used for administrative and fundraising (support services) on the Statement of Functional Expenses. To do this we divide total support services by total expenses. The resulting figure is called the support test (see Table 13-7).

Table 13-7
SUPPORT TEST

Formula	Source of Data
$\dfrac{\text{Total Support Service Expenses}}{\text{Total Expenses}}$	Statement of Functional Expenses

As we saw previously in the Statement of Functional Expenses, the total expenses for this organization are $638,200 while the total support service expenses (management and general and fund-raising) are $122,800. If we divide total support service expenses by total expenses, we find that these support services are 19.2% of the total expenses and conversely, 80.8% of expenses are for programs:

$$\frac{\text{Total support service expenses}}{\text{Total Expenses}} \quad \frac{\$122,200}{\$638,200} \quad = \quad 19.2\%$$

There is no set number that is considered good or bad; generally, the higher the percentage used for program activities, the more efficient the agency. In some cases, a funding source may have a guideline that is used in evaluating agencies, for example it may expect no more than 15–20% of expenses to be utilized for support services. But the support figure must also be viewed in terms of past agency performance, that is, what do the trends show? It must further be viewed in relation to the percentages of other agencies that provide similar services.

Personnel Costs Per Client Served

Personnel costs are the largest expense in the human service organization budget; in fact, some have estimated the percentage to be as high as 80 percent (Hall, 1982). Just as in the health field, the rising costs of providing human services may be partly attributed to rising labor costs. That factor aside, many human service interventions tend to be very labor intensive and often involve staff with advanced degrees. In looking at personnel costs in relation to clients served, one can get an indication of an organization's pattern of growth as well as its efficiency in use of personnel (this formula was discussed in Chapter Nine, Internal Control). If the number of employees is rising this may simply indicate agency expansion or program growth. But if the number of employees is rising in relation to clients served, there are some questions that need to be addressed such as: why is the ratio of personnel to clients increasing? Are the additional personnel identified as program or support staff? What activities are taking place in the agency to account for the change? Has the ratio of program personnel to support personnel changed as well? These questions need to be answered in order to evaluate management practices and organizational efficiency. Of course, they need to be addressed within the context of the long-term plans and goals of the agency as well as current events, such as changes in licensing or staff-client ratio requirements.

Net Asset Mix

An important financial objective is to be able to maintain or increase flexibility in financial operations, to have sufficient current unrestricted operating monies to move where needed quickly. To be able to do this, an agency needs unrestricted assets as a large proportion of total net assets. This may be called asset mix. To measure asset mix, divide current unrestricted assets by total net assets (See Table 13-8).

In examining the Statement of Financial Position in Chapter 12, we

Table 13-8
NET ASSET MIX

Formula	Source of Data
Current Unrestricted Assets / Total Net Assets	Statement of Financial Position

find that this organization has total net assets of $852,500. It also has unrestricted net assets of $794,800. In dividing the unrestricted net assets by the total net assets we see that the asset mix is 93.2%:

$$\frac{\text{Current unrestricted net assets}}{\text{Total net assets}} \quad \frac{\$794,800}{\$852,500} = 93.2\%$$

This organization has a high asset mix. Over ninety-three percent (93.2%) of its assets are available in case it needs to shift funds. A high percentage of current unrestricted assets, for example over 65 percent, would show that the agency has adequate financial flexibility, that is, the organization's ability to respond to short-term needs. However, any asset mix figure must be viewed in relation to past trends within the agency, figures of other agencies offering similar services, as well as current events.

Some have said that quantitative indicators do serve some purposes for interested users, but they must be used sparingly in a careful manner (Drtina, 1982; Hairston, 1985). First of all, not all human service agencies use the same accounting format, although most do use accrual accounting. But they may have somewhat different methods of allocating program costs. This creates problems in trying to compare agencies on some of the measures discussed above. Secondly, applying business ratios to nonprofits is questionable because "neither the range of ratios nor the trends that different types of voluntary agencies exhibit are known" (Hairston, 1985, p. 80). Thirdly, it must be reiterated that these indicators do not measure quality or effectiveness of services.

Quality and effectiveness measures are part of program evaluation and cannot be gleaned from reviewing financial statements. However, financial information is important for planning and decision-making. Some of the measures used here can help users evaluate whether or not a nonprofit has the ability to maintain or increase services at a given level, adapt to a changing funding environment, and creatively adjust to changing socioeconomic and political conditions in its environment by being able to modify its patterns of resource acquisition, allocation, investment, reporting, and service provision.

READING 13-1: Excerpts from *OMB Circular A-133, Audits of States, Local Governments, and Non-Profit Organizations* (revised June 24, 1997). Below are guidelines as to what tasks an auditor should perform in auditing a program receiving federal funds. These include:

1. "Perform an audit of the financial statement(s) for the Federal program in accordance with GAGAS" [generally accepted government auditing standards issued by the Comptroller General of the United States].

2. Obtain an understanding of internal control and perform tests of internal control over the Federal program . . .

3. Performing procedures to determine whether the auditee has complied with laws, regulations, and the provisions of contracts or grant agreements that could have a direct and material effect on the Federal program. . . .

4. Follow up on prior audit findings . . .

5. The auditor's report(s) may be in the form of either combined or separate reports. . . . The . . . report(s) shall state that the audit was conducted in accordance with this part and include the following:

   a. An opinion (or disclaimer of opinion) as to whether the financial statements of the Federal program is presented fairly in all material aspects in conformity with the stated accounting policies;

   b. A report on internal control related to the Federal program, which shall describe the scope of testing of internal control and the result of the tests;

   c. A report on compliance which includes an opinion (or disclaimer of opinion) as to whether the auditee complied with laws, regulations, and the provisions of contracts or grant agreements which could have a direct and material effect on the Federal program; and

   d. A schedule of findings and questioned costs for the Federal program that includes a summary of the auditor's results relative to the Federal program. . . " (OMB A-133, Subpart B, (§_.235).

Reading 13-2: Auditor's Unqualified Opinion

Below is a typical unqualified opinion issued by an auditor regarding a nonprofit's financial statements. Also included in the report is the auditor's opinion about the organization's internal control over its financial reporting and compliance with laws and regulations regarding its governmental contracts and grants. This report would typically be placed at the beginning of the report, before the actual financial statements:

To the Board of Trustees
Human Services Organization, Inc.

INDEPENDENT AUDITOR'S REPORT

We have audited the accompanying statement of financial position of Human Services Organization, Inc. (a nonprofit organization) as of June 30, 2011 and the related statements of activities, functional expenses, and cash flows for the year then ended. These financial statements are the responsibility of Human Services Organization, Inc.'s management. Our responsibility is to express an opinion on these financial statements based on our audit.

We conducted our audit in accordance with auditing standards generally accepted in the United States of America and the standards applicable to financial audits contained in *Government Auditing Standards,* issued by the Comptroller General of the United States. These standards require that we plan and perform the audit to obtain reasonable assurance about whether the financial statements are free of material misstatement. An audit includes examining, on a test basis, evidence supporting the amounts and disclosures in the financial statements. An audit also includes assessing the accounting principles used and significant estimates made by management, as well as evaluating overall financial statement presentation. We believe that our audit provides a reasonable basis for our opinion.

In our opinion, the financial statements referred to above present fairly, in all material aspects, the financial position of Human Services Organization, Inc. as of June 30, 2011, and the changes in its net assets and in its cash flows for the year then ended in conformity with accounting principles generally accepted in the United States of America.

In accordance with *Government Auditing Standards,* we have also issued our reports dated September 30, 2011 on our consideration of Human Services Organization, Inc.'s internal control over financial reporting and our tests of its compliance with certain provisions of laws, regulations, contracts, and grants. Those reports are an integral part of an audit performed in accordance with *Governmental Auditing Standards* and should be read in conjunction with this report in considering the results of our audit.

The audit was performed for the purpose of forming an opinion on the basic financial statements of Human Services Organization, Inc. taken as a whole. The accompanying schedules of expenditures of federal and state awards are presented for purposes of additional analyses as required by U.S. Office of Management and Budget Circular A-133, *Audits of States, Local Governments, and Non-Profit Organizations,* and are not a required part of the basic financial statements. Such information has been subjected to the auditing procedures applied in the audit of the basic financial statements and, in our opinion, is fairly stated, in all material aspects, in relation to the basic financial statements taken as a whole.

Smith & Co.
Certified Public Accountants
September 30, 2011

REFERENCES

American Institute of Certified Public Accountants. (1998), *Statement of Position 98-3: Audits of States, Local Governments, and Not-for-profit Organizations Receiving Federal Awards.* New York: author.

Drtina, R.E. (1982). *The Executive's Accounting Primer.* New York: McGraw-Hill, 1982.

Fraser, L.M. (1988). U*nderstanding Financial Statements* (2nd edition). Englewood Cliffs, NJ: Prentice-Hall,Inc.

Fraser, L.M. & Ormiston, A. (2001). *Understanding Financial Statements* (6th Edition). Upper Saddle River, NJ: Prentice-Hall, Inc.

Gross, M. J. Jr., Larkin, R.F., Bruttomesso, R.S. & McNally, J.J. (1995). *Financial and Accounting Guide for Not-for-profit Organizations* (5th ed.). New York: John Wiley & Sons, Inc.

Hall, M. D. (1982). Financial condition: a measure of human service organizational performance. *New England Journal of Human Services,* 2(1):25–34.

Hairston, C. F. (1985). Using ratio analysis for financial accountability. *Social Casework: The Journal of Contemporary Social Work,* 66:76–82.

Mills, J. R. & Yamamura, J. H. (1998). The power of cash flow ratios. *Journal of Accountancy,* 184(10), Online Issues. www.aicpa.org/pubs/jofa/oct98/mills.htm

Office of Management and Budget (OMB). (1997 Revised). *OMB Circular A-133, Audits of States, Local Governments, and Non-Profit Organizations.* Washington, DC.

Ramanathan, K. (1982). *Management Control in Nonprofit Organizations.* New York: John Wiley.

United States General Accounting Office, Comptroller General of the United States, *Government Auditing Standards* (2003 Revision). Washington, DC

Wilson, E.R., Kattelus, S.C. & Hay, L.E. (2201). *Accounting for Governmental and Non-profit Entities*. Boston: McGraw-Hill/ Irwin.

INTERNET RESOURCES

General Considerations When Planning an Audit. ttp://www.nonprofits.org/npofaq/19/25.html

Office of Management and Budget. http://www.whitehouse.gov/omb

Government Auditing Standards (The Yellow Book). http://www.gao.gov/govaud/yb2003.pdf

Chapter Fourteen

FINANCIAL INFORMATION SYSTEMS

After reading this chapter you should be able to:

1. Understand the functions of a financial information system;
2. Understand the systems development process;
3. Make acquisition/upgrade decisions regarding an organization's information system;
4. Develop the criteria for acquiring or upgrading a system.

INTRODUCTION

"The term *information system* suggests the use of computer technology in an organization to provide information to users. A 'computer-based' information system is a collection of computer harware and software designed to transform data into useful information" (Bodnar & Hopwood, 1995, p. 4). Financial information systems (FIS) are part of the formal information system of an organization; their purpose is to provide data of a financial nature for decision-making and reporting. They are a comparatively recent phenomenon in small human service agencies, spurred by the proliferation of microcomputers. There are many functions that a computer system can perform, but the easiest and simplest are in the area of financial management.

The necessity of mechanizing financial applications such as payroll, inventory, and bookkeeping was often the primary reason for computer acquisition by business organizations and these functions were among the first to be computerized. The desire to automate the financial information system, including accounting, financial reporting, fundraising, and data base management, is often the primary reason that computers are sought by human service organizations.

The kinds of information that a financial management system is concerned with concern all aspects of the agency's activities that can be expressed in monetary terms. "The basis of the financial information system is the flow of dollars throughout the organization . . . "

(Ross, 1976, p. 131). Although most of the data used in a financial information system are historical and internal in nature, a good computer package should be able to provide future projections and simulations if so desired by an organization. The difficulty in converting from a manual to an automated system or upgrading an existing computer system is in designing and/or finding the types of sophisticated programs that will make the computer system a real management tool for planning, operation, and development rather than just a rapid data processor and record keeper. There are three main functions of a financial information system for nonprofit human service organizations:

- To receive and process data regarding the financial activities of the organization in an efficient manner.
- To provide information that will be useful to decision-makers. There are internal and internal users of this information. Internal users of the outputs of the FIS include administrators and boards of directors. Thus an internal informational function is to provide quantitative measures of the organization's performance for purposes of planning, evaluating, and controlling the resources used by the organization.

    External users of the outputs include funding sources, regulatory bodies, community constituencies, and the public at large. An external information system function is thus to provide information of a financial nature to outside funding sources and the public at large for purposes of accountability and fund raising.

- To provide adequate controls so that data and organizational assets are secured (Romney et al., 1997).

In this chapter, an overview of financial information systems will be presented as they apply to the nonprofit human service organization. The discussion presented is meant for the human service manager and staff. Therefore, there will be very little discussion of the technical aspects of computers; that information may be found elsewhere. Rather, this chapter tries to focus on helping professionals make acquisition/upgrade decisions based on some rational criteria, the two most obvious being *cost* and ***product.*** That is, how much will this system cost the organization and what types of products can be expected from a system? Other topics in this chapter include choosing computer consultants and packages. The type of computer system to be discussed revolves around the microcomputer, as they have the speed and storage capacity needed by most organizations. Again, the aim is not to make the reader a computer expert, but rather an informed user.

It must be remembered that computerizing or upgrading an organization's financial information system is not an answer to any of its management or financial problems. There are many things a computer system can do, but one of the things it cannot do is improve an inefficient system. If the organization's financial and accounting system is not very good in its present form, it will be no better computerized except that it will do what it is programmed to do faster.

There is an expression in the computer field: GIGO (garbage in, garbage out), which means that if the data entered into the computer is not good, incomplete, or inaccurate, it will come out the same way. Everyone has heard of various errors blamed on the computer, but a computer just processes what it is given by humans to do. Organizations should bear this in mind in contemplating a new or upgraded computer system, and should be prepared to do the necessary thinking and planning to make it work effectively.

SYSTEMS DEVELOPMENT DECISIONS

The planning and implementation of a computerized information system, of which the financial system may be only a part, is a long, time-consuming process that involves almost everyone in the organization if it is to be successful. The successful implementation of a new system involves commitment of top management to supply the necessary resources, as well as hard thinking on the part of the organization regarding needs, goals, and uses.

Even after an analysis of alternative types of systems, and the acquisition of a system, there is still much work to be done. For a period of time, the old system and the new system have to be run simultaneously to "de-bug" the system. This may entail extra work for staff and they have to be prepared for this. Thus, there may be a long lag time between decision to acquire a computer system, and the actual and final total conversion to the new system.

The decision to acquire or upgrade a computer system in the human service agency involves some initial analysis, study, and planning before the agency even decides whether it should buy, rent, or lease a computer. Some steps in the systems development process include:

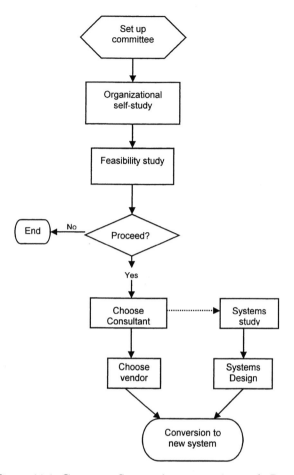

Figure 14-1: Computer System Acquisition/upgrade Process

1) setting up a systems committee; 2) organizational self-study; 3) feasibility study; 4) choosing a consultant; 5) systems study; 6) designing the system; 7) selecting a vendor; 8) conversion of system (see Figure 14-1).

Setting Up Systems Committee

The setting up of a systems committee is a crucial first step in acquiring/upgrading a computerized system. The committee should be made up of board members, administrative staff, and line staff as well. It is important for staff to be involved all along in the decisions to be made in the acquisition/upgrade process. If staff have no input, they will very likely be resistant to the new system, or resistant to filling out the necessary forms that need to be entered in order to be able to generate reports for management and funding sources. Increased performance and improved user attitudes have been found when accounting information system users provide suggestions in a group setting to system developers (Hunton & Gibson, 1999).

The role of the computer committee may be an advisory one in which it may make recommendations for the system. In other cases, the committee may be authorized to make major decisions regarding the acquisition and installation of a new/upgraded computerized system. The committee will represent the agency throughout the process, and in order for it to be effective, staff workloads need to be adjusted so that time is available for the necessary work to be done in the process (Schoech et al., 1981).

Organizational Self-study

Agency staff and board need to do some organizational analysis in order to determine the necessity of upgrading the current information system. For example, are there problems in the processing of data now? Does it take too long for routine records and reports to be processed and received by decision-makers? Is the agency growing faster than its ability to process transactions, so that staff are constantly behind schedule? Does the agency have long-term goals and objectives that include expansion of services, necessitating a new system?

In thinking about the acquisition or upgrade of a computer system, staff must be clear about what they want a computer for and what they want the system to do. Knowing what the computer system is to do for the organization is a crucial question to be answered. Some functions that computers may perform are simple ones such as mathematical and statistical calculations; other functions of a more intermediate nature include such things as word processing, spread sheet applications, and data processing of bookkeeping functions; more complex functions would involve interactive or simulation-type programs.

It is imperative to remember that a computer does not solve organizational problems of efficiency, rather computers perform functions. "The largest mistake made during the implementation of a new accounting system . . . is to redesign the new system to work in the old environment. This is often done without a thorough examination of the effectiveness of existing procedures and an evaluation of where best practices can optimally be employed" (Honig, 1999, p. 5). Acquiring a computer system is not a solution; rather a computer is a tool to be used to solve problems. To be effective, the software that runs the computer system must be able to handle the types of data processing and report generating that organizations can use. Acquiring a system entails hard thinking and planning on the part of the agency staff.

Some questions that have to be answered in planning a new system or upgrading an existing system are:

- What are the information needs of the agency now and in the foreseeable future? Knowing the current and future information needs of the organization is an important issue that needs to be addressed. That is, considering the flow of data in the organization at present, how could a new or upgraded system increase efficiency and/or productivity?
- What are the shortcomings of our current information system?
- What information is not being generated now or takes too long to generate now?
- Does the organization have the type of staff needed to be able to generate organization information efficiently and in a timely manner?
- Does the organization have the time and money to pay for staff training on a new system? The organization must review its willingness and ability to plan for a new system as well as train staff in using it.
- How is the information system being managed now and who will manage the new one?

Feasibility Study

While the organizational self-study is concerned with questions regarding the need for a new or upgraded information system, the feasibility study is concerned with issues regarding the agency's ability to plan for, design, pay for, and implement a new system. Thus, questions of feasibility ask whether a new system is practical, cost-effective, affordable, and able to be implemented successfully at the present time.

In terms of economic feasibility, there are a number of issues related to cost. There are equipment, personnel, development, and operating costs that will accrue to the organization as a result of the acquisition of a new or upgraded system (Schoech, 1985). Can the organization afford the initial upfront cost as well as long-term costs? Does the agency have the financial resources to fund the new or upgraded system as well as the capability to pay for the ongoing maintenance of the system? If it does not have the funds to pay for whatever arrangement is agreed upon (purchase, rental, lease), how will it pay for the system? If the system will be donated, can the agency afford the maintenance and training costs? Donated systems are both a blessing and a curse for small nonprofits. They need the technology on the one hand, but on the other hand, these donations lead to a strange mixture of office computers at different levels of technological capability that may not be compatible.

Another factor to be considered in the feasibility study is whether the organization has the space and personnel to use the computer system. If there are no staff who will know how to use the system, can the agency afford to retrain available staff or hire additional staff to use it? The final question that must be asked is: is this the right time for the organization to embark on this project, knowing the time and expense involved? If the answer is yes, the agency should proceed to the next step.

Choosing a Consultant

Since it is not very likely that many nonprofits have a staff or board member with the necessary expertise in designing and installing computer systems, the organization may have to hire a consultant. One of the problems in choosing a consultant is that most of them are not familiar with the particular needs of the nonprofit human service organization. And while they may have the technical expertise, consultants do not always have the ability to speak clearly and non-technically to computer novices. The danger in this is that there may be problems in communication between the agency and the consultant, resulting in a less than optimal product. Often the consultant may also be a vendor whose aim is not so much to design a system tailored to an organization's needs, but rather to sell computer systems. There are, thus, a number of questions that must be asked in choosing a consultant:

- What is the reputation/experience of the consultant? Reputation can be checked in several ways. One is by checking with the Better Business Bureau to see if there are any unresolved complaints filed against this person or company. This should also be done when screening vendors. Another way to screen a consultant is to check references. Even though references in and of themselves are not always meaningful, they supplement other sources. A third source of information would be other human service organizations that may have utilized the consultant.

- Has the consultant worked with other nonprofits? Are they satisfied with the resulting system? Ask others for the names of consultants who have provided satisfactory service in the planning and installation of computer systems.

After choosing a consultant, the organization should sign a short-term contract, and be specific about what the consultant will do in that time period. The contract should specify outcomes or results. Usually the organization should expect a systems study, a systems design, and some recommendations about hardware and software from a consultant. The consultant may or may not be involved in the actual purchasing of the equipment, but may help with systems installation. On the other hand, if the consultant is not a vendor, s/he may not be involved in the actual implementation of the system. This is because most vendors will not want to guarantee a system that they do not install.

Systems Study

In the systems analysis phase of the conversion process to a new or upgraded system, the consultant must answer a number of questions in order to design a system tailored to the specific needs of the human service organization. Some of the questions that need to be answered in the systems study include: What are the information needs of the organization? What documents are generated by the information system now? What documents does the agency need to be generated by the new system? Who is receiving information from the system now? Who else (key persons, departments, staff) needs to be receiving information from the system? What is the easiest way to capture data that could be used by more than one department for more than one application? What is the volume of processing? How much storage space (CD, tape, disk) does the organization need? What type of expansion capabilities are needed by the new system for future long-term needs?

Based on the consultant's findings to these and other questions regarding the present and future information needs of the organization, the consultant should submit a report detailing:

- Major assumptions used in analyzing the organization's system
- Major organizational/informational problems identified
- Performance requirements for the system (what it should do)
- Recommendations configuration of the system, i.e., hardware and software
- Projected costs and resources required to install the new system (Burch et al., 1979).

The consultant, in doing the systems study or analysis, will also conduct another kind of feasibility study. For the consultant will look at feasibility from a somewhat different view than the agency. That is, besides economic feasibility, the consultant will also be interested in technical and operational feasibility. The final result of the systems study will be a recommendation to proceed with the process, wait, or stop. If the agency decides to proceed, the next step is the design of the system.

Designing the System

Designing the system involves choosing a configuration to meet the current information needs of the agency with capabilities for future expansion as needed. The design of the system should be modular, flexible, simple, and involve all potential users in its preparation. Modular design means that one component of a system is implemented with success before other components are tried. There are a number of factors to take into account in the design of the system. Some of the factors are: hardware, software, human and control.

Hardware

Many people advise that a user should first decide what software s/he wants to run, and then buy the software that will run it. Buying hardware and software is more complex than that, for there are a number of factors that must be considered:

- **Compatibility:** refers to the type of operating system (OS) used by a computer system and whether it will be compatible with the software the organization desires to use. In general, it is better to have a system that is compatible with a wide range of software products so that some software packages may be used "off the shelf", for example, word-processing or mail list programs. Compatibility may also refer to other features of hardware, for example, the ability to attach peripherals such as printers, modems, scanners, video cameras, rewritable CD's and so forth. One of the problems that small nonprofits encounter is that they have donated computer equipment. So that in the design process the committee must decide what to do with a strange assortment of computers variously acquired and whether it is possible that they can be tied together through a LAN (local area network).

- **Capacity:** When microcomputers were first marketed for small-business and home use, they had very little storage capacity, i.e., 64K (kilobytes) or less. Nowadays, capacity is discussed in gigabyte terms. The first microcomputers had no hard disks, now there are hard disks with multi-gigabyte capacity. There are removable hard disks, zip drives, and rewritable CD's that give systems almost infinite capacity. The organization should always try to acquire a system with more capacity than it needs at present.

Software

A fund accounting package is a software program specifically designed to perform the types of accounting tasks unique to nonprofit organizations, that is, separate revenues, public support, and expenses by funds. In addition, it should be able to generate the special kinds of financial statements required for nonprofit human service organizations: The Statement of Position, Statement of Activities, Cash Flow Statement, and Statement of Functional Expenses.

The problem for human service organizations in the past has been not in acquiring hardware, but in acquiring software, or the programs to run the machines. This is because there were very few software accounting packages that were written to fit the unique requirements of the nonprofit human service organization. This left nonprofits with only a few options: 1) have someone write a program specifically for the organization; 2) try to modify an existing general accounting package; or 3) buy one of the few nonprofit accounting packages available.

Some organizations still pay for customized fund accounting programs, but it can be very costly and may not meet the agency's expectations. To successfully write such a program, the programmer(s) would have to be knowledgeable about not just programming, but also nonprofit accounting and nonprofit reporting requirements. How well the job is done depends on finding this unique person as well as being able to communicate agency needs to her/him.

Table 14-1
COMPARISON LIST OF FUND ACCOUNTING/FIS SOFTWARE

Feature	Software Name		
Tutorial provided			
Clear manuals			
Understandable menus			
Interactive program			
Flexible chart of accounts			
Easy to modify data			
Easy to correct mistakes			
Fund accounting			
Appropriate financial statements			
Financial ratios, other statistics			
Agency can design format			
Summarizes data			
Integrated package			
Periodic reports			
Variance budgeting			
Funder accounting			

If nonprofit staff tried to modify an existing general accounting package, its success would depend on whether there were staff with the expertise to do it, or whether it would have to hire someone. If the organization had to hire someone, it would have some of the same problems mentioned above dealing with a programmer. The modified general accounting package approach works best with a small one-program agency.

There are many more fund accounting packages available than in years past (see the end of this chapter for a list of some software vendors). If an agency were to buy an existing fund accounting package, there are a number of features to consider determining whether such a package would be appropriate. Some guidelines in choosing a package include:

- **Tutorial Provided:** there should be a tutorial on disk with an accompanying tutorial in the manual to help the novice learn the program with a minimum of outside assistance (see Table 14-1).

- **Clear Manuals:** Manuals accompanying the package should be clearly written for an ordinary mortal to understand. That is, they should be written in simple English and not "computerese". They should assume minimal knowledge on the part of the reader. The illustrations should be clearly marked and relate well to the text. There should be a complete index and table of contents, with sections easy to find. There should also be an adequate number of copies of the manual and some training of staff so that they will read and use it.
- **Understandable Menus:** Menus are those parts of a program that let you choose what actions you want to do next. They should be understandable enough so that a novice can understand and use them.
- **Interactive Program:** An interactive program is one that responds to an inquiry or answer or converses with the user in some way. Thus an interactive program should have easy to understand prompts and menus and a help key that lets the user ask for assistance form the program itself. It should tell the user when he or she has made a mistake or neglected to do something, and it should have explanations for every action to be taken.
- **Flexible Chart of Accounts:** The program should make it easy to set up and change the chart of accounts and report parameters.
- **Ease of Modification:** It should be easy for the user to go backward and forward during data entry to correct and modify data and descriptions.
- **Error Correction:** It should be simple for the user to correct mistakes.
- **Fund Accounting:** It should include the funds used by nonprofits or be simple enough for the staff to set them up.
- **Prepares Financial Statements:** The program should be able to prepare the necessary financial statements required of nonprofits: a Statement of Position, Statement of Activities, a Cash Flow Statement, and a Statement of Functional Expenses. Watch for programs that purport to be fund accounting programs, yet do not prepare the proper financial statements.
- **Calculates Financial Ratios, Other Statistics:** It is helpful if the program can calculate financial ratios as well as unit costs, cost per client, and so forth.
- **Agency Can Design Own Format for Reports:** The agency may have a need to design different formats for some of its reports, either for internal uses, or for funding sources.

- **Summarizes Data:** The program should be able to summarize data on financial statements and print individually selected schedules and analyses, as needed.
- **Integrated Package:** It should be able to be used with other available programs such as payroll, accounts receivable, accounts payable, and others that may be offered. It especially should integrate budgeting with accounting as well as a fundraising component and a client data component. It should also make it easy to import parts of financial reports or budgets into word-processing programs.
- **Generates Periodic Reports:** The program should generate reports on quarterly basis or for any other period needed by the agency, for example, monthly reports.
- **Can be Set Up for Variance Budgeting:** Variance budgeting can be an important control mechanism. The software package should have the ability to do budgeting as well as variance budgeting.
- **Funder Accounting:** The program should give the agency the ability to set up accounts by funding source, if so desired, and merge these accounts with others in the financial reports (Peskow, 1981)(See end of chapter for a list of fund accounting packages).

Human Factors

Along with considerations of hardware and software, human factors must be considered in the design. There are political and internal control issues as well as physical (i.e., ergonomic) issues. From a political standpoint, as has been mentioned, acceptance and user satisfaction are related to participation in the planning and implementation process (Lin & Shao, 2000). A new information system may change the balance or dynamics of power in an organization because access to information is a requisite for power. So the question becomes, who should have access to financial information in an organization and how does the system restrict access to those who "need to know?"

Need for Controls

While most computer programs have built-in controls for certain kinds of errors, there is always the element of human error in the entry of data to be processed. Therefore, there is a need to establish controls at each stage of the processing to recognize and correct errors. This holds more true for computerized systems because of the speed of processing, as well as the fact that fewer staff will have access to files and therefore, there may be less chance for detection of some types of errors.

There are also internal control issues that must be considered and included in designing and implementing a system. Internal control was discussed in Chapter Nine, here some issues that need to be addressed include control procedures that are " . . . concerned with the safeguarding of assets and reliability of financial statements" (Bodnar & Hopwood, 1995, p. 181). In financial information systems there are *general controls* that affect all transaction processing, for example, equipment control features such as backup and recovery procedures as well as software such as firewalls that protect a networked web-based system from hackers.

In addition, there are application controls that may be applied to individual software applications. These application controls may be input, processing, or output controls (Bodnar & Hopwood, 1995).

Input controls are "designed to prevent or detect errors in the input stage of data processing (p. 187). For example, the program may refuse an entry for a zip code that is not five numerical digits or for a social security number that is not nine numerical digits.

Processing controls are "designed to provide assurances that processing has occurred according to intending specifications. . . " (p. 190). As an example, the program may check to see that the accounts payable subsidiary ledger matches the balance in the general ledger control account.

Output controls are "designed to check that input and processing resulted in valid output and that outputs are properly distributed" (p. 191). For example, the program may attempt to verify balances of clients by sending monthly statements to confirm.

Lastly, one of the most important features of design for financial information systems is the assurance that an audit trail will exist and be available for review. "The audit trail concept is basic to the design and audit of an accounting information system and it relevant to internal auditors, management, systems analysts, and other parties involved in the operation of an accounting information system" (Bodnar & Hopwood, p. 180).

In addition, there are ergonomic factors to consider. Lost work time and disability claims due to carpel tunnel syndrome, eye strain, and back pain due to repetitive hand movement and poorly designed workstations are a major problem for American companies, both for-profit and nonprofit. Many of these problems can be reduced with better planning. There are guidelines for computer workstations that should be included in systems design (Anonymous, 2000; Dzida, 1996; Schulze, 2000).

Finally, a budget should be developed. During the planning and initial implementation stages of conversion to a new system, there will be costs associated with these stages that will not be recouped by the organization for quite a while. In addition, staff and board may not see benefits of the system since it may not be operational during the initial periods. The organization must be prepared for these initial start-up costs, which include such items as the hardware and software for the system, consultant fees, staff training, and so forth.

Selecting a Vendor

With the price of microcomputers so low, it does not make much sense for an agency to rent or lease this equipment. Therefore, the most viable option is to buy a system at the most reasonable price. Remember that nonprofit organizations usually do not pay sales taxes, and that many retailers extend discounts to nonprofits. The vendor may even be willing to make a tax-deductible contribution of all or part of the system itself. A number of software vendors have sought to make their products accessible to nonprofits on a no-cost or low-cost basis; some nonprofits have found hardware vendors in their local communities interested in extending products to them.

Conversion of System

Installing the new computerized system involves conversion of records and files from one system to another. This conversion process entails three aspects: equipment conversion, data processing method conversion, and procedural conversion (Burch, 1978). *Equipment conversion* is changing from handwritten or bookkeeping machine or old computer to new. *Data processing method conversion* means that the person in charge of recording transactions will now enter transactions differently than before. *Procedural conversion* entails instituting new procedures to accommodate the new system. In the conversion stage, the manual system or old computerized system must be run side-by-side with the new computerized system for testing purposes to check for errors and difficulties with software. Each segment of the system should be converted and tested before another segment is introduced. For example, accounts receivable should be tested and then accounts payable, and so forth.

After the new system is totally installed, there should be ongoing evaluation in the operation and maintenance of the system. Modifications should be made, as necessary, in the program that has been acquired by the agency as well as upgrades made to both hardware and software as new technological changes occur.

COMPONENTS OF SUCCESS

This chapter has attempted to point to some of the crucial ingredients in the acquisition or upgrade of a computerized financial information system. The successful conversion from a manual to a computerized information system or an upgraded system entails a number of components. Some of these important components are:

- **Commitment of "Key Stakeholders":** The success of a system is highly influenced by the involvement and commitment of key stakeholders (Sabherwal & Elam, 1995). The commitment of the executive director is crucial, since s/he will oversee implementation of the system. If the executive director is not the project officer, a staff person should be designated responsibility for the overall project and its timely completion. It is important to have some board member involvement in the project since the board will make final decisions regarding the new system. It is useful to have a board member with computer knowledge/expertise or access to it.
- **Involvement of Staff:** Acceptance of the system by staff will be facilitated by involving staff at every stage in the process, especially the design and development stages, and keeping all staff informed of the progress of the project as well as the benefits of it. If staff are not involved in the process, it will be more difficult to generate staff acceptance after the computers have been installed.
- **Long-term Planning:** Installation of a new or upgraded system is an opportunity for the nonprofit to take a hard look at its information needs and ways in which its information system can become a real management information system (MIS). This entails an

analysis of agency goals and operations and its present and future information needs (Wexelblat & Srinivasan, 1999). If the current MIS is inadequate or weak, these problems need to be corrected before implementing a new system. If the inadequacies are not rectified, they will be incorporated into the new system.

- **Documentation:** It is helpful to incorporate some feedback mechanisms in the organization's annual planning cycle to include review and evaluation of the computer system. Documentation at all stages of the process is very important, especially documentation of systems specifications and procedures. All documentation should be kept on hand at the agency for training and reference.
- **Relationship with Consultant:** Users should not let themselves be dazzled by the expertise of the consultant. Two of the biggest implementation problems for organizations are over-reliance on the consultant (thinking s/he knows best) and poor communication between the consultant and user because of the technical jargon of the consultant. The organization should not settle for anything less than the type of system that will best meet its information needs given its financial constraints.
- **Relationship with Vendor:** It is highly recommended that the vendor have staff with experience in installing systems for other nonprofit human service organizations. Some have suggested selecting a vendor through an RFP process, that is the specifications for the system and other requirements are written up in a Request for Proposal, including timelines for completion of each step. A formal RFP may not be necessary but certainly a number of estimates should be solicited.
- **Evaluation:** Periodic reviews and evaluations should be done to make sure that the system is meeting the information needs of the agency and any corrective action or modification should be done promptly.
- **Training:** Adequate training and orientation for staff in system utilization should be planned for and implemented early in the development process (Bowers & Bowers, 1977; DeJacimo et al., 1985; Ross, 1976).

A computerized financial information system can be an asset to the human service organization, helping it to perform needed and important functions more quickly and accurately than ever before. It will also help give needed information useful to agency planning. But before a nonprofit embarks on the task of converting or upgrading a system, it must be prepared to take to time and make the commitment to make it work as an effective tool in the furtherance of its goals.

REFERENCES

Anonymous (2000). Computer workstation ergonomic guidelines. *Occupational Health & Safety,* 69(10): 214–220.

Bodnar, G. H. & Hopwood, W. S. (1995). *Accounting Information Systems* (6th Ed.). Englewood Cliffs: Prentice Hall.

Bowers, G. E. & Bowers, M.R. (1977). *Cultivating Client Information Systems.* Project Share, Human Services Monograph Series, No. 5. Department of Health, Education and Welfare. Washington, D.C.: U.S. Government Printing Office.

Burch, J.G., Strater, F.R., & Grudnitski, G. (1979). *Information Systems: Theory and Practice* (2nd Ed.). New York: John Wiley.

DeJacimo, S., Kropp, D., & Zefran, J. (1985). Success is possible: One agency's experience with a vendor. *Computers in Human Services,* 1(2):85–95.

Dzida, W. (1996). International usability standards. *ACM Computing Surveys,* 28(1): 173–175.

Honig, S.A. (1999). The changing landscape of computerized accounting systems. *The CPA Journal.* http://www.nysscpa.org/cpajournal/1999/0599/features/599p14.html

Hunton, J.E. & Gibson, D. (1999). Soliciting user-input during the development of an accounting information system: investigating the efficacy of group discussion. *Accounting, Organizations and Society,* 24:597–618.

Lin, W.T. & Shao, B.B.M. (2000). The relationship between user participation and system success: a simultaneous contingency approach. *Information & Management,* 37: 283–295.

Peskow, J.K. (1981). How to utilize computers in small and medium-sized accounting firms, pp. 1273–1309 in Jerome K. Perskow (Ed.), *Accountant's Encyclopedia,* volume 2 Revised. Englewood Cliffs: Prentice-Hall, Inc.

Romney, M.B., Steinbart, P.J. & Cushing B.E. (1997). *Accounting Information Systems* (7th Ed.). Reading, MA: Addison-Wesley Publishing Co.

Ross, J.E. (1976). *Modern Management and Information Systems.* Reston: Reston Publishing.

Sabherwal, R. & Elam, J. (1995). Overcoming the problems in information systems development by building and sustaining commitment. *Accounting, Management and Information Technologies,* 5(3–4): 283–309.

Schoech, D. (1985). A microcomputer-based human service information system. In S. Slavin (Ed.), *Managing Finances, Personnel, and Information in Human Services* (pp. 329–344). New York: Haworth Press.

Schoech, D., Schadke, L.L. & Sanchez Mayers, R (1981). Strategies for information systems development. *Administration in Social Work,* 5(3/4): 11–26.

Schulze, L.J.H. (2000). Workstation ergonomics. *Professional Safety,* 45(12): 12,51.

Wexelblat, R.L. & Srinivasan, N. (1999). Planning for information technology in a federated organization. *Information & Management,* 35:265–282.

FUND ACCOUNTING VENDORS

- Accufund, Inc.
    400 Hillside Avenue, Needham, MA 02492
    http://www.accufund.com
- Blackbaud, Inc.
    2000 Daniel Island Dr., Charleston, SC 29492
    http://www.blackbaud.com
- Donor2/Systems Support Services
    http://www.donor2.com
- Dyna-Quest Technologies, Inc., http://www.Dyna-Quest.com
- Executive Data Systems, Inc., http://www.execdata.com
- Fund E-Z Development Corp.
    106 Corporate Park Drive, White Plains, NY 10604
    http://www.fundez.com
- Intuit Public Sector Solutions
    1385 South Colorado Blvd., Suite #400, Denver, CO 80222
    http://publicsector.intuit.com
- Micro Information Products, Inc.
    313 East Anderson Lane, Suite 200, Austin, TX 78752
    http://www.mip.com
- Mirasoft, Inc.
    http://www.mirasoft-inc.com
- Serenic Software, Inc.
    www.serenic.com

INTERNET RESOURCE

To find other accounting software:
http://www.finaccountingsoftware.com

APPENDIX
NOTES TO FINANCIAL STATEMENTS*

The following notes are typical of those that would accompany non-profit financial statements. They help clarify for the reader what is shown in the statements.

HUMAN SERVICE ORGANIZATIONS, INC.
NOTES TO FINANCIAL STATEMENTS

December 31, 2011

NOTE 1: NATURE OF ORGANIZATION

Human Service Organization, Inc. is a nonprofit agency organization organized exclusively for charitable purposes. The Organization provides a wide range of human services through its various programs.

NOTE 2: SUMMARY OF SIGNIFICANT ACCOUNTING POLICIES

Basis of Accounting

The accompanying financial statements of Human Service Organization, Inc. have been prepared on the accrual basis of accounting in accordance with accounting principles generally accepted in the United States

Income Tax Status

Human Service Organization, Inc. is a nonprofit organization ex-

---

* Taken from: *SFAS 116; SFAS 117; Standards . . . (1998).*

empt from federal and sate income taxes under Section 501(c)(3) of the Internal Revenue Code and comparable State law.

Financial Statement Presentation

In accordance with SFAS No. 117, net assets and revenues, expenses, gains, and losses are classified based on the existence or absence of donor-imposed restrictions. Accordingly, net assets of the Organization and changes are classified and reported as follows:

Unrestricted Net Assets: Net assets that are not subject to donor-imposed stipulations.

Temporarily Restricted Net Assets: Net assets subject to donor-imposed stipulations that may or will be met, either by actions of the Organization and/or the passage of time. When a restriction expires, temporarily restricted net assets are reported in the statement of activities as net assets released from restrictions.

Permanently Restricted Net Assets: Net assets subject to donor-imposed stipulations that they be maintained permanently by the Organization. Generally, the donors of these assets permit the Organization to use all or part of the income earned on any related investments for general or specific purposes.

Contributions

In accordance with SFAS No. 116, contributions, including unconditional promises to give, are recorded as made. All contributions are available for unrestricted use unless specifically restricted by the donor. Contributions with restrictions that are met in the same reporting perios as they are received are reported as unrestricted support.

Amounts received that are for future periods, in the form of pledges, or restricted by the donor for specific purposes are reported as temporarily restricted or permanently restricted support that increases those net asset classes.

Functional Expenses

Expenses are charged to each program based on direct expenditures incurred. Any program expenditures not directly changeable are allocated based on management's best estimates.

Fixed Assets

Fixed asset purchases greater than $1,000 are capitalized at cost. Donated assets are recorded at fair market value at the date of the gift. Depreciation is provided on a straight-line basis over the estimated useful lives of the assets as follows:

Buildings and improvements	30 years
Leasehold improvements	30 years
Furniture and equipment	5 years
Automobiles	5 years

Revenue Recognition

Funds received from various federal and state agencies represent grants to the Organization to provide program services. Revenues from these awards are recognized to the extent of expenses incurred under the award terms, Upon completion or expiration of a grant, unexpected funds are not available to the Organization.

Service fees received in advance of service being rendered are reported as deferred revenue and are recognized in the period in which the services are rendered.

Notes and Notes Payable

The Organization routinely enters into notes and loans payable transactions with various state governmental agencies, some of which are forgivable upon the passage of time and th performance of the terms of the loan.

Marketable Securities

Marketable securities consist primarily of equity securities and corporate bonds, They are carried at market value, with unrealized gains or losses included in the operations.

NOTE 3: CASH EQUIVALENTS

For Purposes of the statement of cash flows, the Organization considers all highly liquid investments available for current use with an initial maturity of three months or less.

NOTE 4: ESTIMATED FAIR VALUES

Cash and cash equivalents, receivables (other than pledges) and accounts payable are stated at their fair market values. Investments in equity and debt securities are stated at fair values, based upon quoted market prices.

NOTE 5: MARKETABLE SECURITIES

Investments are comprised of marketable equity securities, binds and investment account cash balances with fair market values of $270,500 on December 31, 20xx. The unrealized loss on the investments amounted to $600 for the year ended December 31, 20xx.

NOTE 6: PLEDGES, AWARDS, AND GRANTS

Unconditional promises to give (pledges receivable) expected to be collected within one year are presented at their net realizable value. Pledges received are as follows:

Unconditional promises receivable (pledges)	$70,100
Less allowance for uncollectibles	11,200
Net pledges receivable	$58,900

NOTE 7: FIXED ASSETS

At December 31, 2011, fixed assets consist of the following:

Land	$59,200
Buildings and improvements	100,000
Furniture and equipment	24,600
Automobile	18,000
Total Fixed Asset	201,800
Less accumulated depreciation	28,000
	$173,800

NOTE 8: DONATED MATERIALS AND SERVICES

Donated materials and equipment are recorded at their estimated values at date of receipt and are reflected as donations in-kind in the accompanying financial statements.

NOTE 9: DEFINED CONTRIBUTION PENSION PLAN

The Organization maintains a defined contribution pension plan for the eligible employees and their beneficiaries. An employee is eligible for participation when s/he has completed two years of service and is at least twenty-one years old. For 2011 the amount contributed was $3,000.

NOTE 10: RESTRICTED NET ASSETS

Restricted net assets are as follows:

Program A	$20,000
Program B	10,000
Program D	15,000
For periods after December 31, 2011	5,000
	$50,000

Permanently restricted net assets are restricted to investment in perpetuity, the income from which goes to support activities. These net assets are as follows:

Program A	$35,000
Program C	50,000
Program D	32,000
Any program activity	3,000
	$120,000

NOTE 11: FEDERAL AND STATE FINANCIAL ASSISTANCE PROGRAMS

In regard to the matching requirement of all agencies, Human Services, Inc. has met the grantee participation level in cost sharing.

NOTE 12: TAXES

All required tax returns have been filed and taxes (including but not limited to payroll taxes) were either paid prior to December 31, 2011 or aid subsequent to year end.

NOTE 13: PAYMENT TO NATIONAL ORGANIZATION

In accordance with the affiliation agreement with the national organization, the Organization remits $82,400 to the national organization. In return, the national organization provides technical assistance and training as well as accreditation to the Organization.

NOTE 14: MORTGAGE

The mortgage is secured by the Organization's land and buildings. It is payable monthly to Commerce Bank, Inc.

GLOSSARY

Accounting: The art of analyzing, recording, summarizing, and reporting the financial activities of an agency using generally accepted accounting principles (GAAP).

Accounting cycle: A fiscal time period in which a similar cycle of events takes place to account for the financial transactions of an organization.

Accounting entity concept: An accounting or business entity is any economic unit that takes in resources and engages in some form of economic activity; it does not include any of the economic activities of any of its employees that are unrelated to, or take place outside of, the main objectives and tasks of the agency.

Accounting equation: Illustrates the relationship between assets and equities by means of a simple equation: Assets = Equities. This means that assets must always equal equities.

Account payable: A type of liability incurred when merchandise or other goods are bought on credit.

Account receivable: A type of asset created when an individual or organization owes money to one's agency.

Accrual basis accounting: Records not only transactions involving the receipt and disbursement of cash, but also transactions in which the agency incurs obligations or others incur obligations to the agency.

Adverse opinion: A type of audit opinion given when the auditor believes that the agency's financial statements are not a fair reflection of its financial position and were not prepared in accordance with generally accepted accounting principles.

AICPA: American Institute of Certified Public Accountants.

Allocation: Funds supplied by federated fundraising and allocation organizations such as the United Way, Jewish Federation, Catholic Charities, Black United Fund, and Women's Way to a nonprofit based on a formula or proposal.

Appropriations: Monies that may be set aside for specific future uses by a nonprofit board.

Assets: Items of monetary value that are owned by an individual or business entity.

Audit: An examination of an organization's financial statements and accounts in order to express an opinion on the fairness of the financial statements, their compliance with generally accepted accounting principles and the consistency of their application.

Audit opinion: An opinion written by an auditor after examining an organization's financial statements and internal controls. Some types of audit opinions are: an unqualified opinion, a qualified opinion, an adverse opinion, and a disclaimer of opinion.

Balance sheet: See Statement of Position.

Bond: A debt instrument, a loan by a person or organization that buys the bond to the issuer of the bond.

Break-even analysis: Determines the break-even point, that is, the point at which revenues match costs.

Budget summaries: A compilation and summarization of all the individual budgets of an organization.

Business risk: The degree of uncertainty associated with an investment's earnings and ability to pay investors returns on their investment.

Capital appreciation: An increase in the price paid for an investment.

Capital gains (or losses): Occur when securities are sold at a price that is higher (or lower) from the original cost. If it is sold at a higher price, there is a capital gain; if at a lower price, a capital loss.

Capital or owner's equity: The rights of the owners of the assets of a firm. Capital represents the residual of the resources of the firm after all the liabilities are satisfied or paid.

Cash basis accounting: Records only those transactions in which cash is received or disbursed.

Cash equivalents: Those cash items held in interest-bearing accounts such as money market or savings accounts with a maturity date of less than three months.

Certificates of deposit (CD's): Time deposits issued banks in which the investor has deposited a specified sum of money for a specific period of time at a guaranteed rate of return.

Chart of accounts: A system for identifying and classifying various account titles and accounting transactions.

Common stocks: Represent shares of ownership in a corporation.

Conservatism principle: Accountants, in choosing among alternative methods or procedures, should choose the most conservative approach.

Consistency principle: An accounting system adopted by an agency will be applied consistently and will not be changed from period to period.

Contributions: Sums of money, or in-kind goods or services donated by individuals or groups to support the work of a nonprofit.

Control: A system for setting standards, monitoring the fiscal activities of the organization, providing feedback regarding these activities, and taking corrective action if necessary in order to minimize risk and assure that organizational goals will be reached.

Control environment: The organizational culture that creates the ambience of an organization, it is seen as the foundation for all the other components of control. It involves board, administration, staff, and others in the philosophy that guides operations.

Corporate bonds: Debt instruments sold by corporations. Investors who buy corporate bonds become creditors of the issuing institution.

Cost principle: Assets are initially recorded in the accounting books of the agency at their actual cost, and no adjustment for inflation or appreciation is made in the books at a later time. The only adjustments made are to allocate a portion of the cost to expenses as the assets expire or depreciate.

Cost-plus reimbursement contract: Payment based on a fixed price with an additional reimbursement for certain costs only.

Current assets: Cash or other assets expected to be converted to cash within one year or less.

Current liabilities: Those debts that must be satisfied in one year or less.

Current unrestricted fund: Used in fund accounting for those resources that have no donor-imposed restrictions on them and may be used to carry out the day-to-day operations of the organization.

Current restricted fund: Used in fund accounting to account for those resources that are expendable only for operating purposes specified by a donor or other funding source.

Custodian fund: Sometimes used in fund accounting to account for assets received by an organization to be held or disbursed only on instructions of the person or organization from whom they were received; a holding or pass-through fund.

Depreciation or amortization: Allocates the cost of an asset over its useful life. Some types of assets that may be depreciated are equipment, buildings, and automobiles.

Disclaimer of opinion: A type of audit opinion that may be given when the auditor is not satisfied with an agency's financial statements.

Disclosure principle: Material and relevant facts upon which outsiders can evaluate the economic activities of the agency should be disclosed either in its financial statements or in the notes accompanying them.

Endowment: A monetary gift that can be invested and the earned interest used by an agency for designated purposes or just general operating expenses.

Endowment fund: Used in fund accounting and is made up of the principal amount of gifts and bequests accepted with the donor-stipulation that it be maintained intact in perpetuity, until the occurrence of a specified event, or for a specified period.

Equities: Claims on assets. There are two components of equities: liabilities and owner's equity or capital.

Expenses: Costs borne by an organization in fulfilling its mission.

Expense variances: The difference between actual and budgeted expenses.

FASB: Financial Accounting Standards Board.

Federal Form 990: An annual form required by the Internal Revenue Service to be filed by all 501(c)(3) organizations that meet certain revenue and asset thresholds.

Fee-for-services: A charge for rendering a service to a client.

Financing cash flows: Transactions related to borrowing and repayment of loans as well as receipt of resources such as permanently or temporarily restricted endowment gifts.

Fixed asset fund: Used in fund accounting and sometimes called the land, building and equipment fund or the plant fund. It is used to account for fixed assets used in the operations of the organization.

Fixed-income investments: Guarantee a given rate of return no matter how the economy fares over the life of the investment.

Fixed-price contract: Vendors receive a set price for specified services performed by a certain date.

Functional basis accounting: An accounting device for separating an agency's expenses into two main categories: program services and support services (management and general and fundraising).

Fund accounting: Separate accounting entities, or funds, are set up to segregate and report on those resources available to be used at the discretion of the board (unrestricted funds); as well as those available to be used for specific purposes only (restricted funds).

Funder accounting: A type of accounting by sources and uses of revenue by funding source.

GAAP: Generally accepted accounting principles.

GAAS: Generally accepted auditing standards.

GAGAS: Generally accepted government auditing standards.

GASB: Governmental Accounting Standards Board.

Going concern concept: An assumption that the accounting entity will not be going into liquidation in the foreseeable future.

Government bonds: Bonds sold by all types of federal, state and local authorities.

Grant: An allocation of funds from a funding source for a specific program or project.

In-kind goods or services: Nonmonetary contributions given to further the goals of a nonprofit.

Interest rate risk: A risk to those who invest in fixed-income securities that inflation may be higher than the interest they receive from their investment.

Internal audit: An examination of the accounting records, compliance, and internal controls of an organization throughout the fiscal year by an agency staff person or audit committee.

Investing: The current commitment of funds in order to receive a future financial gain.

Investing activities: Those cash transactions related to the acquisition and disposal of long-term assets.

Investment income: Return from investments such as interest and dividends.

Joint activities: Activities that combine a fund-raising function with elements of other organization functions, such as program, management and general, or membership development.

Joint costs: Costs that include both fundraising and program components.

Liabilities: The claims that creditors may have on assets. Liabilities are the debts owed by an organization. Some types of liabilities are accounts payable, mortgage payable, and notes payable.

Liquidity: The ability to convert an investment or other assets into cash quickly.

Long-term assets: Fixed assets such as land, buildings, and equipment.

Managed care organizations: Organizations that manage the cost of healthcare, the quality of health care, and the access to health care.

Market risk: The fluctuation in the price of securities due to events perceived to be related to the earning power of the issuing corporation.

Marketable securities: Investments that can be easily converted to cash and whose maturities are less than one year.

Matching principle: In order to measure income accurately, revenue from one accounting period is matched or compared with expenses incurred during the same accounting period.

Materiality: The relative importance of any amount, event, or procedure. If an item is not considered important enough to influence the users of the agency's statements, then it is probably immaterial.

Modified accrual accounting system: Has characteristics of both the accrual and cash bases. That is, an organization may record certain transactions on a cash basis, usually revenue, and record other transactions on an accrual basis, usually unpaid bills.

Monetary principle: States that all financial transactions and statements are reflected in terms of money.

Monitoring: Involves processes and mechanisms that assess the quality of an organization's performance and congruence with planned, measurable benchmarks of achievable outcomes.

Mutual funds: Investment companies that sell their own shares or securities to the public and use the proceeds to invest in other securities.

Net assets: The excess of assets over liabilities. There are three classes of net assets: unrestricted net assets, temporarily restricted net assets, and permanently restricted net assets.

Net income: What remains after expenses have been deducted from revenues during an accounting period, in nonprofits called surplus or excess of revenues over expenses.

Net loss: When expenses exceed revenues during an accounting period, called a deficit of revenues over expenses in nonprofits.

Notes payable: A type of liability or debt incurred by signing a promissory note to repay the monies owed at a definite future time.

Objectivity principle: Objective evidence is necessarily the basis upon which cost and revenue are recorded. Objective evidence is in the form of documents such as receipts, invoices, checks, vouchers, and so forth.

OMB Circular A-11-: *Grants and Agreements with Institutions of Higher Education, Hospitals, and Other Non-Profit Organizations.* Published by the Federal Office of Management and Budget, gives guidelines, rules, and regulations for nonprofit organizations receiving federal funds in the form of grants or contracts.

OMB Circular A-122: *Cost Principles for Non-Profit Organizations.* Published y the Federal Office of Management and Budget, gives guidelines for determining costs of grants and contracts with nonprofits.

OMB Circular A-133: *Audits of States, Local Governments, and Non-Profit Organizations.* Published by the Federal Office of Management and Budget, gives guidelines, rules, and regulations for audits of organizations receiving federal funds.

Operating activities: Those cash transactions related to the day-to-day activities of an organization.

Owner's equity: See capital.

Permanently restricted net assets: Assets whose use is limited by donor-imposed restrictions that are permanent in nature, as for example, an endowment.

Personnel controls: Internal controls involving personnel to minimize risk to organizational assets.

Physical controls: Measures whose objective is the safeguarding of assets and records.

Pledge receivable: Contribution pledged by a donor, but not yet paid.

Preferred stocks: Possess characteristics of both common stocks and corporate bonds.

Prepaid expenses: Expenses that have been paid in advance, for example, insurance or property taxes.

Price-level risk: The risk of losing purchasing power due to inflation.

Principal: The original amount of money put into an investment or donation.

Program specific audit: An audit of organizations that have only one program expending federal award monies.

Psychological risk: The inability of an investor to psychologically cope with the vagaries of the investment marketplace.

Public support: Amounts donated or allocated to a nonprofit.

Purchase of service contract: An agreement in which an organization will provide a specific level and quality of service in exchange for payment.

Qualified audit opinion: Given in those cases in which the auditor thinks that there are certain aspects of the financial statements that vary from generally accepted accounting principles, yet are not material enough to require an adverse opinion.

Rate: Refers to the amounts charged for services and /or products offered by the organization

Realization principle: Revenue is not commonly recognized until it is realized. Two conditions have to be met for revenue to be realized. First, there must be objective evidence that this is so. Secondly, the earning process must be essentially complete.

Revenue: Amounts earned by an agency for providing a service.

Revenue/public support variances: The difference between actual and budgeted revenue and public support.

RFP: Request for Proposal. Information sent, published, or posted for downloading, for potential grant seekers regarding competition for a new grant award.

Risk assessment: Analysis of, and planning for, risks that may hinder achievement of organizational goals.

Safety of principal: An investment goal to retain the principal or amount of money originally invested.

Single audit: Includes an audit of the organization's financial statements as well as a reporting on expenditures of federal awards and a compliance audit.

Socially responsible investing: An approach that integrates personal values and societal concerns with the investment decision-making process.

Statement of Activity: One of the required financial statements for nonprofits. It shows revenues, expenses, and changes in net assets in three classes: *unrestricted net assets, temporarily restricted net assets,* and *permanently restricted net assets.* The statement also includes a total change (increase or decrease) in net assets for the fiscal period.

Statement of Cash Flows: One of the required financial statements for nonprofits. It reflects the amount of net cash given to, and used by, a nonprofit as the result of operating activities, investing activities, and financing activities during the fiscal period being reported.

Statement of Financial Accounting Standards (SFAS) No. 95: *Statement of Cash Flows.* The standard for developing the cash flow budget.

Statement of Financial Accounting Standards (SFAS) No. 116: *Accounting for Contributions Received and Contributions Made.* Provides guidelines on how nonprofit should record contributions and in-kind goods and services.

Statement of Financial Accounting Standards (SFAS) No. 117: *Financial Statements of Not-for-profit Organizations.* The standard for nonprofit financial statements.

Statement of Financial Accounting Standards (SFAS) No. 124: *Accounting for Certain Investments Held by Not-for-profit Organizations.* Provides guidance to nonprofits in the accounting and reporting of their investments.

Statement of Functional Expenses: One of the required financial statements for nonprofits. It is a record of actual expenditures of unrestricted net assets during a fiscal period.

Statement of Position: One of the required financial statements for nonprofits. Also called the Balance Sheet because the Statement of Position is essentially a reflection of the accounting equation: Assets = Liabilities + Capital.

Statement of Position (SOP) 98-2: *Accounting for Costs of Activities of Not-for-profit Organizations and State and Local Government Entities That Include Fund Raising.* AICPA guidelines on accounting and allocating for joint costs and activities.

Statement of Position (SOP) 98-3: *Audits of State, Local Governments,* *and Not-for-profit Organizations Receiving Federal Awards.* AICPA guidelines on nonprofit audits.

Temporarily restricted net assets: Assets whose use is limited due to donor-imposed restrictions, for example, a donation limited to one program or organization activity.

Third-party payments: Payments by agents of patients (or clients) who contract with providers to pay all or part of a bill for a patient (or client). The two most common types of third-party payers are private insurance companies and public payers, such as the federal government.

Time period principle: While an indefinite life for accounting entities is assumed in accounting, this indefinite life is broken into short time intervals for reporting purposes.

Transaction controls: Are concerned with insuring that monetary transactions are executed and recorded properly.

Unit contribution margin: The excess of revenue over variable costs.

Unit cost reimbursement Contract: A contract in which payment for services is based on a computation of the unit cost of the service.

Unqualified audit opinion: Given if the auditor thinks that financial statements were prepared in accordance with generally accepted accounting principles and accurately reflect the financial position of the organization, its operations and changes in net assets.

Unrestricted net assets: All assets with no restriction on them, for example, a donation given to the agency to be used for operations, or fees for services

Variable-income investments: Vary in their rate of return according to how well the company and the economy are doing.

Variance budgets: Show the differences between amounts budgeted and actual amounts spent.

Volume: Refers to the number of units of service offered and/or delivered.

INDEX